CAMBRIDGE STUDIES IN LINGUISTICS

General Editors · W.SIDNEY ALLEN · EUGENIE J.A.HENDERSON
FRED W.HOUSEHOLDER · JOHN LYONS · R.B.LEPAGE
F.R.PALMER · J.L.M.TRIM

The Grammar of Case

Towards a Localist Theory

In this series

THE GRAMMAR OF CASE

TOWARDS A LOCALISTIC THEORY

JOHN M. ANDERSON

*Lecturer in English Language,
University of Edinburgh*

CAMBRIDGE UNIVERSITY PRESS

CAMBRIDGE
LONDON · NEW YORK · MELBOURNE

Published by the Syndics of the Cambridge University Press
The Pitt Building, Trumpington Street, Cambridge CB2 1RP
Bentley House, 200 Euston Road, London NW1 2DB
32 East 57th Street, New York, NY 10022, USA
296 Beaconsfield Parade, Middle Park, Melbourne 3206, Australia

Library of Congress Catalogue Card Number 71-145602

ISBN 0 521 08035 5 hard covers

ISBN 0 521 29057 0

First published 1971
Reprinted 1973
First paperback edition 1976

Reprinted in Great Britain by Redwood Burn Limited,
Trowbridge & Esher

Contents

Part I

PRELIMINARIES

1 Introduction

1.1 A non-localist view of case

In discussing the grammatical role of case inflexions (or pre-/post-positions) it has for some time been the usual custom to talk in terms of different 'functions' or 'uses' of each case, and in particular to separate out 'concrete' (or 'local') uses from 'purely syntactic' ones (and among the 'concrete' to differentiate between (especially) the 'spatial' and the 'temporal'). Also, certain cases are usually considered to be 'characteristically' or 'basically' either 'concrete' or 'syntactic'. Between the 'concrete' and the 'purely syntactic' are often ranged uses which are not obviously or merely spatial (or temporal) and do not seem to be 'purely syntactic' either, but are described in terms like 'dative of possession' or as being appropriate (to mark the 'indirect object', etc.) with certain (semantic groups of) verbs (e.g. 'verbs of giving or putting'). What I have just very briefly outlined can be exemplified from almost any recent traditional classical grammar, or any grammar compiled within that tradition.[1] In terms of such a framework, one might say that the nominative in, for instance, Latin is a case with typically 'syntactic' functions (subjective, etc.), whereas the Latin accusative combines both 'local' (as 'goal'—*Romam ire*) and 'syntactic' (as object—*Romam videre*) uses. A prepositional example like *to* in English shows (among other things) a somewhat 'abstract' use with verbs of 'giving', etc. (*I gave the news to the porter*) and also a more 'concrete' and 'local' function (in sentences like *I travelled to London*). It is doubtful whether there are cases (or prepositions) which are only ever 'concrete' in the strict sense of the word (whatever that might be); this would at least appear to be true of the various accounts of case systems that I have consulted in connexion with the present work. Such is a typical traditional viewpoint, and it continues to inform (though with modifications) more recent discussions like those of Kuryłowicz (1949; 1964: ch. 8).

---

[1] Consider, for example, Gildersleeve & Lodge, 1895: 207–66; Macdonell, 1916: 298–328; or the relevant parts of almost any of the grammars referred to by, say, Havers, 1911. See too Lyons, 1968 a: §7.4.2, for a discussion of such traditional presentations.

1-2

1.11   ...exemplified from Finnish. Within such a framework, then, the cases of, for instance, Finnish[1] might be divided into two groups with regard to their principal uses: the 'syntactic' and the 'local'. The latter indicate location in space (and 'metaphorical extensions' of such), and comprise two main subgroups, the 'internal' and the 'external', each subgroup containing three distinct cases. One case in each subgroup indicates simple location; the internal ('inessive') locates with respect to the inside of some referent, and the external ('adessive') with respect to the surface. The other two represent 'motion from' the interior ('elative') or exterior ('ablative') and 'motion to' the interior ('illative') or exterior ('allative'). We can roughly compare the English prepositions *in, on, out of, from, into, to*. There is a further 'local' case, namely the 'prosecutive' or 'prolative', which expresses 'motion through, along or over'. Also perhaps to be included here is the 'comitative' which indicates typically 'the person along with whom'. Identical in representation to the comitative in many languages but not in Finnish is the 'instrumental' or 'instructive', which represents the means or manner by which some action is performed, and is thus intermediate between 'local' and 'syntactic'.

The typical 'syntactic' cases, which fulfil non-'local' functions, are the nominative, accusative and genitive. The first marks the subject of a sentence and a predicative nominal, and the direct object in imperative sentences (i.e. when no subject is present); otherwise, the direct object is represented by an accusative. The genitive is the (superficial) adnominal case *par excellence*. A further small set of cases blurs this dichotomy, and also, in particular, the preceding description of the syntactic cases. These are the 'essive' and 'translative' which alternate (meaningfully) with the nominative in marking a predicative nominal (the second being used in 'inchoative' sentences), and the 'partitive', which alternates (once again, meaningfully) with the nominative and accusative in representing subjects and objects. This last group, then, introduces further distinctions within the 'syntactic' cases, and also, more interestingly from the point of view of the following discussion, they have in addition 'local' uses, which indeed appear to antedate the 'syntactic' uses. In this respect, essive, partitive and translative constitute a parallel series to adessive, ablative and allative.[2] There is also some

[1] See e.g. Eliot, 1890: particularly 121–62; and for a semi-localist treatment, cf. Sebeok, 1946. For some exemplification of 'syntactic' and 'local' functions, see e.g. Lyons, 1968 a: §§7.4.5–7.4.6.

[2] It is this sort of phenomenon that is perhaps most obviously suggestive of a localist interpretation (as discussed in §1.2—see too §11.62). In other languages (e.g.

evidence (Eliot, 1890: 138) that the Finnish genitive 'incorporates' a former 'dative', which is typically used in many languages to mark the subject with certain ('impersonal') sub-types of verb, and also the 'indirect object' (a further 'syntactic' use). Such an account is, in principle, in Hjelmslev's (1935: particularly 55–61) terms, 'demi-localist', in that these two sub-types of case are recognized, the 'grammatical' or 'syntactical' (or 'logical'—though this is, of course, often used distinctively (cf. §4.31)) and the 'concrete' or 'spatial' or 'topical' (cf. Holzweissig, 1877).

In other languages—e.g. the so-called 'ergative languages'—the non-'local' cases display a somewhat different superficial organization: this will be relevant to our later discussion, and I will postpone an examination of such phenomena until then (§4.6). However, it is worth noting at this point that an account of this kind (involving strict separation of 'local' and non-'local') provides no explanation of why certain cases have both 'local' and non-'local' uses (a point which Hjelmslev, in his argument for a fully 'localist' theory—see §1.21—makes much of). Also, since the number of morphological cases varies from language to language, the uses associated with any particular case label are far from constant: hence some of the problems discussed in §1.3.

Comparability is improved if prepositions or postpositions are included. Thus, I shall want for the purposes of the following discussion of the semantics of case functions to ignore any distinction that might be drawn between 'case' and 'pre/postposition' (cf. e.g. Lyons 1968a: §7.4, particularly §7.4.7), and include under the label 'case' (in somewhat Wundtian fashion) 'functional' elements in general (while not neglecting the fact that prepositions, for instance, appear to be more appropriate to the representation of certain functions than others).

1.2 Localist views of case

Less commonly, attempts have been made, on the one hand, to show a relationship between the 'concrete' and the more 'abstract' uses of the same case or preposition—as, for instance, with the uses of English *to* mentioned above—and, on the other, to reveal common principles

Hungarian—cf. Sauvageot, 1951: 236–47), we must allow for a further series among the non-internal set, such that there is a distinction between a group of three cases indicating location with respect to a surface ('superessive', 'sublative' and 'delative') and a group expressing proximity (adessive, allative and ablative).

underlying both such uses and 'purely syntactic' uses (of the same case, or more generally—as with the Latin accusative (exemplified in §1.1), or with respect to it and the preposition *ad*). I am thinking in particular of the more or less localist accounts (of cases or prepositions) offered by scholars like the Byzantine Maximus Planudes, who appears to have been the first grammarian of note to evolve a coherent (and extant) localist theory of case,[1] Harris (1751: book 2, ch. 3), Condillac,[2] Wüllner (1827—developing Bopp's proposals), Hartung (1831), Key (1850–2; 1874: ch. 18), Madvig (1875), de la Grasserie (1890; 1896: 178–82) and Hjelmslev (1935–7) (and, to a lesser extent, Jakobson, 1936, 1958).[3] The more radical of these attempted to relate all case functions to a small number of universal relations, of which the spatial uses ('location at', 'movement from/to') of (certain of) the cases represent only the most 'concrete' manifestation.

1.21   Hjelmslev's 'la catégorie des cas'

Thus, Hjelmslev—to take a more recent proposal—sets up three semantic dimensions for case systems—'direction' ('éloignement'/'repos'/'rapprochement'), 'cohérence'/'incohérence', 'subjectivité'/'objectivité'—which are intended to characterize the relations expressed by both 'syntactic' and 'local' cases. A number of cases can be differentiated with respect to a single dimension, since Hjelmslev recognizes, apart from the possibility of cases representing the two polar terms and a neutral term (such as 'repos'), complex cases like, typically, the nominative, which can represent both 'éloignement' (as subjective) and 'rapprochement' (as predicative). Further, the dimension is capable of different 'orientations', depending on which case is the 'intensive' (roughly, semantically 'marked' or simplex) one. For instance, Hjelmslev (1935: 45–6, 101) proposes that the Latin ablative is 'intensive' (with respect to the dimension of 'direction'), in that 'l'ablatif latin insiste sur l'éloignement; toute autre cas du système normal du latin est

---

[1] But see the remark of Theodosius quoted by Steinthal, 1863: 623. Planudes' work is printed in Bachmann, 1828: 1–166.

[2] See Le Roy, 1947: 478 a–81 b.

[3] See too Vogt, 1949; Sørensen, 1949; Kuipers, 1962; Velten, 1962. Other works are referred to by Hjelmslev (1935: 1–70) and Brøndal (1948: 49–50). Hjelmslev, indeed, provides a quite extended survey of the development of the various issues surrounding the localist *vs.* anti-localist debate, the comparative neglect of which is a relatively recent phenomenon. For a concise illustration of a localist hypothesis, see particularly Hjelmslev's (1935: 11–13) account of the analysis of the Greek case system proposed by Planudes; and cf., on Hjelmslev's own proposals, §1.21 below.

complexe ou neutre à l'égard de la dimension de direction' (101). In another language (Hjelmslev suggests Greek), it might be a case representing 'rapprochement' that is 'intensive'.

The third dimension, which differentiates between cases which express relations from the point of view of a spectator (typically the speaker—as in a prepositional example like *He is behind the tree*) and those which do not necessarily (*He is underneath the tree*), presupposes the second, but not vice versa. That is, the (morphological) cases of a particular language may not express such distinctions, but if they do, then they will also express those appropriate to the second dimension. This relationship of pre-supposition also holds between the second dimension (which typically distinguishes between, for example, an inessive ('cohérent'—*dans*) and an adessive ('incohérent'—*à côté de*)) and the first. Thus, only the first dimension may be appropriate to the casual system of certain languages.

Other apparent restrictions are more problematic. In general, it is difficult to see the relevance of the second and third dimensions to the 'purely syntactic' cases—except negatively (they are 'incohérent' and 'objectif'?—though see chapter 11, particularly §11.6). It is not clear too how further kinds of 'spatial indication' (Collinson, 1937: 50–4) are to be accommodated. These could no doubt be regarded as essentially nominal rather than casual, so that the markers of such require a complex derivation from a superordinate nominal rather than a simple case or preposition (i.e. are derived by 'casualization'—§2.121); but then this might also be said (as is the case at least superficially in many languages) of, for example, the 'subjectivité'/'objectivité' distinction (cf. *behind* (= 'at/to the back of')). Might not the marking of this distinction simply by case-inflexions be merely superficial (rather than an indication of an underlying casual status) even in those languages where we find this phenomenon?

1.3 'Surfacism'

1.31   ...in localist theories. Such questions are in part a reflexion of a wider deficiency, as a result of which (in particular) such attempts at a localist account can be judged to have been only partially successful; and this was, I think, due especially to the fact that the analyses were applied on the whole to case as a superficial phenomenon—semantic values were, for the most part, attached directly to cases as surface morphological categories. This was despite the fact that such factors as the relationship between casual inflexions, 'word order' and prepositions were recognized (but remained to some extent strangely unexplored in any rigorous way) by, for instance, Wüllner (1827: 6–9) and Hjelmslev (1935: 40–3, 107)—as well as (in some respects at least) by many other scholars in the past, of course,[1] and particularly since the time of Wundt. Certainly, an extension of Hjelmslev's avoidance of a simple 'Grundbedeutung' for nominatives would enable us to overcome the difficulties met by any approach which attempted to characterize the subject–verb relation in terms like 'actor–action' when confronted with sentences like the following:

(i)   *a.* That envelope contains my money
      b. She suffered terribly
      c. John is in the garden
      d. I owe you sixpence
      e. The hams hang from the ceiling
      f. The chalet sleeps six
      g. John got a shock
      h. Ariadne left

Only the last of these would fit without considerable difficulty this particular characterization. As Marache (1967: 292) observes: 'Définir le sujet comme point de départ de l'action a de toute façon l'inconvénient de ramener la fonction au sense de quelques verbes: ceux qui expriment l'action.' However, such an account, while avoiding such difficulties by assigning typically a complex value to nominatives, fails to explain the particular value the nominative has in any one instance. In other words, while it is true that, when we consider such a set of sentences as that in (i), it is impossible to consider that all the subjects have the same semantic function, nevertheless in any one of these sentences (if we ignore the others) the function of the subject is much less ambivalent. Moreover, this proposal does not throw any light on what these diverse elements might have in common—what it is that merits the use of the term 'subject'—apart from identity of superficial marker (positional or inflexional); nor does it explain why the 'actor–action' description is

[1] Cf. e.g. Robertson, 1905: 524–5; Trabalza, 1908: 123; Kukenheim, 1932: 108, 140; Chomsky, 1966: 44–5; Donzé, 1967: 171; Harris, 1751: 25–6; Hjelmslev, 1935: 24, on Bernhardi; Benveniste, 1949; Lyons, 1968a: §7.4.5; Salmon, 1969: 177. On the historical relationship between case inflexions and prepositions, see particularly, e.g., Pott, 1836: 613–51; Velten, 1962.

appropriate for very many active sentences (in English, at least—see Lyons, 1968*a*: §8.1.5). Such inadequacies follow, it seems to me, from a failure to appreciate that there may exist a complex relationship between the underlying semantic (case) relations and their superficial markers (case inflexions or prepositions), due particularly to that interaction with other semantic elements which our syntax will have to provide for.

1.32 ...and in non-localist theories. This kind of failure, however, has also characterized (until very recently—see Fillmore, 1966*a*, 1968*a*, 1968*b*) most non-localist treatments of case—see e.g. de Groot, 1956, or the study of Redden's (1966) discussed by Fillmore (1968*a*: 8–9). And with respect to both positions, this weakened in particular the power of the generalizations concerning cases (as a feature of universal grammar and of particular grammars) that could plausibly be formulated (cf. Fillmore, 1968*a*: §1.2), and thus helped to earn for case grammars the scepticism of scholars like Jespersen (1924: ch. 13; 1930: ch. 30) and Bazell (1937). Consider too the debate concerning the semantic *vs.* the syntactic character of case(-inflexions) referred to by Moreux (1968: 31–2). Such considerations (concerning the inadequacy of attempts to characterize semantically case inflexions) also underlie in part, no doubt, the relegation of case to a very superficial position in 'traditional' transformational grammars (as Chomsky, 1965: ch. 4, §2.2).

Associated with this is the (possible) confusion resulting from the (well-established—cf. Baker, 1931) use of a single term to refer both to case(-relations) and case(-inflexions); part of the reaction against case-grammars is thus merely terminological. An early instance of such a reaction is represented by the remark of Meigret's quoted by Livet (1858: 70): 'Au regard des cas, la langue françoise ne les connoît pas, parce que les noms françois ne changent point leur fin.' Part of the debate between Sonnenschein (e.g. 1927: ch. 1) and Jespersen (e.g. 1924: ch. 13) is concerned with terminological appropriacy. However, the question of terminology is connected with the degree of 'abstractness' accorded to 'case'. I shall opt below for an 'abstract' view of case.

1.4 A statement of intent

Despite such inadequacies in the formulation of localist case grammars in the past, it seems to me that, on the one hand, the study of case functions (whether marked inflexionally or otherwise) has been interestingly renewed (by particularly Fillmore (1968 *a*)) within a framework that allows for a complex relationship between case functions and their superficial representation, and that, on the other, localist studies like those I have mentioned did progress sufficiently towards demonstrating common principles underlying 'spatial' and 'abstract' uses and both of these and 'syntactic' uses, to require the attention of any serious attempt to construct a grammar of grammatical functions (cf. Lyons, 1968 *a*: 301–2). Even in such (for the most part) non-localist discussions as Kuryłowicz's (1964: ch. 8) concerning the Indo-European case-system, the intricate superficial and historical relationships between the representation of 'concrete' and 'abstract' uses are well illustrated— and demand an explanation.[1] A localist conception of case inflexions (and prepositions) and case functions provides in principle an explanation for such, as well as (I am going to suggest) for various other synchronic and diachronic semantic and syntactic phenomena. Moreover, the effect of Fillmore's (non-localist) proposals, if accepted in the following respect, is to remove from consideration at the deepest levels those functions (the subjective and objective, in particular) which represent the most difficult problems with respect to a localist interpretation of case relations. That is, not only different levels of representation are allowed for, but also the traditional 'syntactic' cases, nominative and accusative (the subject and object markers) are to be regarded as (like the genitive) superficial neutralizations of distinct underlying cases (cf. Fillmore, 1968 *a*: 49). Subjective and objective are not among the underlying cases; the non-local underlying cases are of quite a different order, and are thus (I shall suggest) rendered more amenable to a localist interpretation. I shall also argue in what follows that such a conception removes the difficulties noted above (in §1.31), and yet includes what is of value in the demi-localist position, by thus incorporating the 'syntactic' functions as superficial (though some kind of localist interpretation of the surface syntactic functions is not excluded). In sum, then, one of the things I want to argue for most strongly in what follows is that a more abstract view of **case**—taking this term to refer to grammatical relations contracted by nouns which express the nature of their 'participation' in the 'process' or 'state' represented in the sentence (or noun phrase)—cf. Lombard, 1929—and which are repre-

---

[1] For a similar illustration with respect to prepositions, consider, for instance, Sastri, 1968.

sented superficially in various fashions, including inflexionally and by pre- and postpositions—enables us to avoid some at least of the difficulties encountered by earlier studies, and yet to maintain an essentially localist standpoint.

1.41 Prospect. In the following chapter I shall be concerned to formulate a grammatical framework within which to evaluate various sub-parts of a localistic conception of functional relations. As things stand (or fall apart) at present, this will involve me in a number of assumptions and assertions which I cannot hope to fully substantiate in what follows. In particular, at a number of points we are constrained to choose between alternatives whose relative merits I (at least) am in a very poor position to pronounce upon. Thus, I shall for the most part merely try to indicate the nature of the major assumptions being made, some of which are relatively independent of the localist argument (and vice versa). Part II will explore the status within such a grammar (particularly of English) of the case elements nominative and ergative, with respect to both their occurrence in underlying representations and (to a lesser extent) their superficial manifestation. The purpose of the first two parts, then, is to establish a grammatical framework within which case relations can be discussed and to examine (from a non-localist point of view) aspects of the grammar of two cases.

In Part III, two further ('local') case elements, locative and ablative, are introduced (in chapters 6 and 8, respectively) and their syntax examined. Chapters 7 and 9 represent attempts to show that sentences involving various non-spatial relations can plausibly be considered to involve (semantically and syntactically) locative or directional structures, and that they differ from 'concrete' locatives not with regard to the basic case relations involved but in the character of the nouns and (particularly) the verbs that contract the relations. The final section is in part a very tentative attempt to demonstrate that even the most radical localist proposal, namely that there are common (semantic and syntactic) principles underlying both the non-'local' and 'local' cases, can be given some substantiation, even though the incorporation of such 'insights' into the grammar presents for the moment a number of difficulties.

1.42 Wider considerations. This survey of putative 'localist phenomena' is of course far from exhaustive and is intended merely as an illustration of something of the range of phenomena that a localist hypothesis would seek to relate. However, I would like to note that no case categories are envisaged for the clause additional to those that give the second and third parts of the present work their titles; further distinctions can be accounted for in terms of features on these or by reduction ('casualization'—§2.121) of a nominal (*beside*, etc.). Also, I take it that the relationship between both the semantics and the manifestation of temporal and spatial location is well-established. However, an attempt to capture this relationship is faced with special problems that I do not wish to embark upon here—in particular, in so far as I would also want to propose that the surface markers of tense and aspect have their ultimate source in temporal locative structures. For similar reasons, I shall not be taking into consideration rather obviously relevant 'nominal' phenomena—concerning, for instance, the partitive relation or the various categories connected with the notion of 'deixis' (demonstratives, personal pronouns, etc.).[1]

Such a theory of case ought too to be relatable ultimately to the widespread (syntactical and lexical) relationships between 'concrete expressions' and what are usually referred to as 'metaphorical or figurative extensions' of such. Consider examples like Whorf's (1956: 146): 'I "grasp" the "thread" of another's arguments, but if its "level" is "over my head" my attention may "wander" and "lose touch" with the "drift" of it...' However, the extent of (such superficial representation of?) this would appear to vary from language to language, and take rather different forms (cf. Whorf, 1956: 134–59). But such a principle of extension of the concrete to the abstract seems to underlie such diverse phenomena as the Indo-European comparative (for a 'spatial view' of such, see Small, 1924: ch. 1) and the classification of verb stems in Navaho (see Landar, 1959: 303–6). An investigation is required of the synchronic relevance of such relationships; and there are obvious, testable ontogenetic and phylogenetic implications in such a view. A hierarchical relationship between 'concrete' and 'abstract' would argue for a non-innate status for such substantive universals as are involved. I have, indeed, called the present work 'localistic' rather than 'localist', in that I would like to reserve the latter term for a stronger proposal than I shall present evidence for here, namely that not only are there common principles underlying spatial and non-spatial cases, but that also (as is

[1] Certain scholars (Bopp, 1829; Humboldt, 1829) have suggested a locative adverbial (historical) source for pronominal roots. I shall, of course, in what follows regard place adverbs as 'reduced' locative phrases.

implied by the preceding remarks) the spatial variant has ontological (and perhaps chronological—both short- and long-term) priority. My aim in the present context is more modest than this, and I shall not argue from such a position; but the direction such an argument might take is not difficult to discern. The time may not be too distant at which proposals of this kind will permit realistic evaluation (and indeed when concern with the origin, renewal and development of linguistic categories may be accorded the process of renovation recently granted to that other major focus of linguistic debate in the eighteenth century, the notion of 'universal grammar').

2 A sketch of the grammar

Before trying to substantiate the localistic claim embodied in §1.4 (which will concern us in the final three parts of this book), I shall attempt to develop in outline a proposal for a case grammar along lines which are not particularly localist, but which represents (specifically) a modification of the accounts offered in Anderson, 1968a and 1969c. This will be our primary occupation in the second part and what remains of this one, and will form the starting-point for the subsequent investigation of the localist hypothesis. In the present chapter, I want to sketch out a framework within which to discuss the cases, before discussing case as such. In connexion with this it is necessary to state (in a rather informal way, for our present purposes) certain assumptions upon which the following discussion in part depends, and some of which are in their turn supported to the extent that this discussion is fruitful. The first two sets of these I shall indeed discuss immediately; others can be noted in the course of developing our grammar. However, I think that (as suggested in §1.4) the claim can justifiably be made that many of the arguments for a localist position are relatively independent of the particular grammatical framework suggested below.

2.1 Some assumptions concerning the form of the grammar

2.11 The universality of underlying case relations. I assume that the underlying case relations are a universal of language; further, that they are introduced within a set of (at least partially) universal 'base structures'. That is (despite Chomsky, 1968: 57), I concur with Bach's (1968: 14) arguments for adopting initially the 'universalist–unitarian' hypothesis concerning the nature of the base. However, (if we regard the base as semantic—cf. §2.12) such a status is doubtful for many semantic features (despite the fact that many idiosyncrasies can be accounted for in terms of 'lexicalization'—see below (§2.121)) unless perhaps certain distinctions are regarded as merely not being 'utilized' in some languages. Rather, then, features (as opposed to (underlying) categories—see below (§2.2)) are perhaps to be regarded as conforming to a cline of generality, with respect to which implicational

statements (cf. the relation between Hjelmslev's dimensions—§1.21) can be made. Languages may be different with respect to how they divide up minimal semantic fields: cf. e.g. the examples of Weisgerber's discussed by Miller (1968: ch. 4). Also, the referential scope of semantic oppositions may vary. Languages otherwise differ primarily (apart from lexically and phonologically) in the particular transformational operations performed on these underlying representations.

Thus, although my argument will be concerned in detail with sets of examples from Contemporary English (that well-established source of linguistic universals), I shall feel free to draw on illustrations from other languages and from earlier stages of English, particularly where they make clear a distinction obscured superficially in English. Also assumed here is Hjelmslev's ('naturalness') hypothesis (1935: 104) that 'les lois qui dirigent les syncrétismes sont en rapport avec les lois dirigeant la structure du système', as one consequence of a view of linguistic change such as is developed by e.g. Kiparsky (1968) and Schane (1969), following and in reaction to Halle (1962). In particular, the facilitation of the prediction of 'natural' syncretisms and shifts in representation is assumed to be evidence for a hypothesis. I shall not in fact develop this aspect here, except perfunctorily (for example, in §11.22), but it is intended that the argument could be so supplemented.

2.12   Remarks on the organization of the grammar. The structures generated by the 'base sub-component' are to be regarded as semantic (or notional) representations, in the sense discussed in (for instance) the postscript to McCawley, 1968b. I shall therefore prefer here the term **semantic sub-component** (or semantics). These underlying semantic representations form the input to a 'transformational subcomponent' (what were called 'rules of realization' in Anderson, 1968a, 1969c) whose function is to correlate these representations with appropriate surface structures. It now seems not unreasonable to refer to this simply as the **syntactic sub-component** (or syntax). Together, these two sub-components form what one can refer to as a **semantico-syntactic component** (or simply 'grammatical component'?) whose output is the input to the **phonological component** (which it is not my concern to discuss here).[1] It is doubtful whether 'deep structure' in

---

[1] For similar views and argumentation, see e.g. Hockett, 1966: 270–2; Chafe, 1967, 1968a, 1968b; Southworth, 1967; Langacker, 1967: chs. 4 & 5; Bach, 1968: 117–21. Indeed, such a position seems to me a highly traditional one, in a tradition represented, for instance, by Jespersen, 1924: ch. 3, and only recently challenged (Katz &

Chomsky's sense[1]—see e.g. Lakoff, 1968: §o—can be justified (with respect to universal grammar) even as an intermediate unitary (systematic) level. Certainly, I shall assume underlying representations (with respect to which selectional restrictions can be formulated) considerably more 'abstract' than such, which in intention provide (part of) semantic characterizations directly.

This 'abstractness' is manifested in various respects. The differences between the underlying representation for a sentence and its surface structure are often very great—even though the alphabets of elements and the 'construction-types' involved show considerable overlap.[2] This is true particularly of the derivations finally proposed in Part V. Further, the semantic representation underlying 'simple' lexical items is often 'paralleled' by representations realized superficially as configurations of elements.[3] Thus (as observed in Anderson, 1968 b: 308-9), the meaning of a verb like *walk* and certain restrictions on its occurrence (**John walked on foot*) are explicated if we consider the underlying representation for *walk* etc. to be rather like (with various distinctions—see Anderson, 1968 b: 309) that for *travel on foot*. That is, in particular, there is no single category corresponding to *walk* in the underlying structure. The configurational complexity underlying many 'simple' items is perhaps easier to appreciate when there is a surface derivational marker—as in a noun like *driver*—or when, in an unfamiliar language, we find an item for which there is in our native tongue no non-configurational (i.e. lexical) equivalent—as with terms of relationship like the Tlingit *Kik!* ('man's younger brother' or 'woman's younger sister') mentioned by Swanton (1911:196), or the locationals in Koyukon and related languages which involve orientation with respect to the appropriate local river (Henry, 1969), or the variation, in certain Amerindian languages, in the (phonological) shape of the verb in accordance with the character of an associated nominal.[4] Compare English *kick* and *punch* with the French *donner un coup de pied/poing.*

Postal, 1964; Chomsky, 1965)—though Chomsky later (1969 b) appears to be arguing that no such challenge is necessarily intended.

[1] What one might call 'taxonomic deep structure'—cf. Chafe, 1968 a: 120; Fillmore, 1968 a: 88; Bach, 1968: 120; McCawley, 1968 b: 165-9.

[2] I.e., 'stratification' within the semantico-syntactic component is yet to be demonstrated—cf. Chafe, 1968 b.

[3] Cf. e.g. Lakoff, 1965; Bach, 1968: §5; Anderson, 1968 b; Binnick, 1968 b. For further examples like that discussed in what immediately follows, see Porzig, 1934.

[4] Cf. Hoijer's (1945) description of Apachean classificatory verb stems. See too Hoijer, 1959: 367-72; Davidson, Elford & Hoijer, 1963; and more generally, de la Grasserie, 1896: 38-44; 1914 b.

Consider as a further simple illustration from English (suggested to me by some observations of Angus McIntosh) items like *acquaintance* or *stranger*, which are characterized notionally by 'an "inherent" relationship with someone else' which is not present with words like *policeman*— i.e. 'an acquaintance' is 'someone known to some particular person(s)' and 'a stranger' is 'someone not known to some particular person(s)'. Such facets of the meaning of these words, as well as restrictions like that exemplified in **I don't know that acquaintance (of mine)*, are provided for by proposing as their underlying representations configurations which include the appropriate elements I have just represented informally. Other fairly clear instances come from the grammar of 'comparison' (whatever form it might take). McIntosh (1968) has suggested that many simple items (verbs, prepositions, nouns) represent the same underlying relations as 'overt' comparative structures (see too Bach, 1968: 120–1). Consider such different types as *prefer* ('like more'), *darken* ('become darker' or 'become dark'), *exceed* ('be(come) greater than'), *beyond* ('further than'), *after* ('later than'), *top* ('highest point').[1] Once more, an underlying configurational representation for such items seems appropriate; and once again such representations have alternative realizations which, in a sense, retain more of the abstract structuring. This alternation between (superficial) simple item and configuration is quite naturally accommodated within an account which allows for the **lexicalization** of complex structures (or the 'abbreviation (in terms)' of the seventeenth- and eighteenth-century universal grammarians).

2.121 *Lexicalization and suppletion.* One way of interpreting the notion 'lexicalization' is discussed in Anderson, 1968*b*. There, the verb *walk* (as opposed to *move, travel*, etc.) is regarded as being formed by an abbreviatory copying of the specification of an underlying adverbial (which would otherwise appear as *on foot*). That is, a feature (say, 'ambulatory'—which belongs once more to a set whose members are of varying generality) is added to the verb, the presence of which permits the deletion of the underlying adverbial; otherwise, the adverbial ᴀains and *travel on foot*, etc. are the result. (It is no doubt more mplicated than this, since (in particular) *on foot*, as a sub-type of strumental, perhaps involves a complex structure (cf. Lakoff, 1968).)

ᴊlearly, the plea of Campbell and Wales (1969) for more attention to 'comparison' in
˗˗˗˗˗˗˗˗ is fully justified.

I shall refer to this part of the specification for an element as its **derived** (as opposed to **inherent**) **lexical content**.

However, the precise nature of lexicalization is unimportant for our present purposes, though it is worth noting, with Bach (1968: 117), that 'the particular sets of meanings and syntactic features which are given lexical status can vary widely' (from language to language), and that this is a major source of differences between languages;[1] this will be apparent as an assumption throughout the following discussion. This is not to deny that there are constraints on the 'trajectory' for permitted lexicalizations (and grammaticalizations—as with tense—cf. Bopp's 'agglutination'). Typically, under lexicalization, it is a governing element (in the sense of §2.6 below) that incorporates lexical material with respect to a dependent (or set of dependents). Thus, in verbalizations (e.g. *walk*—and see again Porzig, 1934), a dependent case phrase is involved in incorporation, in nominalizations (e.g. *pedestrian*) a dependent clause, and in casualizations (e.g. *beside*) a dependent NP. One can interpret the implicational relationship Hjelmslev posits between his three dimensions (cf. §1.21) as an articulation of constraints on casualization.

More important than exploring the character of lexicalization in the present context is the conclusion to be drawn from such phenomena, namely that many distinct phonological items have in some sense a common underlying (semantic) source, and differ, for instance, in features marking the operation of certain transformations (as above) or indicating the arguments (cf. §4.32). It is necessary to extend such a view and allow for widespread **suppletion** (Anderson, 1968*b*) if one is to match semantic representations with an appropriate paradigm of surface variants. For instance, I shall argue below (§9.6) that *accept* fills a gap in the paradigm for *agree*—in a place where we find no suppletion with the 'negative' *refuse*. Thus:

(ii) 1. *a.* He agreed to have the book
    b. He accepted the book
   2. *a.* He refused to have the book
    b. He refused the book

---

[1] Cf. Boas's (1911*a*: 26) statement that 'every language may be holophrastic from the point of view of another language'. It is perhaps with respect to notions like the variability (over different languages) of lexicalizations and of the distinctions made within minimal semantic fields that one might investigate the linguistic aspects of a modified version of the linguistic relativity principle (see the works referred to in Miller, 1968), whereby languages are conceived of as differing in terms of the 'ease' or 'economy' with which different distinctions can be made or things referred to.

The phenomena of lexicalization and suppletion suggest that certain transformations at least operate independently of phonological information, and that if there is any determination it is rather in the contrary direction. It is indeed quite likely that lexical insertion, which introduces phonologically specified items from the lexicon, should be regarded (if it is a once and for all operation) as following many (at least) of the syntactic transformations (cf. particularly Matthews, 1965; Bach, 1968: §5). These would thus be formulated with respect to semantic (and referential, if necessary) specifications. Such a view would enable us to evaluate the 'semantic naturalness' of the specifications susceptible to particular transformations.

2.13   A schema for the grammar. For our present purposes, something like the following crude schema for the organization of the grammar is suggested (see too Chafe, 1968*a*: 120–1):

(iii)

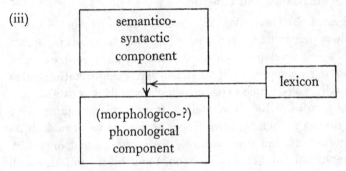

(where such post-lexical transformations as are necessary are included (since they are dependent on phonological information) with morphological distinctions like those concerning declension and grammatical gender in the morphologico-phonological component). Notice that the vertical structure of this diagram indicates what seems to me the only place where anything approaching intra-linguistic 'stratification' has been shown—and even then the division is only 'quasi-stratificational' (cf. Chafe's (1967, 1968*a*) 'symbolization'), since even though the effect of lexical insertion is to introduce representations in terms of a new universal alphabet, the (interpretative) phonological rules nevertheless presuppose syntactic information.[1] However, this schematization ignores

---

[1] Cf. the works referred to by Anderson, 1968*b*: 316–17; Chafe, 1968*b*. Thus, in so far as stratification has been substantiated, it is (Saussuro-)Hjelmslevian (Hjelmslev, 1954; 1961: particularly §13) rather than Lambian (Lamb, 1964*a*, 1964*b*, 1965, 1966) in scope.

the possible incorporation of a 'topicon'—Sampson, 1969—and the place of 'presupposition' with respect to the semantics (cf. Fillmore, 1968c).

2.14 Some omissions. I shall be concerned in what follows almost entirely with certain aspects of the semantic sub-component, to a much lesser extent with the (surface) syntax, only marginally with the lexicon, and (as I have observed) not at all with phonology as such. Moreover, I shall not dwell on the formal implications or insist on any particular aspect of what I am about to outline as a characterization of certain aspects of the organization of the semantico-syntactic component.[1] My main concern is to provide a sufficient framework for the exploration of the localist hypothesis.

2.2 Subcategorization and constituency

I have suggested elsewhere (Anderson, 1968a, 1969a, 1969c) that two types of rule appear to be appropriate to the semantic sub-component: firstly, rules which develop complexes of (**category** and) **features** which we can refer to as complex symbols (CSs)—**subcategorization rules** (SRs); secondly, rules which expand symbols into their constituents—**constituency rules** (CRs). Two points, in particular, require to be made with respect to the respective scopes of these types of rule. Rules of subcategorization, and thus features, are associated not only with lexical or **terminal categories** like N(oun) and V(erb) but also with **pre-terminal categories** like N(oun) P(hrase) and Cl(ause).[2] Also, and connected with this (cf. Hudson, 1967; Anderson, 1969a), the number of non-recursive 'layers' of constituents allowed for by the constituency rules is very small: between the **initial category**, S(entence) and the terminal categories there are at most two 'layers' (Cl and NP). Such a limitation is associated with the notion of 'rank' (Halliday, 1961: 250–4), and (as I have noted), is dependent on the presence of preterminal features[3]—which eliminate the necessity for intermediate layering.[4] We must now look at how these two types of rule 'interact'.

---

[1] These are (as I suggested above) for the most part secondary to the main argument; and anything I suggest is likely to be sacrificed in next month's (last year's to you) revolution.

[2] Cf. Allen, 1956; Weinreich, 1966; Lyons, 1968a: §7.6.9; Chomsky, 1969b.

[3] Or 'systems'—Halliday, 1961: 263–8; 1964: 16–21.

[4] Cf. Chomsky's (1965: ch. 2, §2.3) discussion of the motivations for and consequences of the introduction of 'syntactic features'. A similar reduction in the variety of under-

2.21 Rules of constituency for categories. It is proposed that there are three 'obligatory' CRs (each associated, of course, with a 'step down' in 'rank'), which cannot but apply in the order in which they appear in (iv) (since e.g. rule II presupposes the prior introduction of Cl):

(iv)   I.   S →   # Cl #
      II.   Cl → nom + V
      III.   NP → N

\# is the clausal boundary marker: nom(inative) is a case category (whose status is discussed below—in §3). Such rules are to be construed as stating that the element to the left of the arrow (wherever in the course of a derivation it occurs) is replaced by (or rewritten as) the string to the right; the element(s) of that string are its (immediate) constituents. There is a rule (which we shall discuss below) which inserts a NP after (in English) any case category (and whose operation therefore must precede that of III). Thus, if we take this last rule into account, the rules in (iv) will provide (in terms of the usual conventions for tree-formation) for the aspects of the structure of, say, *John sneezed* represented in (v):

(v)

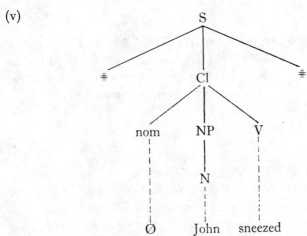

lying relations allowed for can be achieved in terms of the reduction of most (or all) of these to the 'sentential' (NP⌒VP)—i.e., in particular, in terms of analyses involving 'abstract verbs' (Lakoff, 1965). The proposals formulated in Part V represent a combination of these two possibilities. A major problem in both instances ('featurization' and 'sententialization') is to determine the constraints appropriate to such powerful devices.

In the papers referred to above, I suggested that Det(erminer) was introduced with N in the rule equivalent to III in (iv). However, it is clear that 'determiners' as such represent a rather superficial phenomenon: see, for instance, particularly on the so-called 'indefinite article', Perlmutter, 1969; the 'definite article', in its turn, is a sub-type of 'demonstrative' (cf. e.g. Key, 1844; 1846–7; 1874: ch. 25), which would appear to have their source in a (embedded) locative.[1] This category is thus excluded from rule III. NP is retained as a pre-terminal category to allow for noun modifiers (via, in particular, the embedding of S—'noun phrase complementation' (Rosenbaum, 1967a; Rosenbaum, 1967b: particularly chs. 1 and 2) and 'relativization'). In a similar way, there was in these papers a CR parallel to III which expanded V(erb) P(hrase) as T(e)ns(e) + V, VP having been introduced in II in place of V. For similar reasons, too, Tns is omitted from the present rules: like the markers of 'aspect', it is likely that tense markers derive from super-ordinate temporal locative clauses (cf. Darrigol, 1829; Garnett, 1846–7). Further, in this instance, VP can probably be eliminated as a pre-terminal category—since the evidence for the notion of 'verb phrase complementation' (as originally formulated by Rosenbaum, at least—though see §12) is rather tenuous (Rosenbaum, 1967b: preface; Bowers, 1968; Wagner, 1968).

2.22   Rules of subcategorization. Associated with each of the pre-terminal categories (S, Cl, NP) is a set of rules of subcategorization which develop CSs with S, Cl and NP (respectively) as the initial element. These rules are of the general form represented in (vi):

(vi) 1. category$_a$ → ± feature$_i$
     2. + feature$_i$ → ± feature$_j$

wherein each rule is to be interpreted as stating that any CS that is already specified with respect to the element on the left of the rule is to be replaced by a CS containing the previous specification together with either a + value or − value for the feature on the right; and, once more, the relative order of e.g. SRs 1 and 2 in (vi) is determined by the elements involved. Depending on the selections made in (vi), various CSs are developed, as indicated in (vii):

[1] With 'speaker'/'addressee' reference—cf. McCawley, 1968b: 155–61; Lyons, 1968a: §7.2.3.

(vii) *a.*
$$\begin{bmatrix} \text{category}_a \\ +\text{feature}_i \\ +\text{feature}_j \end{bmatrix}$$

   b.
$$\begin{bmatrix} \text{category}_a \\ +\text{feature}_i \\ -\text{feature}_j \end{bmatrix}$$

   c.
$$\begin{bmatrix} \text{category}_a \\ -\text{feature}_i \end{bmatrix}$$

Thus, the categories are merely the initial elements in (potential) CSs.[1] Such SRs specify the semantic alternatives (such are the feature opposi- tions) appropriate to each category, and their ordering explicates the (hyponymic) relationship between the individual oppositions. Certain semantic oppositions have a sentential domain, others a clausal, and so on.

2.23   Rules of constituency for features. Observe further that the SRs also control the development of the structures immediately domi- nated by the category which initiates the CSs formed by these rules. For instance, one might have a SR for the clause of the following form:

(viii) Cl $\rightarrow \pm$ locative

which distinction underlies (in a fairly obvious way) part of the (notional) difference between, say, the clauses in (ix):

(ix) *a.* John lay on the floor
    b. John sneezed

(ix.*a*) is 'semantically' a 'locational' clause in a sense which (ix.*b*) is not. Moreover, the effect of selecting + locative is to introduce another case phrase—assuming that the subjects in both of the clauses in (ix) are nominative; i.e., the Cl in (ix.*a*) has an extra case constituent. Such a possibility is allowed for if we modify the notion of CR (cf. the examples in (iv)) to include (after II in (iv)) rules like that in (x):

(x) + locative $\rightarrow$ loc$//$V—

which is to be understood as stating that if the feature specification + locative occurs in a CS, then a category, loc, is inserted in the string of elements immediately dominated by that CS. The place of insertion

---

[1] This distinction between category and feature is analogous to that drawn within the phonology by e.g. Kohler (1966: 340) in terms of sequential *vs.* componential elements. Cf. too particularly Chomsky, 1965: ch. 2, §2.

is indicated to the right of a double slash, as in (x). That particular rule requires the prior operation of rule II in (iv) to provide the appropriate environment. In the proposed sets of rules which follow (in Parts I, II and III) I shall suggest that each element be introduced in what can be shown to be its 'neutral (or unmarked) position' in English (from which it may be shifted by subsequent syntactic (i.e. transformational) rules); but I shall review the nature of such a concept in more detail in Part IV. If − locative is selected in (viii), then obviously rule (x) does not apply, and the structure dominated by the CS is unaffected (as in (ix.*b*)). Clearly, the rules in (iv) can be regarded as a sub-type of such rules, which refers only to categories, instead of a feature and a category—as in (x). Their formal nature thus becomes much more mysterious than the gloss of them proposed above (following (iv) in §2.21) implies. I want to allow too for CRs which refer only to features, i.e. CRs whereby a + feature 'introduces' a feature which is added to a terminal category (see Anderson, 1968*a*: 5–7; 1969*a*: 131–3), which thus once again represents (potentially) a CS. We can thus make a distinction (within the part of the grammar we are concerned with) between pre-terminal or **primary** features (which are introduced by SRs) and terminal or **secondary** features (which are introduced by CRs). Such CRs can be represented as in (xi):

$$\text{(xi)} \quad +\text{p.f.}_i \rightarrow \text{s.f.}_j // \left[\overline{\begin{matrix} \text{category}_k \\ \end{matrix}} \right]$$

I.e. the presence of (primary feature) + p.f.$_i$ in a CS initiates a CR which introduces (secondary feature) s.f.$_j$ into the CS initiated by category$_k$ and immediately dominated by the CS that contains + p.f.$_i$. Secondary features are not specified as to + or −, since only + specifications for primary features appear in rules like (xi).[1] Thus CRs 'expand' CSs like those in (vii) in terms of their constituent categories and features.

2.3   Syntactic (transformational) rules

Associated with each pre-terminal category, then, is a set of SRs and a (subsequent) set of CRs which develop constituents for each CS initiated by the category, in accordance with the particular selections represented in the CS. These two sets comprise the semantic sub-

---

[1] This does not mean to say that (transformational) rules which refer to the absence of such a feature cannot be formulated (if necessary).

component—at least, those parts of it that are directly relevant to the present study. Defined upon the specifications which form the output to these rules is a set of syntactic (transformational) rules (TRs), which associate with the appropriate semantic representations a class of well-formed (surface) syntactic structures. However, I have suggested elsewhere (Anderson, 1968*a*: 20; 1969*c*) that it is possible that certain TRs follow immediately the semantic rules for (e.g.) Cl, rather than all the semantic rules. They would thus intervene between the successive sets of semantic rules associated with the respective pre-terminal categories. Since (as is remarked on above) the transformational rules are conceived of as operating with respect to 'abstract' (not phonologically specified) representations in general, this would not present any fresh problems. But the evidence so far adduced for such a requirement is somewhat tenuous, in that, in particular, the interpretation of the imperativization phenomena mentioned in Anderson, 1968*a*: 19–21, is rather complex (cf. Boyd & Thorne, 1969: 58–62), and also the rule which introduces a NP for each case, which might be formulated as in (xii):

(xii)   case → case + NP

(where case is defined as any immediate constituent of Cl apart from V) and which is a TR that clearly must precede the rules for NP, is eliminated as such by a modification to the grammar I shall propose below. Nevertheless, I shall allow for the insertion of a set of TRs between each bloc of semantic rules; and we shall consider what evidence for such emerges from the discussion which follows in other chapters.

2.4   Overview of the semantico-syntactic component

Accordingly, the rules of the semantico-syntactic component fall into three successive sets. The first set of SRs, CRs and (perhaps) TRs is associated with S; they allow for the semantic oppositions and the variety of structures that are relevant to the notion of coordination of clauses (cf. Anderson, 1969*c*: 307–8), and introduce one or more clauses (and conjunctions where appropriate) as constituents of S. The rules for Cl define the semantic oppositions associated with the introduction of the various constituents of clauses, including particularly the cases. NPs are also introduced, as we have seen, by a TR which operates at this stage. NPs have then, in their turn, a set of rules associated with them which accounts for the appropriate semantic alternatives and structural variety. Each successive set presupposes (the elements introduced by) the previous set. Thus, we have three ordered sets of rules:

(xiii)   I. S → ...

             . . . .

      II. Cl → ...

             . . . .

    III. NP → ...

             . . . .

Within I, II and III there are three further subsets of rules: of subcategorization, of constituency and (perhaps) of transformation—each set presupposing (the elements introduced by) the previous one. So:

(xiv)   I. i. $\hat{S}$ → ± ...

             . . . .

      ii.   S →   Cl

             . . . .

     iii.   . . . .

    II. i.   Cl → ± ...

          etc.

Within each of the subsets indicated in (xiv) the rules are partially ordered. They are thus assigned integers (from I to n) to represent this order; 'simultaneous' rules (i.e. which operate at the same point in the sequence) are paired with the same integer and distinguished by a letter (*a*, *b*, *c*, ...). An exemplification of such is presented in (xv):

(xv)   II. i. 1.   Cl → ± feature$_i$

          2. *a*.   + feature$_i$ → ± ...

            b.   − feature$_i$ → ± ...

      ii. 1.   Cl → nom + V

         2.   + feature$_i$ → ...

             . . . .

     iii. 1.   case → case + NP

Associated with such rules are structural descriptions like that abbreviated in (xvi):

(xvi)

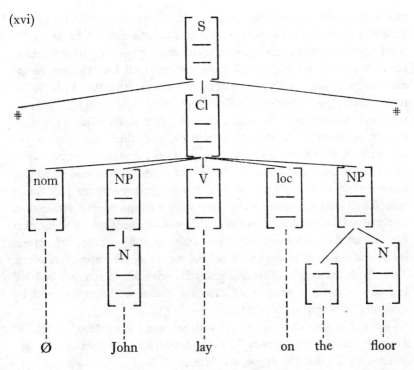

Notice that it is only the rules within iii in each of I, II and III (the TRs)
that display any 'significant' ('extrinsic'—Chomsky, 1965: 223, note 6)
ordering, in the sense that the ordering of the rules within i and ii and
the ordering of I, II and III is simply dictated by the elements that
appear in the rules (cf. McCawley, 1968*a*). For instance, an element
that is required as an environment for a rule must have been introduced
by a logically previous rule. (Some instances of ordering within ii are
perhaps significant (cf. II. ii in (iii) in §3.3), but this property is removed
by the proposal made in chapter 10). It may be that one should regard i
and ii as simply constituting well-formedness conditions on semantic
representations.

2.5   Some inadequacies of constituency rules

However, there are various inadequacies, particularly with respect to the
specific sub-parts we are primarily interested in, to be found in such a
sketch for a grammar. I want now to consider a possible modification
which is intended to remedy one defect in the characterization of

phenomena that are at the centre of our area of enquiry; and this concerns the relation between a case and its associated NP. As I have tried to indicate briefly elsewhere (Anderson, forthcoming *a*), it seems to me that an account like that I have just outlined fails to capture the essentially 'relational' character of cases—the fact that they indicate the functions in the clause which their respective NPs contract. In (xvi), nom and its associated NP (introduced by rule II. iii. I in (xv)) appear merely as co-constituents of the clause, and there are further co-constituents which are not related to them in the same intimate way in which they are related to each other. Of course, one could introduce some sort of auxiliary marking which would represent the fact that a rule like II. iii. I had operated by indicating a relationship between nom and the following NP. However, this would constitute a somewhat mysterious device imposed on the results of the operation of certain rules, and does not emerge in a natural way from the rules themselves. Thus, both the degree of intimacy of relationship between case and NP and the relational character of case are inadequately represented by structural descriptions like (xvi).

Given this, one alternative that suggests itself is to introduce NP as a constituent of case, together with a co-constituent—say prep(osition)— realized (in English) as *at, on*, etc. Thus:

(xvii)

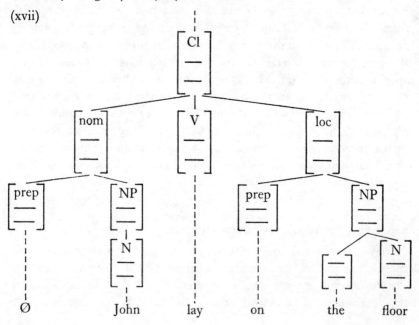

A similar viewpoint (on the relevant aspect of the representation in (xvii)) is adopted by Fillmore (1968a: 32-3).[1] There are at least two related deficiencies in such accounts, despite the fact that the dominating position of nom, loc, etc. with respect to NP comes closer to capturing their 'relational' status. It seems to me misleading, however, to suggest a constituency relationship for, say, loc and NP; loc is not a constitute of which NP is one constituent, but rather it expresses the function which a particular NP has in the clause. Certainly, with regard to representations like (xvii), it can be shown that a particular (many-to-one) sub-type of constituency is involved; but it would still seem to me that the 'relational' character of case is being given only an indirect expression. The inappropriateness of regarding NP as a constituent of case is revealed by the fact that an extra (otherwise unnecessary) category is introduced in (xvii) (as compared with (xv))—namely prep, which, together with NP, will have to be marked as locative, etc., depending on the nature of the dominating case. The two types of categories, case and preposition, are needed only because of the fact that case as a pre-terminal category can be provided with a phonological representation only indirectly, via a terminal category (prep) introduced specifically for this purpose. In this respect, the account underlying (xvi), which introduces cases as terminal categories, is to be preferred—although, as we have seen, it is rather more inadequate in other respects. The crux of the problem is then this: it is to characterize an element which in some sense indicates the functions of NPs with respect to what is denoted by the V but which is nevertheless a terminal category.

2.6 Dependency as an alternative to constituency

I proposed in the paper referred to above (Anderson, forthcoming *a*) (and Fillmore (1968a: 87) mentions such a possibility) that certain at least of these problems are resolved if underlying representations are interpreted in terms of **dependency** (in the sense of, for instance, Hays (1964), Gaifman (1965), Heringer (1967)). Instead of (xvi) and (xvii), in particular, I suggest a representation like that in (xviii):

---

[1] Compare too the relation between (say) adjunct and prepositional phrase allowed for by Halliday (1961)—though the difference is described as not merely one of constituency ('rank'); Fillmore (1968a: 88) also compares the case representations he proposes with tagmemic formulae.

(xviii)

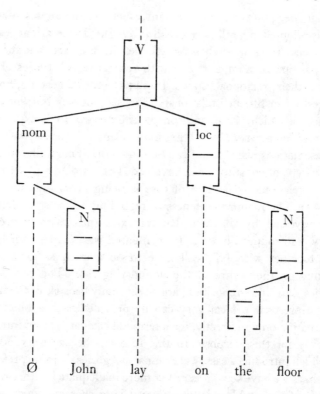

Pre-terminal categories have been eliminated, and in place of the constituency relationship, the categories are 'hierarchized' with respect to dependency. Loc and nom are dependent on V (which thus **governs** them); and they each have dependent on them (i.e. they govern) a N. Thus, the case elements can be interpreted quite naturally as expressing the relation contracted between their dependent Ns and the governing V (which replaces the Cl of the constituency grammar), and they are nevertheless terminal categories.[1] The governing (and 'hyper-rela-

---

[1] The relation of such a proposal to various traditional concepts like 'rection' is briefly discussed in Anderson, forthcoming *a*: particularly notes 4, 5 and 6. Such an interpretation of case also appears to be close to the *kārakas* of the Sanskrit grammarians, or the Greek notion of (oblique) cases as indicating the nature of the noun's dependence on the verb. Cf. particularly, the concepts of 'actant' and 'valence' in Tesnière (1959) and the works referred to by Droescher (1969). Notice, however, that the suggestion of a dependency grammar for this part of the grammar does not necessarily exclude the possibility of constituency elsewhere (e.g. perhaps in the morphology, or in terms of late syntactic rules imposing a surface structure bracketing). I shall not touch on such questions here. My aim is merely to argue that case relations can be given a more natural expression with respect to the notion of dependency.

tional') position of V within the clause can be justified in various ways,
including in particular that as such it will be assigned the clause subcategorization rules—which allow for the various combinations of cases,
among other things—and it would be necessary anyway to subcategorize
verbs with regard to the cases they co-occur with. The following
discussion will provide, I think, further support for this interpretation.
In this way, too, the essentially relational (notional) role of V is con-
trasted with the basically 'thing'-referential N[1] (which governs in underlying representations only by recursion).

I am suggesting then that rules like those in (xv) be replaced by such
rules as are presented schematically in (xix):

(xix) II. i. 1. $V \rightarrow \pm \text{feature}_i$

2. *a.* $+ \text{feature}_i \rightarrow \pm \dots$

b. $- \text{feature}_j \rightarrow \pm \dots$

. . .

ii. 1. $V \rightarrow \text{nom}//\text{—}V$

2. $+ \text{feature}_i \rightarrow \dots$

. . .

iii.   . . .

The rules in ii are dependency rules (DRs) which introduce a dependent
category (or a secondary feature), given the presence of a particular
element in the governing CS—which latter is indicated to the left of the
arrow. The position of the dependent category with respect to its
governor is indicated to the right of the double slashes. In this way,
II. ii. 1 requires the introduction of a dependent nom before a V.[2] Thus,
the rules in (xix) differ from those in (xv) in the substitution of V for Cl
and the replacement of the CRs in II. ii in (xv) by the DRs of (xix).

2.61 N and NP. A further difference between the two accounts is that
N appears in (xviii) in place of NP. The modifiers of N which form

---

[1] Cf.: 'nouns are primary, in the sense that they are linked referentially with "things"
(in the "nuclear" instances)' (Lyons, 1966: 230). It is possible to accommodate this
'referential primacy' of nouns without acceding to Lyons' subsequent argument
concerning the purely surface centrality of the verb. Within the dependency framework outlined here, verbs (or 'predicators') and nouns are 'basic' with regard to
different aspects of the semantic representation. Verbs are central relationally: they
govern the case functions contracted by nouns. Nouns are primary referentially (and
perhaps selectionally—but cf. Seuren, 1969: §3.2.2); they terminate (non-recursive)
dependency trees.

[2] The obvious redundancy of the notation has been introduced in the interests of
clarity to the reader.

within a constituency framework co-constituents of NP with the N are regarded within a dependency account as elements governed by the N. Some arguments against the treatment of the relationship between a N and its modifier(s) as one of co-constituency of a NP are put forward by Lyons (1968 *a*: §§6.3.7, 6.4.3, 7.6.8). He suggests that CRs fail to provide an adequate expression of the notion of endocentricity fundamental to such a construction, just as they are inappropriate to the exocentric type that has been our concern in the immediately preceding discussion.

2.7   Revision of the semantico-syntactic component

Note further that the rule introducing N after each case category (conceived of as a TR in (xv)—rule II. iii. 2) can now be conceived of as a DR of the form presented in (xx):

(xx)   case → N//case—

The rules of the semantico-syntactic component must then be regrouped in four rather than three blocs. Set II is as proposed in (xix), i.e. with the rules for the clause reassigned to V; set IV (previously III—in (xiii)) are the SRs, DRs and TRs for N (previously NP). (I shall however retain the terms 'NP' and 'clause' to refer to whatever is governed by a N and a V, respectively; and I shall employ 'case phrase', etc. in a similar fashion.) Set I accounts for coordination of clauses. Set III includes the DR presented in (xx) and presumably (e.g.) SRs and further DRs (parallel to those in I) to provide for 'NP-conjunction'—since the evidence that at least some superficial instances of such are not derived by a reduction of a sentence-conjunction would appear to be quite strong.[1] Thus more than one N may be associated with each case category, as also there may be more than one clause per sentence.

2.71   Further omissions. I shall not explore here the nature of the

rules or elements appropriate in I, except that I shall assume that the rules are responsible for the introduction of V. I shall thus avoid as much as possible invoking instances displaying coordination of clauses. Sentences involving questions, commands and modals will also be eschewed, in that they introduce a wide range of considerations outside

---

[1] See e.g. McCawley, 1968 *b*: 148–55; Dik, 1968: particularly ch. 5; Hudson, 1969; but cf. Matthews, 1969: 351–6.

our main topic.[1] I shall, for our present purposes, assign questions and commands to the discarded rag-bag of I. Distinctions relating to the further mysteries of tense and aspect will be ignored in what follows. The rules within III and IV will also in the main not be our concern— apart, of course, from the DR in III which introduces N. I want, then, to focus our attention on the SRs, DRs and TRs within II which account for the introduction, interrelation and distribution of the case elements which form the object of the present investigation.

[1] Cf., e.g. Boyd & Thorne, 1969; Ross, 1969; Anderson, 1969*b*.

Part II

NOMINATIVE AND ERGATIVE

3 *Nominative*

3.1 Preliminaries

Let us take as our starting-point the skeleton for II proposed in (xix) in
§2.6. If no further cases are introduced and, of the relevant DRs, only
II. ii. I is operative, then there is generated the structure underlying a
clause like *John died* or *John sneezed*:

(i)

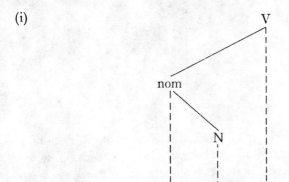

which involves a 'process' with a single 'participant' (cf. Lombard,
1929), which is moreover non-agentive—since there is, for instance, no
normal imperative possibility (*Die, John*) outside specialized contexts—
see further §4.1. This single participant is governed by **nominative**,
which term is used here for a semantic (case) element and is not to be
confused with the label commonly used (as in §1.11) for the subjective
(and predicative) case inflexion in languages like Latin. I am suggesting
that nom is the notionally most neutral case. What is intended by this
will only become clear, I think, as other cases are introduced, and we
shall return to the question of characterizing nom in the following
chapter, where I shall also be proposing that nom is the only obligatory
case, in that the others may be absent from any particular clause: nom is
introduced by a DR with V on the left, the others by one with a
+feature.

3.2   Stative and non-stative

However, before turning to this, I want to note that there is another kind
of clause involving a single 'participant' but not a 'process' but rather
a 'state' or 'quality'—i.e. which has a structure like that in (i) but in
which V is +stative rather than −stative. Such are clauses containing
'adjectives' like *John is dead*. Apparently, we can associate with the
selection of +stative (in English) a DR which introduces a cop(ula).[1]

(ii)

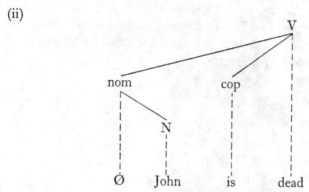

Thus, I am assuming (with the more Aristotelian of the Arabic grammarians) that 'verbs' and 'adjectives' are categorially identical, and
that they differ with respect to the feature ±stative. We shall see below
that, as cases other than nom are taken into account, the situation is
somewhat more complex than this; however, this extension also provides
evidence for categorial identity, in that in particular we shall find
'verbs' and 'adjectives' with parallel combinatorial possibilities with
respect to cases, and entering into (intrinsically) suppletive (see §4.32)
sets.[2]

[1] No copula is necessary in, say, Navaho (Hoijer, 1959: § 6), in which, even superficially,
'adjectives' are clearly a sub-type of V. We shall indeed (as noted below) have
occasion to return to the relation between stativity and the presence of the copula
below (particularly in §§4.81 and 6.42).

[2] They constitute underlying (Aristotelian) *rhémata* (cf. Robins, 1966). See too Harris,
1751: 23–6; Beauzée, 1767: vol. 1, 403; Tooke, 1798–1805; de la Grasserie, 1914*a*:
32–5; the various accounts referred to by Hjelmslev (1928: 14, fn. 2). A somewhat
similar position has been argued for, within more recent terms of reference, by, for
instance, Lakoff, 1965: app. A; Lyons, 1966: 221–3; 1968*a*: §7.6.4; Fillmore, 1968*a*;
Anderson, 1968*a*: 15–18; 1969*c*.

3.3 Fragment of grammar, 1

The rules necessary to allow for the relevant parts of the structures in
(i) and (ii) can perhaps be formulated as in (iii):

(iii) *Fragment of Grammar, 1*
 II. i.   V → ± stative
   ii. 1. V → nom//—V
        2. + stative → cop//—V
 III. ii.   nom → N//nom—

The fact that II. ii. 2 is ordered after II. ii. 1 allows for the fact that cop
immediately precedes V. The difference between (i) and (ii) is attributable to the particular selection made in II. i, such that only in the case of
(ii) is II. ii. 2 operative.

 In the chapter which follows immediately, we shall be looking at the
rules introducing a second case element, representing another kind of
'participant'; this will entail other modifications to the grammar in (iii)
besides mere addition.

4   Ergative

4.1 Preliminaries

At the end of the previous chapter, a fragmentary grammar was proposed (in (iii)) which would allow for clauses containing one case element nom, and which correlated the semantic opposition between stative and non-stative with the distinction between 'adjective' (V preceded by cop) and 'verb' (V without cop). It is now my intention to begin to introduce other case elements, and to examine the viability of the +stative/'adjective' correlation with regard to clauses containing more than one case. This will involve us initially in the present chapter in a consideration of 'transitive' clauses, and in particular of the major subset of these which can be said to contain the case category **ergative**, which introduces the N that is regarded as the initiator of the 'action‑ associated with the V in such clauses.[1]

4.2 Some syntactic correlates

Such (ergative) clauses are those in (iv):

(iv)   *a.* Egbert read the book
      b. Egbert killed the duckling

but not those in (v):

(v)   *a.* Egbert knew the truth
     b. This bag contained the money

I want to suggest that the (superficial) subjects (but not the objects) in the clauses in (iv) represent underlying ergatives, and that neither the subjects nor the objects in (v) are such. Let us consider, in relation to this suggestion, various sorts of phenomena that we can associate with the presence of erg(ative) as opposed to other cases, including in particular nom.

---

[1] Cf. Fillmore's (1966*a*, 1968*a*) 'agentive' (though I would prefer to say that the ergative N is typically rather than necessarily animate).

Notice first of all that the verbs that I am suggesting take (in 'active') clauses) an ergative subject (those in (iv)) also appear in imperative sentences like those in (vi):

(vi) *a.* Read the book!
      b. Kill the duckling!

(where presumably a vocative ergative subject (cf. e.g. Thorne, 1966) has been deleted). Whereas the sentences in (vii):

(vii) *a.* *Know the truth!
       b. *Contain the money!

are somewhat peripheral, at best. (Even if we imagine a human subject for *contain*—*The party contains two psycholinguists*—a 'corresponding' imperative remains anomalous.) Further, 'intransitive' verbs like *sneeze* and *die* also do not permit the ordinary imperative possibility, but must be given special interpretations:

(viii) 1. *a.* Egbert sneezed
           b. Egbert died
        2. *a.* *Sneeze!
           b. *Die!

I am suggesting that such restrictions are related to whether or not the subject with the verbs is ergative; only *read* and *kill* take an erg as subject. Another difference between the verbs in (iv) and those in (v) concerns compatibility with 'progressive aspect': *know* and *contain*, like 'adjectives', do not normally appear in 'progressive' clauses,[1] and therefore are usually termed 'stative verbs' (cf. e.g. Godel, 1950). Thus:

(ix) 1. *a.* Egbert is reading the book
         b. Egbert is killing the duckling
      2. *a.* *Egbert is knowing the truth
         b. *This bag is containing the money

In this instance, the 'intransitive' are like the 'ergative' verbs:

(x) *a.* Egbert is sneezing
     b. Egbert is dying

And this is also true with respect to certain of the question–answer

---

[1] Cf. e.g. Goyvaerts, 1968; Allen, 1966: apps.; and the works referred to therein.

restrictions exemplified in (xi)—since, once again, all the questions demand 'non-stative' answers:

(xi) 1. What did Egbert do?
- a. He killed the duckling
- b. *He died
- c. *He knew the truth

2. What happened to Egbert?
- a. *He killed the duckling
- b. He died
- c. *He knew the truth

3. What happened?
- a. Egbert killed the duckling
- b. Egbert died
- c. *Egbert knew the truth

It seems to me that the type of verb exemplified by *know* emerges as distinctive enough to warrant detailed separate study of its syntax; and I shall be suggesting below (in chapter 6) that the character of this is connected with the presence (in associated underlying representations) of a particular case element. Such a three-way distinction, and its connexion with aspect, etc., has long been recognized; Velten (1931), for instance, attempts to trace Indo-European aspectual distinctions to an earlier three-term classification of verbs—into those expressing 'physical or mental states' (*hate*) those representing 'transition between states' (*die*) and those representing 'action proper' ('caused by the volition of the subject'—*seize*). However, having established their distinctiveness, I want for the moment to lay aside clauses involving the 'stative' verbs,[1] and to examine in more detail phenomena connected with the other types of clause, which show an interesting overlap in the restrictions we have surveyed, and, as I shall suggest, other interrelations.

4.3 Ergative and nominative

Thus, *die* and *kill* clauses have in common compatibility with 'progressive aspect' and appropriateness as answers to questions like that in (xi. 3). They differ in that an imperative is unusual with *die* and that such a verb is inappropriate in the answer to (xi. 1). We can associate these differences with the character of the subject—ergative with *kill*, nominative with *die*. This also accounts for the distinction in acceptabi-

---

[1] I shall also neglect for the moment (but see §11.6) any examination of the nature of question clauses like those in (xi). Their function in this and the following chapter will be merely 'diagnostic'.

lity with regard to the answers in (xi. 2). But notice that both of the answers in (xii) are appropriate:

(xii)   What happened to the duckling? $\begin{cases} a. \text{ It died} \\ b. \text{ Egbert killed it} \end{cases}$

as also is (xiii):

(xiii)   It was killed (by Egbert)

That is, the object in the active transitive clause and the subject in the passive appear to 'behave' in this respect like the subject in the intransitive clause. The semantic parallel is clear: in each case the referent of the N involved 'undergoes' the 'process' denoted by the V—as opposed to the subject of the active clause, which (as ergative) is the initiator of the 'process'—which indeed 'converts' the 'process' into an 'action'.[1] Accordingly, it seems reasonable to regard all these non-ergative Ns as sharing a case function—viz. nom. We might represent the (appropriate parts of the) structures underlying (xii. *b*) and (xiii) as in (xiv. *a*) and (xiv. *b*), respectively:

(xiv) *a.*

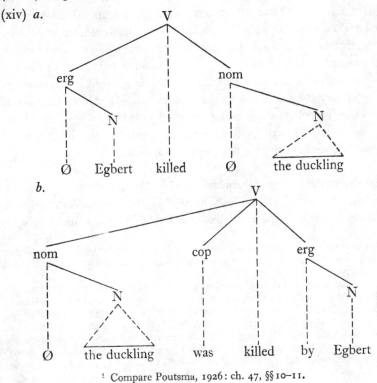

---

[1] Compare Poutsma, 1926: ch. 47, §§ 10–11.

Whereas nom both before and after V (as subject or object) has no phonological representation, we find the preposition *by* as the marker of erg in those instances where it has not been converted into the subject ('subjectivized').

4.31 Some remarks on the formation of subjects and objects. We shall not be concerned here with the details of subject- and object-forming, except with regard to questions of sequence; it may be that for English something like Fillmore's (1968 *a*: §3.5) rules for deleting the subject and object prepositions (and subjoining the relevant N directly to V) are involved. However this may be, I shall regard the functions 'subject-of' and 'object-of' as 'neutralized relations' (Hofmann, 1968: 35), in that the nominals which come to contract these functions have diverse underlying case relations.[1] Such a notion of 'subject' and 'object' is closer to Chomsky's 'surface subject' and 'object' than to their deep equivalents (where these are distinct), which latter have not been shown to have any systematic status. However, I shall for the moment assume that the rules placing case phrases in subject-position (e.g. (xvii) below) operate within II, i.e. before the development of NPs (see further below); and I shall not deal here in any systematic fashion with phenomena connected with what Halliday (1967: §4) calls the 'information structure' of the clause and Fillmore (1968 *a*: 57) refers to as 'secondary topicalization' ('subjectivalization', which in general determines verbal concord, being regarded as 'primary')—i.e. particularly 'superficial' variations in 'word order', and presumably 'clefting' and intonational markers with a similar function.[2]

4.32 Ergative and non-ergative verbs. We have been discussing latterly a 'transitive' and an 'intransitive' verb (*kill* and *die*) which one could regard as a quasi-suppletive set: *kill* differs from *die* only with

---

[1] Hofmann (1968: 52) associates the formation of subjects with the provision, within embedded sentences, of a 'slot from which things are deleted and into which they can be reconstructed'.

[2] Cf. the distinctions discussed in terms of different kinds of 'subject' in the tradition represented by, e.g. Paul, 1886: ch. 16; von der Gabelentz, 1891: 348–57; Wundt, 1900: ch. 7, §3; or, more recently, accounts like those in Bolinger, 1952; Hatcher, 1956; Koch, 1965; Uhlířová, 1966; Halliday, 1967: §4; Lyons, 1968 *a*: §8.1.2; Kirkwood, 1969; Chomsky, 1969 *b*; and the numerous works initiated by Mathesius concerned with 'functional sentence perspective'—e.g. Mathesius, 1929, 1964; Daneš & Vachek, 1964: 22; Firbas, 1964; Daneš, 1964; Sgall, 1967; etc. For earlier studies, see e.g. the references in Hjelmslev, 1928: §30.

respect to a feature like, say '+ ergative'. And if we differentiate between those features of the verb which merely serve to introduce other elements like cases (and thus to subcategorize V with respect to these) and those features which are **intrinsic** to the verb (cf. Fillmore's (1968*c*) distinction between 'basic sense' and 'arguments'), then we can say that *kill* and *die* are intrinsically the same (or intrinsically suppletive). In many cases, we find a single item with a distribution equal to that of *kill* and *die*—as *open, move, grow*, etc. On the other hand, there appear to be 'ergative verbs' with no 'non-ergative' equivalent, and vice versa: perhaps *read* and *sneeze* are (respectively) examples of such. However, we can plausibly interpret *read* as like *kill* and *sneeze* as like *die* in the set of cases they require—though it should be noted that examples with *read* which would form natural answers in (xii) and (xiii) are difficult to find. We shall indeed have to return below to an examination of the nature of the distinction between verbs like *read* and verbs like *kill* of which this restriction is a reflexion.

4.33   Rules for ergatives. Let us add then to the rules proposed in (iii) in §3.3 a subcategorization rule of the form of (xv):

(xv)   II. i.   V → ± ergative

which serves to differentiate between clauses containing *die* and *sneeze* (− ergative) and those with *kill* and *read* (+ ergative). It is necessary now to consider the associated dependency rule, and also the character of the distinction between 'actives' and 'passives'—as represented in (xiv). We need to introduce into the grammar a dependency rule which inserts erg appropriately. Erg, however, appears both before the V (in 'active' clauses) and after it (in 'passives'). Nom, conversely, is subject in 'passive' and object in 'active' clauses. And it is also subject in clauses in which erg does not appear—as *He died*. It seems best in such circumstances to leave rule II.ii.1 (in (iii) in §3.3) as it is—i.e. introducing nom preverbally—and to propose a rule introducing erg post-verbally, with a subsequent (permutation) rule 'switching' nom and erg in active clauses. So:

(xvi)   II. ii. 1. *a.*   V → nom//—V
           b.   + ergative → erg//V—

The structure represented in (xiv. *a*) is the result of the subsequent permutation; (xiv. *b*) is unpermuted.

4.4 Ergative clauses

4.41 'Actives' and 'passives'. Despite the arguments for post-verbal introduction of erg, it seems to me that the sequence in (xiv. *a*) is in some sense less 'marked' than that in (xiv. *b*)—and most past treatments of 'passives' have indeed interpreted them as more complex than the corresponding 'active' clause (see e.g. Katz & Postal, 1964: §4.2.1). This suggests that if we maintain (for the above reasons) that the underlying sequence is as in (xiv. *b*), then the permutation rule ought to be so formulated as to operate unless certain conditions are met: non-operation of the permutation should emerge as the marked possibility. And this is supported by certain further considerations concerning the structure represented in (xiv. *b*). Notice in particular that (xiv. *b*) is also superficially more complex in containing cop (which is lacking in (xiv. *a*)). Perhaps then we can associate the operation of the permutation with the absence of cop, such that the rule could be formulated as in (xvii):

(xvii) $\text{nom} + \alpha + V + \text{erg} \rightarrow \text{erg} + \alpha + V + \text{nom}$
$$\text{CONDITION}: \alpha \neq \beta + \text{cop} + \gamma$$

(α, β, ... are variables over any (including the null) subsequence). The condition requires the operation of the rule unless cop has been introduced. I shall assume that the rule in (xvii) belongs to II. iii, i.e. precedes the rules for N, though the evidence so far presented for this is perhaps not very strong (though the development of subjects and objects appears to be presupposed by the rules allowing for different kinds of embedding (see Reich, 1969)—and otherwise cf. Anderson, 1968*a*: 19–21).

Observe that this rule in (xvii), despite the intention of (xvii), suggests a post-verbal position as 'neutral' for erg, a decision which (in itself) it would be difficult to motivate. An alternative is to introduce erg pre-verbally. However, if a pre-verbal position is retained for nom, we would then have to substitute two (albeit simpler) rules for that in (xvii), one to postpose nom in actives, the other erg in passives. Moreover, how is the relative underlying (pre-verbal) sequence of erg and nom to be selected in a non-arbitrary fashion? This sort of dilemma can be resolved in terms of the proposals made in Part IV.

4.42 The status of cop. The representation in (xiv. *b*) embodies another claim which we shall have to discuss at this point. Both the *be* which appears in 'passive' clauses (like (xiv. *b*)) and the one which appears before 'adjectives' (cf. §3.2 (ii)) are interpreted as representing a single category, cop. In view of the considerable parallelism with respect to superficial syntactic 'behaviour' between them (see Anderson, 1968 a: 14–16), and despite one traditional preference (which e.g. Lees (1960: 6, 34) incorporates) for deriving the two instances of *be* in rather different fashions, this seems just; and it enables us to avoid suggesting that the occurrence of *be* in both these environments is merely 'accidental'. However, it is necessary then to investigate whether this represents a deeper (semantic) parallelism, in that, in particular, a single subcategorization selection underlies the presence or absence of cop. I want to suggest that this is indeed the case and that cop is in both cases introduced by rule II. ii. 2 in (iii) in §3.3, which inserts cop before a +stative V. I shall propose further below (in §6.3) that other instances of *be* (as in *John was in the garden*) are also related to +stative (and it could be argued that the derivation of 'progressive aspect' involves a sub-type of such (locative) clauses). Thus, ±stative is simultaneous with ±ergative:

$$(\text{xviii}) \quad \text{II. i.} \quad V \rightarrow \begin{bmatrix} \pm \text{ergative} \\ \pm \text{stative} \end{bmatrix}$$

4.43 'Long' and 'short passives'.

Despite the above interpretation of cop, it is clear that only the 'short form' of passive clauses can have a semantically 'stative' interpretation—and this is true of only some of these. Thus, a clause like (xix. *a*), containing a 'short passive':

(xix) *a.* The lights were dipped
       b. The lights were dipped by the oncoming driver

is (as has often been noted in the past—see e.g. Kruisinga, 1931: 38–40; Hasegawa, 1968: §3) ambiguous between 'stative' and 'non-stative', whereas the 'long passive' (xix. *b*) is unambiguously 'non-stative'. Only the 'non-stative' version has a corresponding 'progressive':

(xx) The lights were being dipped (by the oncoming driver)

Compare here the distinction drawn by Chanidze, with respect to Georgian, between 'static' and 'non-static' passives (Lafon, 1963), the former being limited, as (less markedly) in English, to certain verbs. I suggest that the 'non-stative' version of (xix. *a*) involves a deleted ergative phrase, and that the 'stative' one is like a simple 'adjectival'

clause in lacking such. The two structures can be represented as in
(xxi)—the *a* instance being 'stative' and the *b* 'non-stative':

(xxi) *a.*

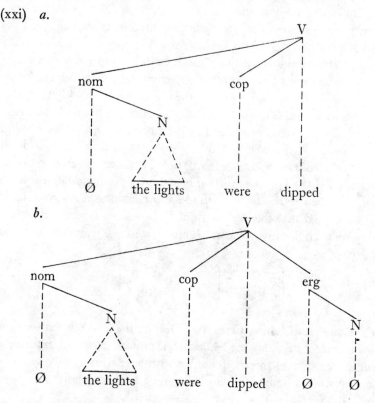

b.

Henceforth, I shall regard instances like (xxi. *b*) as shortened forms of
'long passives'; only examples like (xxi. *a*) will be referred to as 'short
passives'. It would seem then that if we are to maintain the position
that the introduction of cop is always related to +stative, we must allow
for the 'stative' character of +stative to be 'overruled' by co-selection
of +ergative: only when erg is absent is a clause containing cop
semantically 'stative'.[1] And we shall see below that we appear to have
to allow for this anyway in the case of certain 'adjectives'.

[1] This notion of 'over-ruling' can perhaps be supported with respect to a concept of
hierarchy for semantic elements like that proposed (Lass, 1969) for the phonetic
features. It would also seem that if the 'stative' character of +stative is 'over-ruled',
then it becomes available as a 'topicalizing' feature permitting subject position to
nom in ergative clauses. However, this looks like a statement of a diachronic rather
than a synchronic process; and it thus perhaps suggests an inadequacy in the present
account.

4.5   Reflexive ergative clauses

If such a position is accepted, then (the relevant aspects of) both 'active' and 'passive' ergative clauses are allowed for by adding the rules in (xv) (as part of II. i), II. ii. I. *b* in (xvi) and (xvii) to those proposed in (iii) in §3.3. However, we must now take account of the fact that there are 'intransitive' clauses which nevertheless appear to partake of certain of the characteristics of 'transitive' clauses with ergative subjects. Compare with the examples in (vii) and (xi) those in (xxii):

(xxii)   I. *a.* Work!
        b. Leave!

2.   What did Egbert do? $\begin{cases} a. \text{ He worked (harder)} \\ b. \text{ He left} \end{cases}$

(Cf. too *Egbert is working, Egbert is leaving*.)

I propose that these be allowed for by introducing a rule which attaches erg to nom in such cases, producing structures like that in (xxiii):

(xxiii)

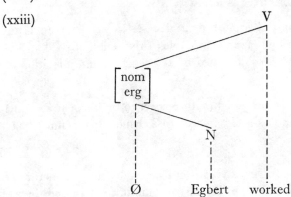

Ergative clauses can thus be either **reflexive** or non-reflexive: if they are reflexive, then erg is attached (as in (xxiii)) to nom; if they are non-reflexive, it is introduced as a separate category (as in the ergative clauses we looked at above—see particularly (xiv) and (xxi. *b*)). Thus, (xxiv. *a*) is reflexive, and (xxiv. *b*) is not:

(xxiv)   *a.* Egbert moved
        b. Egbert moved the couch

(Clauses with *move* can also, of course, be −ergative.) *Egbert moved himself* is a non-reflexive ergative clause which contains a reflexive nominative N. That is, I am distinguishing between clausal and phrasal reflexives. This enables us to reflect the fact that in reflexive ergative clauses the agent 'operates' in some sense upon itself, without our having to suggest that all such clauses contain deleted (reflexive) nominative NPs.[1] This latter proposal might be appropriate in the case of (xxiv. *a*)—though it would leave unexplained the difference between this and the clause with overt reflexive pronoun—but appears to be much less plausible in the case of, say, *work* or *leave*. A clause like *Egbert worked himself hard* is indeed semantically very unlike the clause in (xxiii).[2] We shall return to a proposal for an explanation of this below.

4.51   The unique status of nom. Such considerations underlie the adoption of the proposal embodied in (xxiii) rather than an alternative one in which nom would be absent from such clauses (cf. Fillmore, 1968 *a*: particularly §3). Nom is thus universally present (as implied by rule II. i. 1. *a*). It is clear anyway that nom (cf. Fillmore's 'objective') is rather unlike the other cases in other respects also. Fillmore (1968 *a*: 25) describes the 'objective' as follows:

(xxv)   ...the semantically most neutral case, the case of anything representable by a noun whose role in the action or state identified by the verb is identified by the semantic interpretation of the verb...

This uniqueness is characterized (with respect to the present account) in terms of the unique status of nom as a case element that is universally present in the clause.[3]

4.52   Revised rules for ergatives. Let us consider now the nature of the rules necessary to allow for the distribution of nom and erg in the

---

[1] Cf. Huddleston, 1969; and, for further examples, see Vendryes, 1932.

[2] See further Anderson, 1968 *a*: *postscript*.

[3] One possible kind of exception is represented by *It's hot in this room*, with an 'expletive' subject—cf. *This room is hot*, with locative subject. If this analysis is accepted, then apparently nom is optional (in locative clauses, at least). However, it may rather be that the subject in the former sentence represents an underlying (though perhaps 'empty') nom (i.e. it has a structure like (in this respect) that for *The temperature is high in this room*), whereas the nom of the latter has been deleted and the loc subjectivized. So too 'weather' clauses—cf. Postal, 1966 *b*: 98, fn. 8. Notice too that these present less of a problem if loc and nom are identified (§11.6). However, it may indeed rather be that we should allow for clauses which contain only either nom or loc; this would not be unnatural in terms of the relationship (between nom and loc) suggested in Part V, particularly §12.3.

manner I have suggested. Nom is already adequately allowed for. The requirement is to provide for erg to be introduced both as a separate category and as a feature on nom. I propose in this connexion the following rules, involving the notion 'clause reflexive':

(xxvi)   II. i. 2.   +ergative → ±reflexive

$$\text{ii. 2. } b. \quad +\text{ergative} \rightarrow \text{erg}// \left\{ \begin{bmatrix} \text{nom} \\ \overline{} \\ \text{V}\text{—} \end{bmatrix} \Big/ \begin{bmatrix} \overline{} \\ +\text{reflexive} \end{bmatrix} \right\}$$

In terms of (xxvi), ergative clauses (like certain NPs) can be +reflexive or −reflexive. If they are +reflexive then erg is added to nom; if not, then it appears as a separate category after V. In rule II. II. 2. *b* in (xxvi) we thus have two sorts of environment indicated: '$\begin{bmatrix} \text{nom} \\ \overline{} \end{bmatrix}$' and 'V—' indicate the (alternative) environments into which erg is introduced; '$\begin{bmatrix} \overline{} \\ +\text{reflexive} \end{bmatrix}$' is a 'left-hand side' environment—it indicates the context for +ergative in which erg is added to nom. '+reflexive' does not appear itself on the left of a DR; its function in such is to allow for alternative placements of erg. These rules provide for 'clause reflexives'. Further rules for N involving ±reflexive will allow for 'phrasal reflexives'. Rule II. ii. 2. *b* in (xxvi) is a revised version of rule II. ii. I. *b* in (xvi). The re-ordering (from ii. I to ii. 2) is necessary because 'nom' has now been introduced into the rule as an environment, and thus must have been already inserted (by II. ii. I). These additions to the grammar will provide for the structure in (xxiii) suggested for *Egbert worked*. We must consider rule II. i. 2 more closely below, in particular with respect to whether it operates independently of whether the V is +stative or −stative. For the moment, I want to consider how the distribution of erg and nom is reflected inflexionally in various languages.

4.6   The morphological representation of erg and nom in various languages

We have allowed within our rules for three possible combinations of the cases nom and erg: nom appears alone; nom and erg form co-components of a single CS; nom and erg occur as separate categories. Different aspects of these combinations appear to be relevant to determining the shape of the surface markers of the cases and the nature of verbal concord in different languages.

4.61 'Ergative languages'

Thus, in Basque and other so-called 'ergative languages', erg as category has a distinct shape from nom (whether with erg attached or not), and verbal person–number concord also operates on this basis. Consider the following examples, adapted from Lafitte, 1962:

(xxvii) 1. Gizonak ogia jan du ('The man has eaten some bread')
       2. *a.* Gizona ethorri da ('The man has come')
          b. Ogia ona da ('The bread is good')

Here the -*k* suffixed to *gizona* in (xxvii. 1) is the marker of the ergative category; the other instances of nominals (*ogia* in 1 and 2. *b*, *gizona* in 2. *a*), as nominatives, lack the -*k*. On verbal concord, which shows a similar distinction, see e.g. Martinet, 1958; Anderson, 1968*a*: 9–10. A similar situation is attested in a number of other languages, including (to take something of a geographical sample) Tibetan, Eskimo, Samoan and Chinook.[1] Various scholars indicate the further relation between the ergative marker and (one type of) the 'genitive'—a connexion we shall be unable to explore here.[2]

4.62 'Active languages'

The labels 'ergative' and 'nominative' are usually used with respect to such an inflectional (and concord) system; alternative terms are 'actif'/ 'nominatif' (Lafitte, 1962), 'agens'/'patiens' (Troubetzkoy, 1929), 'casus activus' (or 'transitivus')/'casus passivus' (or 'intransitivus') (Jespersen, 1924: 166), 'casus energeticus'/'casus inertiae' (Uhlenbeck, 1916*a*). However, Uhlenbeck's distinction represents a conflation of the sort of system we have been discussing so far and another in which any case CS containing erg, whether as category or feature, is represented

---

[1] For examples and discussion, see for instance Matthews, 1953:404–5; Lyons, 1968*a*: §8.2; on Tibetan, etc., Maspero, 1947–8; on Eskimo, Pott, 1873: 89–94; Jespersen, 1924: 166; Finck, 1930: §3; Thalbitzer, 1930; Velten, 1932*b*: 217–21; Erichsen, 1944; Hill, 1958: App. A, §8; on Chinook, Boas, 1911: §§15, 16 and 18; on Basque, Uhlenbeck, 1907*a*; 1949; Lafon, 1960; Martinet, 1962*b*. On the Caucasian group, see Čikobava, 1969, and the works referred to therein. See too the examples and references in Anderson, 1968*a*: 11, fn. 12.

[2] See, however, de la Grasserie, 1890: 12–13, 65–6; 1901: 1–13; 1914*a*: 34–45; Schuchardt, 1921; Lewy, 1928; on Eskimo, Hammerich, 1951; Sauvageot, 1953; Schmitt, 1956; on Tibetan, Eskimo and Indo-European, Hammerich, 1956 (see too Jespersen, 1924: 166); on Indo-European, van Wijk, 1902; on Basque, Naert, 1956. Cf. too discussions like Müller, 1876: particularly 123–5; Winkler, 1889: 96–100; these are concerned with the development of the so-called 'objective' conjugation (cf. p. 67, n. 1).

differently from nom (without erg attached)—as appears to be the case in Dakota, for instance.[1] Consider the Dakota examples in (xxviii) (taken from Boas & Swanton, 1911):

(xxviii) 1. *a.* oma'hiⁿħpa'ya ('I fall into'—Teton Dialect)
       b. maya'k'te ('You (*sg.*) kill me'—Santee dialect)
    2. *a.* ćowapa ('I wade'—Santee)
       b. wakaksa ('I cut off'—Santee)

in which *ma* in 1 represents the first person 'inactive' (Boas & Swanton's 'objective' form), and the *wa* in 2 the first person 'active' (Boas & Swanton's 'subjective'). ('Stative' verbs take the 'objective' form: *maśi'ca* ('I am bad').)

4.63 Other possibilities. Other possible relationships between (particularly pronominal) inflexional distinctions and underlying cases are noted (with respect to various Amerindian languages) by Sapir (1916*a*: particularly 86) and, following him, Fillmore (1968*a*: §4.1). For instance, there are languages like Takelma in which the nom in 'intransitive' clauses (with erg attached or not) is represented differently from both erg and nom in 'transitive' clauses, which are in turn distinct from each other. Thus, for example, we find in Takelma (according to Sapir, 1922: 284) the following distinct first person singular aorist forms:[2]

(xxix) 'intransitive': $-t'e^\varepsilon$
    'subjective transitive': $-(a')^\varepsilon n$
    'objective transitive': $-xi$ ('subject' in 'passives')

Clearly, in other languages (like Yana) there are no nominal inflexional distinctions attributable to the distribution of nom and erg, or even more superficial case distinctions. In yet others, the determining factors are rather the distribution into subject and object: in English, for instance, there is a separate pronominal form (in most instances) for subjects from that we find elsewhere (with the possible exception of predicatives), and verbal concord presupposes this division. I.e. pronominal morphology is determined after and with respect to the results of subjectivization.

---

[1] And Sapir (1917*a*) takes Uhlenbeck (1916*a*) to task for conflating the two distinctions in pursuit of his—and Uslar's and Schuchardt's (cf. e.g. 1905–6)—'passive nature of the transitive verb' hypothesis. On this cf. Fillmore, 1968*a*: §4.4.

[2] For discussion and full exemplification, see Sapir, 1922: §§59–67.

4.64 Co-existent morphological systems. English also reveals that more than one inflexional system may co-exist in a single language, in that no such distinction is drawn between non-pronominal subjects and objects. In Navaho (see Hoijer, 1964: 147–8), the pronominal prefixes to the verb are distinguished as subjective or objective, whereas the verb classification system operates with respect to the nominative N, whether subject (in intransitive clauses) or object (in transitive). Sapir (1916*a*: 84–5) comments on co-existing inflexional systems within various other Amerindian languages. And certain of the Caucasian languages (e.g. Georgian) show an alternation between a subject–object system and an ergative–nominative one, in accordance with 'tense' differences.[1] Consider the following Georgian examples cited by Sommerfelt (1937: 183):

(xxx)   *a.* Ķaci h-ķlav-s megobar-s ('The man kills his friend')
        b. Ķac-ma mo-ķla megobari ('The man killed his friend')

In the present tense (*a*), *ķaci* ('the man') is in the 'nominative' and 'his friend' in the 'dative'/'accusative'; in the aorist (*b*), *megobari* ('the friend') is in the 'nominative' and 'the man' is what Vogt, for instance, refers to as the 'narrative' and what others have called the 'ergative' (though verbal concord operates as for (*a*)).[2] It has also been suggested[3] that although Indo-European, as usually reconstructed, shows a subject–object inflexional system, there are signs (e.g. in the system of gender) that at an earlier period the inflexions may have been (in the relevant respect) more Basque-like. (However, 'ergative constructions' in various of the Indo-European dialects seem to be attributable to the influence of other languages[4]—in those cases where indeed it is reasonable to interpret the phenomena involved as such.)

In sum, the relationship between the underlying distribution of nom and erg and surface inflexional distinctions, verbal concord, etc. is a

---

[1] See e.g. Schuchardt, 1896; Sommerfelt, 1937; Tagliavini, 1937; Vogt, 1938.
[2] The further alternation in Georgian, whereby, in the perfect, 'the man' would be in the 'dative' and 'the friend' in the 'nominative', is relateable to the derivation of such 'tenses' from underlying locative clauses—see chapter 7, and cf. e.g. Meillet, 1924; Finck, 1930: §9; Benveniste, 1952; Allen, 1964; Lyons, 1968*a*: §8.4.6; for a convenient summary, see Lafon, 1963. On 'affective' verbs, which show a rather different distribution of case inflexions, see §§7.1–7.2.
[3] Though still controversially—cf. e.g. Uhlenbeck, 1901, 1907*b*; Finck, 1907; Velten, 1932*a*: 268, 1932*b*: 218–22; Vaillant, 1936; Lehmann, 1958: 190. For a concise account, see Martinet, 1962*a*: 149–54.
[4] Cf. Pedersen, 1906; Zubatý, 1906; Velten, 1932*b*; Matthews, 1953; Laroche, 1962; Benveniste, 1962.

complex one. And there are further complications of a somewhat different nature from those we have been considering. In Basque, for instance, it is not merely underlying ergs that are represented by the -*k* inflexion but also underlying animate locatives (datives) that have at some stage been converted into ergs (just as different cases may be subjectivized).[1] The surface inflexional reflexion of nom and erg is thus usually interconnected in various ways with that of other cases (particularly the dative) as well as with (and often as a result of) the process of subjectivization and objectivization, the 'neutralizing' effect of which was mentioned above. Systems of inflexion and concord accordingly provide only rather indirect indications of the underlying distribution of cases, though clearly we must require of a theory of case relations that, together with certain other relevant considerations, it should enable us to account for such systems in a natural way. It seems to me that, although we have not explored this explicitly, the account I have outlined above (in §§4.1–4.5) will in principle allow for the sorts of variation in inflexional systems that we have briefly surveyed (in §4.6).

4.7 Stative reflexive ergative clauses

I have argued for the introduction of rule II. i. 2 in (xxvi) in §4.52 (distinguishing between reflexive and non-reflexive ergative clauses) with regard to −stative clauses. We must investigate whether the rule must be so restricted (i.e. to $\begin{bmatrix} +\text{ergative} \\ -\text{stative} \end{bmatrix}$ clauses) or whether it is appropriate to +stative clauses also. We have associated 'adjectives' (if we include the 'verb' in 'short passives' (xix. *a*)) with the selection of +stative and −ergative; and this underlies the absence (under the normal interpretation) of 'progressive aspect' with items like *dead*, as compared with *die* or *work*:

(xxxi) *He was being dead

Notice however that certain 'adjectives' do permit normal 'progressive' forms—as in (xxxii. *b*):

(xxxii) *a*. Egbert was cautious
       b. Egbert was being cautious

How are we to account for this? The clauses in (xxxii) still contain the *be* we have associated with +stative, yet notionally and syntactically they

---

[1] Cf. Anderson, 1969*c*: fn. 5; and §§7.23, 7.25 and 11.44 below.

are 'non-stative'. But notice that we have already encountered such a situation in the case of 'long passives'. They contain cop (introduced as a result of the selection of + stative in rule II. i in (iii) in §3.3), and they also are nevertheless notionally and syntactically 'non-stative'. We associated this in their case with the co-selection of + ergative (which 'over-rules' + stative in these latter respects—though not blocking the introduction of cop). This suggests that erg is also present in clauses like those in (xxxii), and is presumably attached to nom: the clause is + reflexive. That is, we can account for such clauses by an extension of rule II. i. 2 in (xxvi) (in §4.52) to + stative clauses. It can remain in the more general form it is stated in there, and need not be limited by adding − stative to the left-hand-side specification:

(xxvi)   II. i. 2.   + ergative → ± reflexive.

Accordingly the relevant structure underlying (xxxii. *a*) can be represented as in (xxxiii):

(xxxiii)

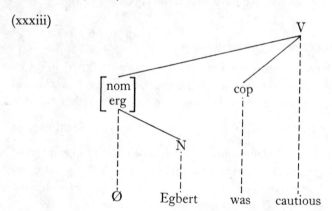

This interpretation is supported by the fact that we find such adjectives in imperative clauses:

(xxxiv)   Be cautious!

which again suggests that they have an ergative subject. Note too that *He was cautious* is appropriate as an answer to both *What did Egbert do?* and *What was Egbert like?* Certain adjectives (*curious, suspicious*) can be ambiguous between a 'stative' and a 'non-stative' interpretation—i.e. (in terms of the present proposal) with respect to whether erg is present or not—as in *He is a suspicious old man.*[1] Thus, *Egbert killed the duckling* is −reflexive and −stative, *The duckling was killed by Egbert* −reflexive and +stative, *Egbert worked* +reflexive and −stative, and *Egbert was cautious* +reflexive and +stative. They are all +ergative.

4.8   Oblique stative ergative clauses

However, consider now the pair in (xxxv):

(xxxv)   *a.* Egbert was careful with the vase
        b. Egbert was being careful with the vase

These are notionally and syntactically 'non-stative', and once more nevertheless contain the cop introduced as a result of the selection of +stative. Notice too the imperative possibility represented in (xxxvi):

(xxxvi)   Be careful with the vase!

Once again it would appear that the subject in such a clause is ergative. Indeed, it seems not unreasonable to regard (xxxv) as the 'transitive' equivalents of (xxxii): compare the 'intransitive use' in *Be careful!* That is, the structure underlying (xxxv. *a*) might be represented as in (xxxvii):

(xxxvii)

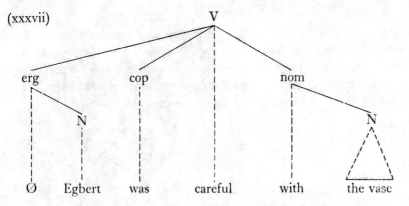

---

[1] Observe however that a clause like *Joe is being sick* (in British English) appears not to be accountable for in this way: **Be sick.* But this is idiosyncratic in other ways, in that (in particular) the notional relation between *Joe is being sick* and *Joe is sick* is not simply that of 'progressive' to 'non-progressive' (however this is characterized). There are further exceptions to the association of 'non-stative' copular clauses with the presence of erg if one has to allow for 'pseudo-passives' (Mihailović, 1967) as distinctive.

(in which post-'adjectival' (as opposed to post-'verbal') nom has not been objectivized and is represented as *with* (cf. Fillmore, 1966*a*)). But let us reflect on the consequences of adopting the structure in (xxxvii) as appropriate for (xxxv. *a*). Presumably the clause is +ergative (to account for the presence of erg), −reflexive (erg is not attached to nom) and +stative (cop has been introduced). But this is precisely the specification for 'long passives'. Yet clauses like (xxxv. *a*) differ from 'long passives' in the items that manifest V, and in particular in the relative sequence of erg and nom. It would appear that in (xxxv) something like rule (xvii), which permutes nom and erg, has operated; however, the condition for the operation of (xvii) is not met, in that cop is present before the verb. Presumably, whatever it is in the specification underlying (xxxv. *a*) that differentiates it from a 'long passive' is also associated with the sequence of nom and erg in (xxxvii).

These facts can be accounted for in terms of a modification to the rules which will receive further support in Part III. I suggest that +stative does not introduce cop directly, but rather adds to a case element a feature, stat. Cop is then introduced before V only when the subject case is marked as stat.[1] Further, rule (xvii) will be reformulated to operate unless the CS containing nom also contains stat—so:

(xxxviii)   nom + V + erg → erg + V + nom
             CONDITION: stat ∉ [nom]

(where the condition is to be interpreted as stating that the rule is operative unless stat is included in the same CS as the nom in the structure index on the left of the arrow). To exploit this, I am proposing that the structures underlying a 'long passive' and a clause like (xxxv. *a*) can be represented as in (xxxix. *a*) and (xxxix. *b*) respectively:

(xxxix)   *a.*   *b.*

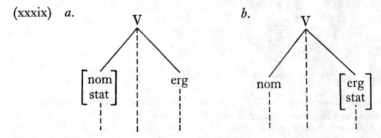

---

[1] We shall find in chapter 6 instances where a clause though +stative, nevertheless does not contain cop; and I shall associate this with the post-verbal position of the case which has stat attached.

Thus, in the case of the 'long passive' ((xxxix. *a*)) the condition for rule (xxxviii) is not met, and no permutation takes place; whereas in (xxxix. *b*), in which stat is attached to erg rather than nom, the condition is met, and the sequence represented in (xxxvii) results.

4.81 The revised status of cop. What is required now is a rule introducing cop after a subject case which is marked as stat. If we order this rule after (xxxviii) then in both the 'long passive' and the 'transitive adjective' instances cop will (correctly) be introduced. We can number rule (xxxvii) as II. iii. 1; and the rule introducing cop will be II. iii. 2:

(xl)   II. iii. 2.   stat + V → stat + cop + V

(I.e. any subject case CS containing stat will have cop introduced after it.) As I have mentioned, further instances supporting such a (more devious) interpretation of the introduction of cop will be discussed in §6. However, it is worth indicating at this point that the fact that cop is introduced only 'indirectly', via a TR dependent on pre-verbal stat, is perhaps in itself a pleasing consequence, since clearly the introduction of cop in such sentences is not a universal feature of language. (Consider those languages (like Japanese or Navaho) in which there is no distinction of this sort between 'adjectival' and (active) 'verbal' clauses.) Therefore, it seems appropriate that cop is not introduced directly in the semantic subcomponent (whose degree of universality is thus enhanced) but as a consequence of the operation of various TRs. In terms of these proposals, 'adjectives' in English are that sub-class of V which appears after cop in the absence of a following erg; this includes those items that occur in 'short passives'.

4.82 Revised rules for stativity. It remains to allow for the distribution of stat as a feature either on erg or nom. This can be accomplished by rules analogous to those providing for the placement of erg. In clauses which are − reflexive and + stative, there are two places in which stat can appear: I shall introduce a feature ± **oblique** which determines this. So:

(xli)   II. i. 3. $\begin{bmatrix} -\text{reflexive} \\ +\text{stative} \end{bmatrix}$ → ± oblique

(which must be ordered, as indicated, after the rule involving ± reflexive). The relevant DR can be formulated as in (xlii):

(xlii)   II. ii. 3. $+\text{stative} \rightarrow \text{stat}// \left\{ \begin{bmatrix} \text{erg} \\ - \end{bmatrix} \Big/ \begin{bmatrix} \underline{} \\ +\text{oblique} \end{bmatrix} \atop \begin{bmatrix} \text{nom} \\ - \end{bmatrix} \right\}$

(in which, once again (cf. '+reflexive'), '+oblique' does not introduce
an element directly, but merely serves as a left-hand side environment).
In this case, the ordering is determined by the fact that erg is required
as an environment.

4.9   Fragment of grammar, 2

Let us indeed reformulate at this point the partial grammar whose
development forms a major aim of our discussion, incorporating the
various modifications that have been proposed in the course of the
present chapter.

(xliii)   *Fragment of grammar, 2*

II. i. 1. $V \rightarrow \begin{bmatrix} \pm\,\text{ergative} \\ \pm\,\text{stative} \end{bmatrix}$

    2. $+\text{ergative} \rightarrow \pm\,\text{reflexive}$

    3. $\begin{bmatrix} -\,\text{reflexive} \\ +\,\text{stative} \end{bmatrix} \rightarrow \pm\,\text{oblique}$

  ii. 1. $V \rightarrow \text{nom}//\text{—}V$

    2. $+\text{ergative} \rightarrow \text{erg}// \left\{ \begin{bmatrix} \text{nom} \\ - \\ V\text{—} \end{bmatrix} \Big/ \begin{bmatrix} \underline{} \\ +\text{reflexive} \end{bmatrix} \right\}$

    3. $+\text{stative} \rightarrow \text{stat}// \left\{ \begin{bmatrix} \text{erg} \\ - \end{bmatrix} \Big/ \begin{bmatrix} \underline{} \\ +\text{oblique} \end{bmatrix} \atop \begin{bmatrix} \text{nom} \\ - \end{bmatrix} \right\}$

  iii. 1. $\text{nom} + V + \text{erg} \rightarrow \text{erg} + V + \text{nom}$
       CONDITION: stat $\notin$ [nom]
    2. $\text{stat} + V \rightarrow \text{stat} + \text{cop} + V$

The range of structures allowed for by these rules is likewise represented
in (xliv):

(xliv)   *a.*

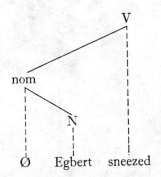

b.

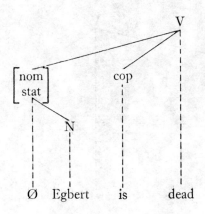

c.

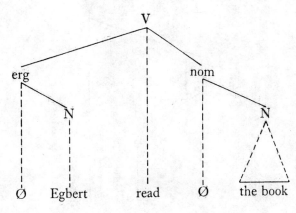

d.

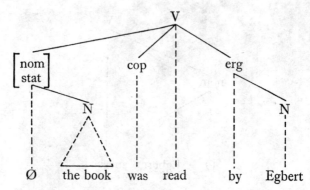

e.

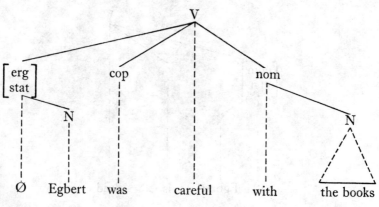

f.

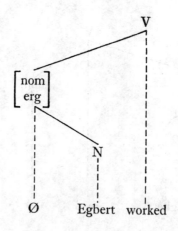

g.

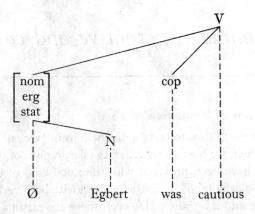

It is perhaps also potentially of interest—though the drawing of any firm conclusions would clearly be premature—that the structures in (xliv) in whose derivation most positive terms are selected (i.e. *e* and *g*,

$$
\begin{bmatrix} +\text{ergative} \\ +\text{stative} \\ -\text{reflexive} \\ +\text{oblique} \end{bmatrix} \quad \text{and} \quad \begin{bmatrix} +\text{ergative} \\ +\text{stative} \\ +\text{reflexive} \end{bmatrix}, \text{respectively})
$$

are also those which seem intuitively to me to be semantically the most 'marked'.

5 Nominative, ergative and causatives

5.1 Two kinds of 'transitive' verb

I would like now to turn to certain distinctions in 'verbal' clauses containing erg which we have so far failed to take account of. Clauses with *kill* and *read* have been provided with the same kind of derivation in terms of the rules in (xliii); I have associated with both verbs structures like those in *c* and *d* in (xliv). However, there are reasons for thinking that though they may have this much in common, we are dealing with two systematically different sub-classes of verb. Notice first of all the rough indication of difference provided by our question–answer frames:

(xlv)   What did Egbert do to the book? $\begin{cases} a. & \text{He damaged it} \\ b. & \text{*He read it} \end{cases}$

'Reading' is not something one 'does to' a book (though it is perhaps something one 'does with' it). The restriction represented in (xlv. *b*) (and a parallel one with *happen to*) seems to me to be a reflexion of a notional distinction between verbs like *kill* or *damage* and verbs like *read*, such that some sort of 'change of state' in the object is a necessary consequence of the action denoted by the former—whereas there is no such necessary implication in the case of *read*. 'Change of state' is to be interpreted rather widely: it can refer to a change in the 'physical or mental condition' of the nominative N—as with *damage, dismantle, repair, kill, revive, terrify*; or in its 'physical or abstract location'—as with *move, turn, lift*. With *read*, although in the case of a book as opposed to an inscription on a tombstone it is necessary to 'change the state' of the book in various ways (in particular by turning pages) in order to read it, the action of reading in itself has no such consequences.

5.2 'Transitive' and 'intransitive' uses

Many 'do to' verbs have intransitive equivalents—i.e. verbs which refer to the same 'process' without mentioning an agent. These verbs in English may have the same phonological shape as the 'transitive'—as in (xlvi. 1) (and cf. Poutsma, 1926: ch. 46, §37–41)—or be different—as in (xlvi. 2):

(xlvi) 1. *a.* The landscape has changed
           b. They have changed the landscape
        2. *a.* Bill died
           b. John killed Bill

For further examples like *change*, see Jespersen, 1928: §§16.4. Sundén (1916: 108–86) classifies a large number of verbs with both an 'intransitive' and a 'transitive' (mostly 'do to') use.

5.21 'Transitive' suffixes in various languages.

In many languages, the 'transitive' form is marked by a suffix, as in the Turkish equivalents of (xlvi. 2) quoted by Lyons (1968*a*: 353):

(xlvii) *a.* Bill öldü
         b. John Bill-i öldürdü

The formation of 'transitive verbs' in this way (by suffixing *-dür-* (and its phonological equivalents) to an 'intransitive') is a productive process in Turkish. In other languages the relationship is not productive: the phonological difference between *cwelan* ('die') and *cwellan* ('kill') in Old English is attributable to the absence *vs.* the presence of such a suffix, but 'transitive verbs' were no longer freely formed in this way. As further examples of 'transitive' suffixes, consider Coos *-t* and *-ts* or Takelma *-(a)na-*, illustrated respectively by (xlviii. 1) (taken from Frachtenberg, 1922: 328) and (xlviii. 2) (taken from Sapir, 1922: 136):

(xlviii) 1. *a.* x·pī ('It burned down')
            b. ṇx·pît ('I burned it')
          2. *a.* hãx ('It burns')
            b. hãxna ('He burned it')

(See too, for further examples, Tesnière, 1959: ch. 113.) It is possible for an affix with such a historical origin to spread to other 'uses' or become confused in phonological realization with affixes with distinct functions, or (as we have noted) cease to be productive. Which is only to say that the superficial morphology is (once more) not always a reliable indication of such underlying relationships. All of this is illustrated by the distribution (whatever its history) of the same Old English suffix (but see Jespersen, 1928: §16.51).[1] Consider too Sapir's

---

[1] Cf. too Old English *ge-* and *be-*: Visser, 1963: §§134, 144.

A G C

(1922: §45) discussion of the -(*a*)*n* suffix illustrated above (including the intriguing relationship between *waĩt'e*ᵉ ('I shall sleep') and *gel-wa-ina'n* ('I shall sleep with her')). I shall, however, not explore these surface complications here.

5.3 On causative verbs

Such 'transitive verbs' are usually termed 'causatives', and such an affix (where it occurs) is usually referred to as a 'causative' or 'transitive' affix. I propose to adopt the term **causative** with reference to 'transitive' verbs of the 'do to' kind—i.e. not only for those which bear an appropriate affix (as in the *b* examples in (xlvii) and (xlviii)) or are phonologically the same as the corresponding 'intransitives' (as *move* in English). Moreover, I want to include not only those verbs which have an (notionally) obvious 'intransitive' equivalent (like *kill*) but also verbs like *dismantle* or *repair* to which there does not appear to correspond any particular 'intransitive verb'. This requires (as a preliminary formulation) a rule dependent on (at least) +ergative of, say, the form in (xlix):

(xlix)   +ergative → ± causative

These verbs, then, are +causative; *read* and the like −causative. In many instances, as we have observed, there is no phonological distinction between the causative and the corresponding 'intransitive' (if there is one); in other cases, the presence of +causative is associated with a distinct 'lexical item' (as *kill*/*die*). Presumably in a language like Turkish there is a 'segmentalization rule' (cf. Postal, 1966*a*; Jacobs & Rosenbaum, 1968: ch. 11) which 'segments out' the +causative feature as a suffix to the verb. There are causative equivalents for 'intransitive' clauses with ergative subjects as well as those with simple nominatives— as in (l) (and cf. some of the examples in Poutsma, 1926: ch. 46, §37):

(l)   1. *a.* They marched to the station
        b. Egbert marched them to the station
      2. *a.* They work hard
        b. Egbert works them hard

(though the existence of examples lacking phonological identity is doubtful). Compare the distinction between *o*-causativization and *ni*-causativization in Japanese (Kuroda, 1965).

5.31 Causative and inchoative. There does occur in English what might appear to be a causative suffix with causative verbs which correspond to 'intransitive adjectives'—as *slacken/slack*. But we find this same *-en* form as the simple 'intransitive verb' corresponding to *slack* (its 'inchoative' equivalent), as illustrated in (li):

(li) *a.* The rope was slack
    b. The rope slackened
    c. Egbert slackened the rope

This suggests that *-en* is a 'verbalizing' suffix rather than specifically causative. There is a general correspondence in shape between such inchoatives and causatives—as *increase, decrease, age, blacken, lie/lay* (see Poutsma, 1926: ch. 46, §§20, 42; Jespersen, 1928: §§16.5, 16.7). Note the inchoative and causative uses of *grow*, etc. (*It grew, He grew it, It grew tall*) and *get* (*It got taller, He got it ready*). Such an inchoative/causative correspondence is not surprising; in general, it would appear that 'inchoatives' are merely the non-'verb'-root 'intransitive' equivalents of causatives—they express the 'change of state' that the causatives effect. A perhaps more promising candidate as a quasi-productive causative suffix in English is *-ize*, added particularly to 'adjectives' and nouns; *legalize, characterize*. Note too examples like *synthesize*. However, in this instance also we find inchoatives like *materialize*.

5.32 Other 'transitive' and 'intransitive' pairings. Clearly there are other superficial 'transitive'/'intransitive' pairings than that we can associate directly with causativity. There are a large number of surface 'intransitives' that result merely from the deletion of the object (which may be of various types):[1]

(lii) *a.* Egbert is painting
    b. He drinks
    c. He undressed
    d. They kissed
    e. They always change for dinner

---

[1] See further e.g. Poutsma, 1926: ch. 46, §§7–10, 26–9; Jespersen, 1928: §§16.0–16.3; Visser, 1963: §§155, 159–62; Lyons, 1968a: §§8.2.9–8.2.11. In (for instance) Hungarian, intransitive clauses show the same set of subject pronoun affixes on the verb as transitives with deleted indefinite object: the so-called 'indefinite' (Csink, 1853: 265–7) or 'subjective' (Sauvageot, 1951: 68–75) conjugation. However, verbs with a definite object (deleted or not) take the 'definite' or 'objective' conjugation. This provides a further possible source for such morphological variations unconnected with underlying cases (cf. §4. 64).

However, there is a further kind of 'transitive'/'intransitive' example which is rather more problematic; and this results from what Jespersen (1928: §16.8) calls the 'activo-passive use of some verbs', as exemplified in (liii):[1]

(liii)   The book sold quickly

A sentence like *It washes well* is ambiguous between an interpretation associated with an ergative subject and a deleted object and an interpretation like that for (liii), with respect to which an underlying nominative appears as subject. That is, (liii) looks superficially as if it should have a corresponding causative (like *John sold the book quickly*). But these two clauses are clearly not related as are (xlvi. 1. *a*) and (xlvi. 1. *b*) (nor are the two interpretations of *It washes well*), and a clue to this is provided by the obligatory presence of an adverbial with the V in (liii)), which expresses 'either a qualification of it or a generalization about its feasibility' (Halliday, 1967: 47—see too Erades, 1950: 156). This 'modal' quality, the associated 'habitual' aspect, and the fact that in such instances an agent appears to be presupposed (though the 'modality' is associated with the 'process' denoted by the verb—it is 'process-oriented' rather than 'agent-oriented' (Halliday, 1967: 47-8)) make it tempting to try to relate clauses like (liii) to 'modal transitive' clauses like *It was possible to sell the book quickly* (Anderson, 1968a: 29, fn. 42). Compare too the examples in (liv):

(liv)   *a.* It polishes easily
       b. It can be polished easily

But consider an example like *The book sold well*. With it there are no such corresponding 'modal transitives', and this is because more obviously in this case (and, I would suggest, with (liv. *a*)) the adverbial is 'associated' with the subject, whereas in (liv. *b*) and the like it relates

---

[1] Cf. too Sundén, 1916: particularly 187–216; Poutsma, 1926: ch. 46, §§32–3; Hatcher, 1943; Kirchner, 1959; Visser, 1963: §§163, 168; Lyons, 1968a: §8.2.13; Anderson, 1968a: 12–13. This phenomenon appears to fall within the scope of Tesnière's (1959: chs. 115–16) 'diathèse récessive', which refers to clauses in which the number of 'actants' (cases) normally associated with a particular verb-type is reduced, and within which he includes passives with deleted agent, 'impersonal passives' (*Itum est*) and 'reflexives' like *Cet objet se vend bien*. Thus, with respect to 'passives', we must allow for the fact that, in certain languages (e.g. Turkish—Lyons, 1968a: §8.3.4), this form of the verb appears to be a reflexion of the denial of subject position to and deletion of an indefinite agent (whether in a transitive or intransitive clause). However, I shall be unable to explore here the principle underlying this surface intersection of 'passive' and 'reflexive'.

rather to the agent. Kandiah (1968) suggests that such a distinction is characteristic in general of the relation between causatives and their corresponding intransitive (and this would be explicable with reference to the view of causatives proposed below in Part V). Consider too the examples cited by Hirtle (1967: 53): *This shirt irons well, His plays act well, Food spoils quickly in summer, It washes like cotton.* And notice the notional similarity of clauses with two surface nominals like *Oysters make a good meal.* The derivation of such clauses remains (for me) something of a mystery, as does a characterization of the range of verbs that permit such a 'use' (see too Jespersen, 1928: §16.8). However, for a discussion of further examples of the various kinds of verbs that can be either 'transitive' or 'intransitive', see Sundén (1916: 218–362), Maejima (1958) and the works referred to there.

5.4 Causatives with 'sentential' nominative

We should also note that certain (minimally specified) causatives take a 'sentential' nominative, as in (lv):

(lv) *a.* Egbert made them leave
      b. Egbert allowed them to leave
      c. Egbert prevented them from leaving

or with more complex verbs involving lexicalization of typically 'speech as an instrument':

(lvi) 1. *a.* He persuaded them to leave
          b. He dissuaded them from leaving
       2. *a.* He ordered them to leave
          b. He permitted them to leave
          c. He forbade them to leave

There seems to be a tendency (to put it no more strongly) for *make* (as opposed to *allow* and *prevent*) to require an ergative subject in the subordinate clause:

(lvii) 1. *a.* *He made John die
           b. *He made John's death
        2. *a.* He allowed John to die
           b. He prevented John's death

Some non-ergative subjects appear under *make*: *He made John fall/cry*. But *cause* appears normally to fill this 'slot':

(lviii)   He caused John's death

Have similarly pre-supposes some agency other than that of the subject of the superordinate clause, but in its case the subordinate ergative need not be subject:

(lix)   1. *a.* He had them leave
        b. He made them leave
        2. *a.* He had them killed
        b. *He made them killed

(and even in lix 1. *a* the involvement of the superordinate ergative seems more 'indirect' than in the corresponding sentence with *make*). Partly because of this, a clause like *He had a book stolen* is ambiguous. On the derivation associated with the alternative interpretation, see §9.3; and for a discussion of the differences between such constructions with *have*, compare Lee, 1967. Notice too 'quasi-causatives' like *require*, which can take a *that*-clause as nominative rather than the 'reduced' forms demanded by *make*, etc. (Cf. the discussion of the distinction between *demand* and *command* by Boyd & Thorne, 1969.) We shall have occasion to return to the relationship between these various types of causatives with sentential nominative and 'simple' causatives below, particularly in Part V.

5.41   A problem in the grammar of antonymy. As an aside, I would like to note that the forms in (lv) and (lvi) raise two further considerations that will recur in our discussion. Firstly, there is the question (which I shall merely raise) of accounting for the relation between polar terms and the negation of their respective antonyms, such that the 'comparative' and 'scalar' properties of *big/not big/not small/ small* and the like require expression. The problem becomes acute with 'overt comparatives':[1] *John is bigger than Bill* does not imply that 'John' is 'big' or 'Bill' is 'big' (or even 'small'), but merely indicates their relative positions on the *small/big* scale. With the present examples, the situation is slightly more complex, as is illustrated by the 'equivalences' tabulated in (lx):

[1] Cf. Small, 1924; Jespersen, 1949: 388; Vendler, 1967: 180–1; McIntosh, 1968; Seuren, 1969: 128–30.

(lx) 1. *a.* Egbert made them leave
   b. Egbert didn't allow them not to leave
   c. Egbert prevented them from not leaving
  2. *a.* Egbert didn't make them leave
   b. Egbert allowed them not to leave
   c. Egbert didn't prevent them from not leaving
  3. *a.* Egbert made them not leave
   b. Egbert didn't allow them to leave
   c. Egbert prevented them from leaving
  4. *a.* Egbert didn't make them not leave
   b. Egbert allowed them to leave
   c. Egbert didn't prevent them from leaving

A further such set is obtained when we substitute *remain* for *not leave* and *not remain* for *leave*.[1] The formulation of a non-*ad hoc* account of all this is not immediately obvious (to me, at least), but there are some reasons for regarding *make* as the 'unmarked' form, and some sort of notion of 'inherent negation' will perhaps take us part of the way towards a solution. One reason for thinking this is connected with my second observation, namely the association we find here (as elsewhere) between the 'negative' form and the occurrence of *from* rather than *to* (or *in*). Compare *absent from/present in*, and the further examples we shall encounter in the following chapters. I shall, in this instance, also, consider some of the implications of this for our present investigation in Part V.

5.5 'Intransitive' causatives

So far we have been discussing causatives in relation to 'transitive' clauses only. We must consider now whether they are limited to these, or whether the ± causative distinction is also appropriate to reflexive clauses. Must the specification on the left of the rule in (xlix) be further qualified (in particular, as −reflexive), or can it be left to apply in the more general way indicated there? Notice to begin with that (notionally) it would seem not unreasonable to regard *Egbert moved* as causative, given that *Egbert moved the stone* (and *Egbert moved himself*) has been so interpreted. So too with most other reflexive verbs, which appear to

[1] I have noted elsewhere (Anderson, 1969b: part 2) a similar situation with respect to 'modal verbs' in English—and also (parenthetically) with 'quantifiers' (as too Jespersen, 1924: 324–5; Householder, forthcoming: ch. 6; Leech, 1969: §3.5).

involve the subject effecting a 'change in his state' (in the rather broad sense in which this was interpreted above)—consider e.g. *leave, swim,* etc. The question is to determine whether there are any non-causative reflexives. The number of non-reflexive non-causatives is apparently rather small—I am not even sure that *read* is a very good example. So too with the reflexives. Perhaps *work* is an example. 'Changes of state' for the subject are usually associated with most kinds of working, but it is not clear that these are intrinsic to 'work' itself. Notice that, as we observed above, the semantic difference between *They worked* and *Egbert worked them* (*hard*) is much greater than that between *They moved* and *John moved them.* Let us, for the moment at any rate, leave open the possibility of such a distinction with respect to 'verbal' reflexive clauses, and thus leave rule (xlix) unmodified in this respect.

5.6   'Adjectival' causatives

An even more difficult decision (for my part) is posed by 'non-verbal' clauses. As rule (xlix) stands, it allows for $\begin{bmatrix} +\text{reflexive} \\ +\text{stative} \end{bmatrix}$ clauses to show a $\pm$ causative distinction. *He is cautious* and the like seem fairly straightforwardly non-causative. But consider examples like those in (lxi) where we have *get* rather than *be*:

(lxi)   1. *a.* He got tough
        b. He got aggressive
     2. *a.* Get tough!
        b. Get aggressive!

The examples in (lxi. 2) can be read as injunctions to the subject to bring about a 'change of (mental) state' in himself. In this case, the causative feature is reflected in the shape of the copula (and its associated surface syntax): cf. *He was tough.* Once again, as remarked on above, there is a correspondence between causative and inchoative:

(lxii)   He got old(er)

In 'long passives', the overriding effect of the presence of erg is such that any distinction between *get* (inchoative) and *be* is considerably attenuated—cf. *He got/was killed.*[1] The relevance of the $\pm$ causative

---

[1] Thus, there are two rather different ways on the surface of marking inchoatives—as in (lxii), or by 'verbalization' (cf. *He aged*—see too (xlviii)). This may be merely the result of alternative segmentations. I.e. it may be possible to have a general con-

distinction to oblique stative clauses (*He was careful with the book*, etc.) is even more doubtful, and I shall not allow for such in the sets of rules that are discussed in what follows: ± oblique will be dependent on − causative. If one also wanted to exclude the ± causative possibility from reflexive stative clauses, then the rules could be ordered appropriately—e.g. by making ± reflexive dependent on $\begin{bmatrix} +\text{oblique} \\ -\text{stative} \end{bmatrix}$ as well as + ergative.[1] However, for the present discussion I propose that we add rule (xlix) as it stands to II. i. 2 in (xliii), and modify the left-hand side of II. i. 3 to include − causative.

5.7 Rules for causativity

Thus, II. i would now read as in (lxiii):

(lxiii) 1. $V \rightarrow \begin{bmatrix} \pm\,\text{ergative} \\ \pm\,\text{stative} \end{bmatrix}$

  2. $+\,\text{ergative} \rightarrow \begin{bmatrix} \pm\,\text{reflexive} \\ \pm\,\text{causative} \end{bmatrix}$

  3. $\begin{bmatrix} -\,\text{reflexive} \\ -\,\text{causative} \\ +\,\text{stative} \end{bmatrix} \rightarrow \pm\,\text{oblique}$

There is no DR (in II. ii) for + causative; it is intrinsic to V and has no effect on the array of case elements or the subsequent subcategorization of their dependent Ns. (This means that *kill* and *die* now differ by an intrinsic feature; however, the effect of the proposals made in Part V is once more to remove this intrinsic difference.) This allows for the various (more and less certain) causative possibilities we have discussed.

5.8 Clauses of result

There is a further distinction that would appear to be relevant here. In the various 'active transitive' clauses we have been discussing, all the objects have belonged to the traditional category of 'affiziertes Objekt' ('Richtungsobjekt', 'objet affecté')—though as Jespersen (1928: §12.12)

vention allowing a subclass of + stative verbs to be inserted with respect to a − stative, − ergative V, with associated segmentalization of the − stative feature as a distinctive copula (*become*) or as a suffix. However, cf. Lakoff, 1965: §§4.15, 9.2.

[1] I leave the reader to construct this set of rules for himself, if he so wishes. This would also entail changes in II. ii.

points out, 'neither the names given to these objects...nor the definitions usually given are comprehensive enough'. This is associated with Fillmore's characterization of the 'objective' case ('the semantically most neutral'—1968 *a*: 25) quoted above. However, there is one of the traditional sub-types of object which is semantically and syntactically sufficiently distinct to have been differentiated by definition and name from other kinds of object. This is the 'object of result' ('effiziertes Objekt', 'Ergebnisobjekt', 'objet effectué'). Notionally, such an object is the result of the action of the verb, as in the examples in (lxiv):

(lxiv)   1. *a.* Egbert built the house
              b. Egbert wrote a book
          2.   Egbert painted a picture

Verbs like *paint* (cf. Jespersen, 1928: §12.22) also take an 'ordinary' object, as in *Egbert painted the ceiling* (though this may be indeed an underlying locative). Consider the possible ambiguity (noted by Fillmore, 1968 *a*: 4) of *John paints nudes*; cf. too *grind corn/grind flour*. The fact that the 'object of result' does not ante-date the action of the verb underlies the restriction illustrated in (lxv):

(lxv)   What did Egbert do to the shack? $\begin{cases} a. & \text{*He built it} \\ b. & \text{He demolished it} \end{cases}$

Like non-causative clauses, clauses with an 'object of result' (or 'subject of result' in 'passives') are not appropriate as answers to 'do to' questions. But they are notionally unlike non-causatives, in which I have suggested the action of the verb does not necessarily impinge at all on the state of the object. Clearly, 'result' clauses are more like causatives in that the action of the verb is intimately bound up with the object; it is not merely a play on words to say that both types of clause express the effect of an action, effective in the one case and affective in the other. The object is 'brought into existence' (in some sense)—*build, create, produce*—or 'put out of existence'—*demolish, destroy*—or has its 'physical or mental state or location' modified in some other way— *change, move*. The sequence *build/dismantle/rebuild* reflects a series of 'causative' actions—effective, affective (or 'diseffective'), (re)effective.[1] Notice that *make*, as well as being a causative which takes a sentential nominative (cf. (lv. *a*)), also takes an 'object of result'—as in *He made*

---

[1] I leave aside the interesting questions of reference (see e.g. the works referred to and discussed in Sampson, 1969) raised by such a sequence.

the toy. If both such uses are interpreted as 'causative' (as I am proposing), then the distribution of *make* is revealed as systematic, rather
than merely haphazard. Thus, I would like to regard clauses with an
'object of result' as a sub-type of causative, as expressed (for the
moment) in a rule like that in (lxvi):

(lxvi)   II. i. 3. *b.*   +causative → ± resultative

It may be that +resultative should introduce (in II. ii) a feature on nom.
Also, if there are no reflexive resultative clauses (I am unable to con-
struct any), then − reflexive should be added to the left-hand side of
II. i. 3. *b* in (lxvi).

5.9   Causativization of 'nominal' clauses

I shall in the next few chapters neglect this distinction among what I
shall henceforth term simply causatives—referring to both *build* etc. and
demolish etc. But before leaving this area, one particular question remains
to be considered. I have suggested that resultative clauses are a sub-type
of causative, and that in particular no case category additional to those
we have considered is involved in such clauses. However, there are
clauses in which we appear to find an 'ordinary object' together with an
'object of result', as in (lxvii):

(lxvii)   *a.* We elected him president
          b. They appointed him treasurer

(Cf. the examples in Jespersen, 1940: §3.2.) The 'archi-causative' *make*
(and *create*) is also one of these verbs: *They made Egbert an observer.*
From such examples, it might be argued that the effect of selecting
+resultative is to introduce a distinct case category, say 'result', which
is manifested as *president* in (lxvii. *a*) and *treasurer* in (lxvii. *b*), and
presumably as *the house* in (lxiv. 1. *a*). (The universal presence of nom in
clauses would then be difficult to maintain.) However, I would prefer to
interpret (lxvii. *a*) and (lxvii. *b*) as the causative equivalents of respectively (lxviii. *a*) and (lxviii. *b*).

(lxviii)   *a.* He was/became (the) president
           b. He was/became (the) treasurer

That is, the clauses in (lxvii) represent the causativization of 'nominal'
clauses. Compare the parallelism in number etc. restrictions instanced

by **He was the presidents*/**We made him presidents*, **He was the waitress*/
**We made him the waitress*. Note too **President was elected him (by us)*:
unlike a 'result' NP, such nominals do not show 'passivization'. If the
relevant structure of (lxviii. *a*) can be represented as in (lxix. *a*), then
that for (lxvii. *a*) and the 'passive' (*He was elected president by us*) is
perhaps as in (lxix. *b*):

(lxix)   *a*.

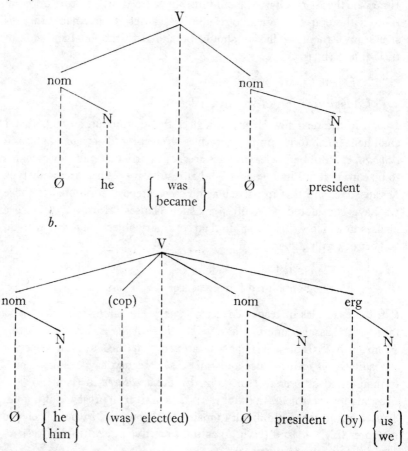

   b.

However, the interpretation of clauses like those in (lxviii) presents a
number of problems which I do not wish to broach at this point. The
fact that in (lxix. *a*) *was* directly represents V will be allowed for by a
modification to the rules for cop proposed in §6.3. The interpretation
of (at least some) predicate nominals as a second nominative phrase I

would not urge strongly here, particularly as it leaves all sorts of problems unsolved, but it seems not too implausible in view of the nature of their surface inflexional marking in many languages and the various restrictions associated with the co-referentiality of the two Ns involved.[1]

5.10 Prospect

I shall touch upon this area briefly again in Part V. Also in Part V we shall be reviewing the interpretation of causative clauses presented here in the light of the full range of phenomena surveyed in this and the following part. Already, it seems likely that an interpretation of causatives involving some kind of superordination (such that the structures underlying causatives with sentential nominatives and 'simple' causatives are rather more alike) is to be preferred. Jespersen (1940: ch. 3), for instance, suggests that examples like (lxvii) represent a sub-type of 'simple nexus as object of result'.[2] The fact that a combination of two nominatives is permitted only either in clauses lacking an ergative or in ones which are causative suggests this: if causatives involve superordination, then it would be possible to generalize in terms of restricting two-nominative combinations to non-ergative clauses, since the ergative in causative sentences would then appear in the clause superordinate to that containing the two noms. We shall find similar restrictions in the distribution of locatives, which thus provide further support for such an interpretation of causatives. Notice too that we find clauses very like (lxvii) (semantically and in surface syntax) which must involve two clauses: consider 'resultative' clauses of the type of *Anderson drives me mad* listed by Jespersen (1940: ch. 3) (and cf. Visser, 1963: §§644 ff.). We find once again in such clauses the omnipresent *make* (*He makes me sick*), though without the restriction to ergative subordinate subjects (cf. (lvii. 1)). A unitary treatment of causatives would favour a two-clause derivation for (lxvii) and the like—and even, as we shall see, for other 'simple' causatives (resultative and non-resultative), as has been argued in rather different terms by Lakoff, 1965: §§4.16, 9.1–2. However, in the following Part, rather than develop directly such an argument, I want to bring in some further phenomena relevant to our main theme, and try to account for such within the framework developed in this and the preceding part.

[1] Cf. e.g. Lehiste's (1969) discussion of the distribution of the 'nominative' and 'essive' in Estonian.
[2] Cf. too e.g. Sechehaye, 1926: 160–1; Anderson, forthcoming *b*.

Part III

LOCATIVE AND ABLATIVE

6 *Locative*

6.1 Preliminaries

In this chapter I propose (among other things) to take up again the question of the analysis of those 'non-adjectival' verbs which tended preferentially not to co-occur (superficially at least) with 'progressive aspect', i.e. 'stative' verbs like *know, possess* and *contain*. In order to do this, it is necessary first of all to consider the introduction into our grammar of the notion of **locative**, as a further case element whose syntax I propose now to examine.

I suggest that in clauses like those in (i):

(i)   *a.* The statue stands on a plinth
     b. He remained in London
     c. We keep the money in a box

there is (whatever else there may be) a locative phrase, which contains a noun indicating the spatial location of the nominative (and the associated 'process'/'state'), and is characterized in these particular examples by the occurrence of the superficial case markers *in* and *on*. Clearly since *in* and *on* (and *at*, etc.) are not semantically equivalent (though *in* and *on*, for example, may overlap in 'extension'—Bennett, 1968: 164), the locative category would appear to be subject to more extensive sub-categorization than seemed to be obviously appropriate to the cases we have studied so far, and this is recognized in traditional terms like 'inessive' and 'adessive' (as subtypes of locative)—and by Hjelmslev (1935) with respect to the dimension 'cohérence'/'incohérence'. This is not to deny that many (at least) such 'prepositional' distinctions can be considered (even without the ingenuity of a Horne Tooke) to involve (underlying) nominals—*beside, in front of*, etc. This is particularly transparent in the 'postpositions' of Basque—as *etchearen aldean* ('beside the house'; *etche*—'house', *alde*—'side'; *etchearen* is (definite) genitive, *aldean* (definite) locative).[1] I do not intend here to investigate

---

[1] See further Lafitte, 1962: 168–72; cf. too similar phenomena in e.g. Hindi, Turkish, Twi. On such (historically) in Indo-European, see the works referred to in Brugmann, 1911: §§ 594 ff. (and cf. §§ 551 ff.). See also, more generally, de la Grasserie, 1890: 98 ff.

in any detail such phenomena, an account of which for English would have to reckon with surveys like those of Blake (1930), Lindkvist (1950) and Hill (1968)—though Lindkvist's account, for instance, suffers from over-differentiation with respect to polysemy (as pointed out by Bennett (1968: 156)), in that it incorporates distinctions into the description of prepositions that are marked rather in the accompanying noun phrase. I shall take into consideration only such aspects as are necessary for the account I am going to propose below of the relation between the locative and other case categories. Thus, overlooking these differences of sub-categorization with respect to the locative category, we can represent the structures underlying the examples in (i) as in (ii):

(ii)   *a.*

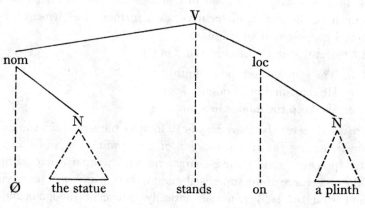

b.

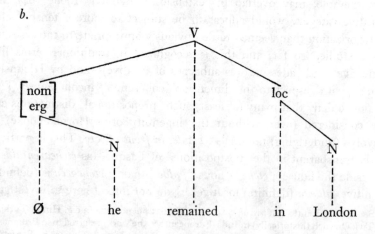

c.

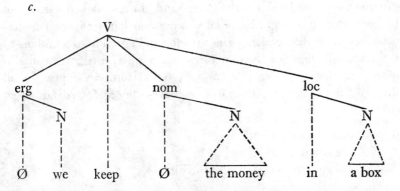

(The structure of (i. *c*) as represented in (ii) presupposes, of course, the prior operation of rule II. iii. 1 in (xliii) in §4.9. The verb is also causative, as, of course, is that in (*b*), a point to which I shall have to return below.) In the examples in (i), the verbs chosen all 'strongly select' loc; i.e., allowing for deletion, loc is necessarily part of the frame into which such verbs are inserted (and we might thus call them 'locative verbs'). It is clear that there are many verbs with respect to which this is not the case—verbs, that is, which co-occur with loc, but not necessarily. I shall not propose here an account of the occurrence of loc with these latter verbs.[1] I shall be concerned primarily with 'locative verbs'.

6.11   Rules for locatives. We could allow for such clauses as those in (i) by the simple addition of a subcategorization rule in II. i, and a matching dependency rule in II. ii, of the form represented in (iii):

(iii)   *a.* X → ±locative
        b. +locative → loc//V—

where X stands for the as yet undetermined left-hand side of the first rule. Presumably (iii. *b*), intended to introduce loc in its neutral position, is ordered early in II. ii (i.e. in II. ii. 2), in order that the rule introducing erg can be ordered after it, so that erg will be placed before loc, where both are present—*The money is kept by us in a box*—if indeed the reverse

---

[1] It is likely that in such instances loc is derived rather differently (cf. Fillmore, 1968: note 64), probably via some type of superordination. On the other hand, it may rather be that the distinction between 'locative' and 'non-locative' verbs is a feature of the subcategorization of verbs. However, a decision in this area is not crucial to the present discussion.

order is more 'marked'. On the other hand, if such markedness cannot be motivated, this might be suitably represented in terms of simultaneousness of the dependency rules for loc and erg. These additions to the rules will allow for the structures represented in (ii). We can also note here that it is possible for one verbal form to appear in all three different locative structures we have allowed for so far, as in (iv):

(iv)   *a.* It stood on a plinth
       b. He stood on the chair
       c. He stood it on the top of the piano

Compare here clauses with *lie/lay* (and see Jespersen, 1928: 340–6).

6.2   Stative locative clauses

However, the clauses we have looked at so far (though they show that loc co-occurs freely with nom and erg) are apparently all non-stative, in that (e.g.) cop is absent; we must now determine whether the new subcategorization rule in (iii) is dependent on (the selection of) − stative, or whether it will be possible to regard the selection of loc as independent of ± stative—i.e., we must determine further the composition of X in (iii. *a*). There are indeed apparently clear instances of stative clauses which contain a locative, as in (v):

(v)   The post was fixed in the ground

This example is either 'adjectival' or 'non-adjectival', depending on whether the underlying structure lacks an ergative category or not (as emerged from the discussion in §4.4); and it differs from the examples in (i) in that the nom category is marked as stat (and the copula is thus subsequently introduced). This suggests that rule *a* in (iii) might be incorporated as a sub-part of II. i. 1, as simultaneous with ± ergative and ± stative (though the verbs appearing in clauses that are both + stative and + locative seem to be restricted to non-adjectival roots—as in (v)— unless *close by* and the like are taken as simple examples of adjective plus loc). However, the occurrence of locative verbs seems to be limited to clauses which either lack an ergative or are causative (as I observed above with particular reference to the examples in (i)): loc and erg are mutually exclusive in non-causative clauses. Accordingly, rather than appearing in II. i. 1, the subcategorization rule allowing for locatives

should apparently be ordered at II. i. 3, with a left-hand side specification
$\left\{\begin{array}{l} -\text{ergative} \\ +\text{causative} \end{array}\right\}$ [1].

6.3   Clauses with copula + locative

We should now note that there are also certain locative clauses which
(superficially, at least) contain a copula and no verb element. So (vi):

(vi)   His house is in the country

The question arises: how are we to interpret such clauses with respect to
their structure?

6.31   Interpreted as 'verbless.'   We could allow for them by modi-
fying our set of rules in such a way as to generate locative clauses without
verbs (adjectival or not), with the copula presumably introduced once
more superficially (to 'carry' the tense marker, etc.). And this is perhaps
how we could interpret in part recent suggestions by Lyons (1966: 229;
1968a: §8.4). That is, the base rules for the clauses would have to allow
for clauses with a verb and without a locative (*John sneezed*), clauses
lacking a verb but containing a locative (*His house (is) in the country*) and
clauses with both a verb and a locative phrase (*The statue stands on a
plinth*)—unless this last possibility is interpreted as involving some sort
of co-ordination or subordination, with *stand*, etc. perhaps representing
lexicalizations of a copula with respect to underlying 'manner' phrases
indicating 'posture'. However that may be, two types of clause would
be envisaged, one type characterized by the presence of a verb, the other
by the absence of such. And the copula is introduced either in the
absence of a verb (but the presence of a locative) or after an occurrence
of stat (when a verb is present).

6.32   ...as involving deletion of a pro-verb.   However, we also have
to account for clauses like that in (vii):

(vii)   His house is situated in the country

---

[1] Such a specification suggests that an account of causative locative clauses in terms of
superordination (cf. §5.10, and see further Part V) may eventually prove preferable.
In this case, the locative and ergative would not appear in the same (underlying)
clause, but the locative in a subordinate and the ergative in the superordinate—thus
accounting for the restriction embodied in the specification $\left\{\begin{array}{l} -\text{ergative} \\ +\text{causative} \end{array}\right\}$. Compare
the discussion of causative 'nominal' clauses in §5.9.

which I presume we would want to show as closely related to (vi). Now, (vii) could perhaps be derived in the same way as I have just sketched out for (vi), with the addition of a rule introducing a verb that is present only superficially—since this verb is lexically empty. Consider too the examples in (viii):

(viii)   *a.* Father was in his favourite chair
         b. Father was seated in his favourite chair

where the lexical content of *seated* can perhaps be regarded as derived from the locative phrase. But such an explanation is inappropriate in cases like (v) or (ix):

(ix)   *a.* Father was seated on the ground
       b. Father was sunk in his favourite chair

where the verb in a locative clause does have some independent lexical content. This situation suggests rather that we should try to extend the account proposed earlier for (v) (and thus (ix)), in which a verb is present in the underlying structure, to the clauses in (vii) and (viii. *b*). Such an account, however, leaves us in its turn with the problem of bringing out the relationship between (vi) and (vii) and (viii. *a*) and (viii. *b*), respectively. The most obvious solution seems to reside in regarding the superficial absence of a verb in (vi) and (viii. *a*) as resulting from the deletion of an underlying pro-verb (rather than as a reflexion of the underlying lack of a verb), a verb which remains superficially in (vii) and (viii. *b*). It is the 'predictability' of the content of such verbs that permits the deletion. Notice that in cases like (ix) there is no corresponding form with deleted verb, since the content of such a verb is not unambiguously recoverable in this way—cf. *Father was stretched out on the ground. Father was on the ground* is not more closely related to (ix. *a*) than to this latter clause; it involves the deletion of some pro-verb less delicately specified than the verbs underlying either of these. *Seated* is thus 'unmarked' only in certain restricted environments; and it is not the case that other stative verbs do not co-occur with such locatives, but merely that *seated* is in this instance the 'neutral' one, which matches the lexical content of the locative noun phrase. *Situated*—or *located*— (the maximally unspecified locative verbs), is rather more generally 'unmarked'. It should be noted, however, that there are clauses containing superficially copula + locative phrases which do not appear to have a corresponding clause with the verb represented; and the clause just quoted is such, as is the example in (x):

(x)   Your uncle is in the garden

Thus, in many instances of the occurrence of the minimally specified stative locative verb (which with certain (inanimate) types of nominative and locative phrases is represented when not deleted as *situated, located,* etc.—though the restrictions on these are rather different), it is obligatorily deleted.

Accordingly, with respect to this latter account, in all of examples (v) to (x), I suggest that we have an underlying structure that can be represented schematically as in (xi):

(xi)

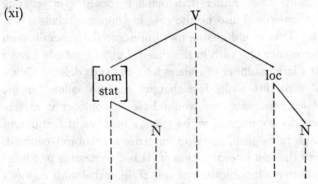

Such an account has the following pleasing consequences: (1) the diversity of (underlying) clause types is reduced, and thus the complexity of the relevant base rules; (2) the copula is in all these instances introduced before a V in the environment of a preceding stat, rather than in two different sorts of context. (Something like consequence (2) can be achieved (at least in part) in terms of a 'verbless locative' interpretation by regarding such clauses as a subtype of stative clause, cop thus being introduced in their case too with reference to a preceding stat, but only at the cost of a special rule permitting verbless locatives only in stative clauses, thus aggravating the degree to which consequence (1) is not met.) These simplifications are achieved at the expense of a rule deleting the verb where appropriate; but this is offset by the fact that it is no longer necessary to have a rule introducing a surface verb in certain circumstances.[1] If such an account is accepted (and it seems to be the

---

[1] This latter sort of rule would also appear to involve us in difficulties with respect to derived constituent structure, at least in terms of an account of the type discussed by Lyons (1968a: §8.4).

preferable one, given the assumption that a V is present at all in the underlying structure of clauses), superficially verbless locative clauses can thus be accommodated in terms of the base rules already proposed.

6.33 ... as involving non-segmentalization. However, with respect to the introduction of cop, another, I think preferable, possibility—assuming the availability in the grammar of segmentalizing rules like those proposed by Postal (1966 a)—is rather to introduce it initially as a feature added to V, a feature which is segmented out except in those cases in which, under the previous interpretation, the verb was deleted—in which instances, within the present interpretation, cop will merely be retained as a feature of V rather than being preposed as a separate segment. (And such would also be the case in 'nominal' clauses—cf. (lxix. a) in §5.9.) This would enable us to preserve the generalization concerning the presence of a verb in the clause, but without our having to consider that a large number of clauses have the verb deleted after a copula. Linked with this is the fact that we can now allow for the 'verbalness' of be; otherwise, we would have to consider it merely coincidental that the copula and verbs share a number of features of their syntax—e.g., in English, marking for tense and subject-concord. I shall thus adopt this last interpretation of clauses containing be + locative, and shall assume a modification of rule II. iii. 2 that adds cop as a feature to V (cf. (xl) in §4.81). Accordingly, the structure represented in (xi) can be developed as either (xii. a) or (xii. b):

(xii)   a.

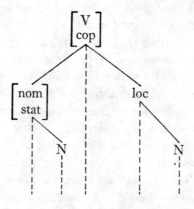

b.

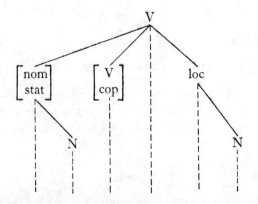

the former underlying *His house is in the country*, etc., the latter *His house is situated in the country*.

6.4   Subjectivization of locatives

6.41   A preliminary formulation. It would further seem to be the case that clauses containing a certain subset of locative verbs are the result of the operation of a permutation rule like II. iii. I with respect to nom and loc rather than nom and erg—and this involves at least some of the verbs like *contain* that we have noted as being problematic in some respects. Consider the *a* examples in (xiii):

(xiii)   1. *a.*   That box contains the apples
         b.   The apples are contained in that box
         c.   The apples are in that box
    2. *a.*   Our group includes many Eskimos
         b.   Many Eskimos are included in our group
         c.   Many Eskimos are in our group

(The selection of *contain* vs. *include* is apparently a function of the subcategorization of the relevant NPs. Also, after *included, among* appears to be the preposition appropriate with plural (as opposed to collective) NPs.) The *c* clauses differ from the *b* in showing the lack of the operation of the locative verb segmenting rule proposed above. The *a* clauses differ from both *b* and *c* in sequence (loc preceding nom) and in lacking a copula. A verb like *abound* (as noted in Jespersen, 1928: 214) appears in clauses both showing and lacking such a subjectivization of the locative, as in (xiv):

(xiv)   *a.* This area abounds $\left\{\begin{array}{l}\text{in}\\\text{with}\end{array}\right\}$ wild life

        b. Wild life abounds in this area

Compare too *Wild life is abundant in this area*, with $\begin{bmatrix}\text{nom}\\\text{stat}\end{bmatrix}$. (For further examples see Sundén, 1916: 91–2.) This situation could in part be explained in terms of an extension of rule II. iii. 1 to locative clauses, with nom in *b* and *c* in (xii) marked as stat and nom in *a* not so marked. Thus, II. iii. 1 can be reformulated as in (xv):

(xv) $\text{nom} + V \left\{\begin{array}{l}\text{erg}\\\text{loc}\end{array}\right\} \rightarrow \left\{\begin{array}{l}\text{erg}\\\text{loc}\end{array}\right\} V + \text{nom}$

        CONDITION: stat $\notin$ [nom]

Unlike those with subjectivized ergatives, such locative clauses naturally do not allow for imperatives (**Contain the apples*). We can also now associate the lack of the 'progressive' possibility in clauses like those in *a* with the presence of a locative subject. But we shall return to this below.

6.42 Cop, stat and subjectivization. In various respects, then, locative clauses can be accommodated by rather obvious extensions of the rules proposed so far. But a problem has arisen. Consider again example (i. *a*) (or (xiv. *b*)). This shows the same sequence as the *b* and *c* examples in (xiii) (i.e., nominative phrase + verb + locative phrase), but like the *a* instances it lacks a copula. Thus, if we suggest that a clause like (i. *a*) contains $\begin{bmatrix}\text{nom}\\\text{stat}\end{bmatrix}$ because of the sequence, then we shall also have to make rule II. iii. 2 (introducing cop after stat) optional in locative clauses to account for both *b* and *c* in (xiii) (with copula) and (i. *a*) (without). This would constitute an undesirable complication. Moreover, a number of further problems are evident when we consider (i. *b*) and (i. *c*), corresponding to which there are no clauses with subjectivized locatives. Thus, under such an interpretation, the formulation of II. iii. 1 and II. iii. 2 would require additional complexities. It would seem preferable to propose a rather different explanation for the occurrence of both *That box contains the apples* and *A statue stands on the plinth*, whereby the latter of these does not contain $\begin{bmatrix}\text{nom}\\\text{stat}\end{bmatrix}$ and it is unnecessary to modify II. iii. 2. I suggest that we add to the subcategorization rules in II. i a rule of the form presented in (xvi):

(xvi)   II. i. 2. *b.* $\begin{bmatrix} + \text{locative} \\ - \text{ergative} \\ - \text{stative} \end{bmatrix} \rightarrow \pm \text{subjective}$

The effect of + **subjective** is (via a dependency rule) to add the feature subj to loc; and it is only when loc is so marked that it will undergo rule II. iii. I—which will have to be re-modified in accordance, as in (xvii):

(xvii)   II. iii. I. $\text{nom} + \text{V} \begin{Bmatrix} \text{erg} \\ \text{subj} \end{Bmatrix} \rightarrow \begin{Bmatrix} \text{erg} \\ \text{subj} \end{Bmatrix} \text{V} + \text{nom}$

   CONDITION: stat $\notin$ [nom]

(The condition is vacuous in the case of subj, since it will automatically be fulfilled, in that ± subjective is dependent upon (the selection of) − stative.) These rules account for the restriction of locative subjectivization to non-ergatives, and do not involve us in a modification of II. iii. 2 to allow the introduction of a copula after stat to be optional in locative clauses. Moreover, the subjectivized locative is shown as the marked possibility, which is reflected in the restricted set of verbs to which subjectivization is appropriate. Thus, the structure underlying (xiii. I. *a*) (after the operation of II. iii. I) can be represented as in (xviii):

(xviii)

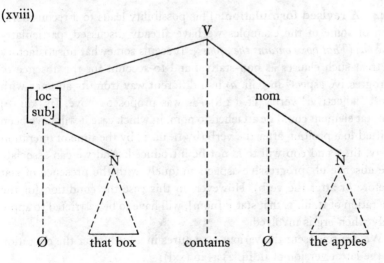

That for (i. *a*) remains as in (ii. *a*): in the absence of subj, II. iii. I has not operated.

6.43   Stat on loc. However this does not exhaust the possibilities. Consider now a clause like that in (xix):

(xix)   The ground was strewn with litter

in which *the ground* represents an underlying locative and *with litter* a nominative (with the *with* which characterizes (among other things) nom). Compare the clause in (xx):[1]

(xx)   Litter was strewn $\left\{ \begin{matrix} \text{on} \\ \text{over} \end{matrix} \right\}$ the ground

The difference between (xix) and (xx) consists in the presence versus the absence of subjectivization of the locative. However, in both cases, we find a copula. The occurrence of such is already in part allowed for by the rules we have considered so far, but if we are to account for the presence of cop in (xix) in terms of rule II. iii. 2 then stat must be attached to the subjectivized loc which precedes the verb at the time at which II. iii. 2 operates. Thus, (xix) and (xx) would differ not only in the presence versus the absence of subjectivization but also in the location of stat.

6.44   A revised formulation. This possibility leads to a reconsideration of some of the examples we have already discussed, particularly (xiii. *a*) (*That box contains the apples*). It seems somewhat unsatisfactory to treat such clauses as non-stative, and to account for the absence of 'progressive aspect' in (xiii. *a*) in a different way from its absence with most 'adjectival' verbs (cf. §4.8)—as was proposed above. In (xiii. *a*) the stat element could be attached to nom, in which case it will have been shifted to a position after the verb (by II. iii. 1) by the time of operation of IV. iii. 1 and cop will thus not be introduced. And we can associate the absence of 'progressive aspect' uniquely with the presence of stat (before or after the verb). However, in this case the condition for the operation of II. iii. 1, that stat ∉ [nom], will have to be restricted to apply only when erg is involved.

We can represent the various structures involved (after the operation of the latest version of II. iii. 2) as in (xxi):

---

[1] And see too Jespersen, 1928: 214; and, once more, Sundén, 1916: 91–2.

(xxi)   *a.*

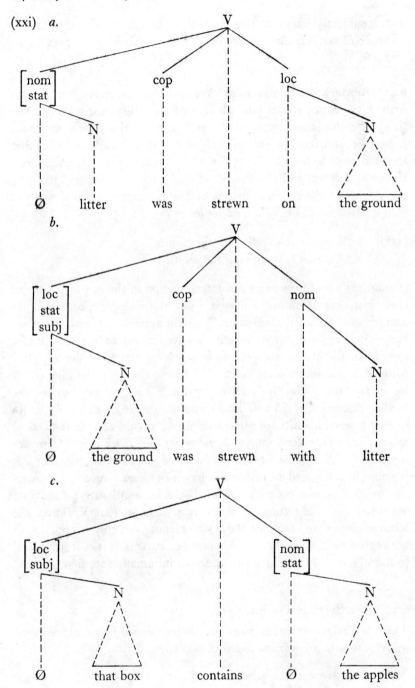

b.

c.

Thus, subjectivization of the locative is always associated with the presence of stat, attached either to loc (as in (xxi. *b*)) or to nom (as in (xxi. *c*)).

6.45   Remarks on 'stativeness'. We have thus associated 'stativeness' with the presence of stat (and absence of erg). But clearly clauses like (i. *a*) (*A statue stands on the plinth*) and (xxiv. 1. *a*) are, in some sense, notionally 'stative' also, and it is only in the presence of an ergative that they too cease to be such. They are 'static' rather than 'dynamic'. Yet, if we associate stat with the absence of the 'progressive aspect', then our decision to interpret such clauses as lacking stat seems just in view of the comparative normality of the examples in (xxvi):

(xxvi)   *a*. A statue is standing on the plinth
         b. A statue is occupying the plinth

(though we should note that the interpretation of the *be + ing* clause in such instances is rather different from those appropriate to other occurrences). From this situation, it would appear that, just as clauses containing stat are not notionally 'stative' when an ergative is also present in the clause, so a clause which lacks stat (and also erg) but contains loc is nevertheless 'stative'. That is, clauses containing either loc or stat are notionally 'stative' in the absence of erg (but see the further discussion in §8.11). This common feature no doubt underlies in part historical shifts from locative phrase to stative verb (adjective) exemplified in the development of *asleep* (or *alive*) in English. Compare too pairs like *She is exhausted/She is in a state of exhaustion*. Whether it is possible to show a more intimate relation between 'adjectival' clauses and locative clauses (as with 'nominal' clauses and locative clauses), I am uncertain. We return briefly to this point in Part V. Thus, the locative clauses we discussed above which contained only a copular verb are a sub-type of those clauses which contain two markers of 'stativeness' (stat and loc—and no erg), with the verb minimally specified.

6.5   Objectivization of locatives

There is a relevant further possibility to be allowed for, as represented in a clause with an ergative like that in (xxii):

(xxii)   John strewed the ground with litter

Compare *John strewed litter on the ground*, and consider too the paradigm in (xxiii):

(xxiii)   *a.* John planted the garden with apple-trees
      b. John planted apple-trees in the garden
      c. The garden was planted with apple-trees
      d. Apple-trees were planted in the garden

In cases like (xxii) and (xxiii. *a*), the locative is objectivized (and the nominative, displaced as object, is marked with *with*), rather than sub-jectivized as in (xix) and (xxiii. *c*). Consider too *fit with* vs. *fit in/on/to*. We could allow for these by considering loc to be marked optionally (via sub-categorization and dependency rules) as **obj(ective)**; and we can associate the difference in implication between the members of pairs like (xxiii. *a*) and (xxiii. *b*) ('focus'—Fillmore, 1968*a*: 48—where further examples of such phenomena are provided) with the presence versus the absence of obj. Such a locative will then undergo object-forming rules. Similar (but without erg (as in 1), or with reflexive erg (2)) are the clauses in (xxiv):

(xxiv)   1. *a.* A statue occupies the plinth
      b. The plinth is occupied by a statue
    2. *a.* The enemy occupied the country
      b. The country was occupied by the enemy

with the *a* examples containing an objectivized locative and the *b* examples a stative subjectivized loc. Compare too *live in/inhabit*, with similar differences in implication to those we noted immediately above. We can represent the structure underlying (xxiv. 1. *a*) as in (xxv):

(xxv)

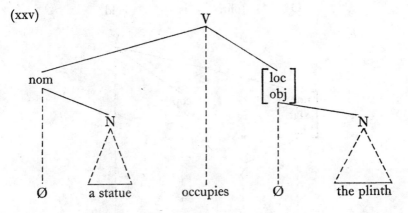

6.6   Reflexive locative clauses (loc on nom)?

Before attempting to formulate the necessary modifications to the rules, I would like to consider one further distinction that is perhaps relevant here. We have already allowed for erg, as well as appearing as a separate category, also to be attached as a feature to nom (by rule II. ii. 2 in (xliii)) in §4.9. We should now consider whether such a distribution is characteristic of loc too, i.e., whether there are clause-types explicable in terms of a conjunction of nom and loc. Indeed, it may be that the ambiguity of a clause like that in (xxvii) can be related to such a possibility:

(xxvii)   John is cold

This may refer either to John's sensations or to someone else's (who, for instance, has just touched John). If we relate the second interpretation to a simple stative structure, we can perhaps account for the difference in the first one in terms of the notion 'reflexive locative'.

(xxviii)   *a.*

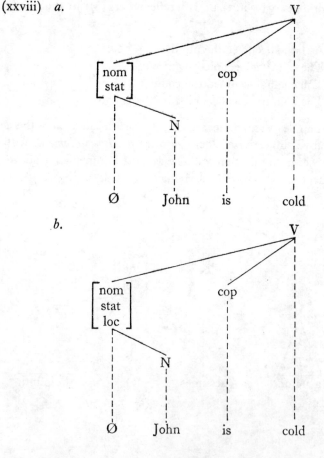

b.

(Or perhaps the relevant distinction is concerned with the attribution of a contingent rather than an inherent quality: see Gardiner, 1927: §141.) This makes a certain amount of sense, intuitively. Compare more obviously locative constructions like German *Es ist mir kalt* (with 'formal' subject). (It may be too (though what follows is even more speculative) that we should also make allowance for a non-stative equivalent to structures like that in (xxviii. *b*)—underlying, say, *John suffered*.) Compare also the Georgian examples in Chanidze, 1963: 18–20, where a form like *mciva* is paraphrased as 'à moi il y a froid'. *I am hungry* and the like may have an underlying structure of the type represented in (xxviii. *b*)—compare the Old English construction *Him hingrian* with 'dative subject' (see Visser, 1932: §29). In view of the uncertainty with respect to such an interpretation of these forms (they are certainly much more restricted than the comparable ergative phenomena), I shall not include the appropriate rules among those proposed below. Consideration of such clauses also leads on to the question of non-spatial locatives, which is what I want to consider next in a more general fashion. Let us at this point, however, incorporate into our grammar the rules allowing for locative clauses.

6.7   Fragment of grammar, 3

In this respect, I propose the revised set of rules presented in (xxix):

(xxix)   *Fragment of grammar, 3*

II. i. 1. $V \rightarrow \begin{bmatrix} \pm \text{ergative} \\ \pm \text{stative} \end{bmatrix}$

2. $+ \text{ergative} \rightarrow \begin{bmatrix} \pm \text{causative} \\ \pm \text{reflexive} \end{bmatrix}$

3. *a.* $\left\{ \begin{array}{l} - \text{ergative} \\ + \text{causative} \end{array} \right\} \rightarrow \pm \text{locative}$

b. $\begin{bmatrix} - \text{causative} \\ + \text{stative} \\ - \text{reflexive} \end{bmatrix} \rightarrow \pm \text{stative-ergative}$

4. $+ \text{locative} \rightarrow \left\{ \begin{array}{l} \pm \text{subjective}/ \begin{bmatrix} \overline{} \\ + \text{stative} \end{bmatrix} \\ \pm \text{objective} \end{array} \right\}$

5. $\begin{bmatrix} + \text{subjective} \\ - \text{ergative} \end{bmatrix} \rightarrow \pm \text{stative-locative}$

ii. 1. *a.* $V \rightarrow nom//\!-\!V$

   b. $+ locative \rightarrow loc//V\!-\!$

2. *a.* $+ ergative \rightarrow erg// \left\{ \begin{bmatrix} nom \\ - \\ V- \end{bmatrix} \Big/ \begin{bmatrix} \overline{} \\ + reflexive \end{bmatrix} \right\}$

   b. $\left\{ \begin{array}{l} + objective \rightarrow obj \\ + subjective \rightarrow subj \end{array} \right\} // \begin{bmatrix} loc \\ - \end{bmatrix}$

3. $+ stative \rightarrow stat// \left\{ \begin{array}{l} \begin{bmatrix} erg \\ - \end{bmatrix} \Big/ \begin{bmatrix} \overline{} \\ + stative\text{-}ergative \end{bmatrix} \\ \begin{bmatrix} loc \\ - \end{bmatrix} \Big/ \begin{bmatrix} \overline{} \\ + stative\text{-}locative \end{bmatrix} \\ \begin{bmatrix} nom \\ - \end{bmatrix} \end{array} \right\}$

iii. 1. $nom + V \left\{ \begin{array}{l} erg \\ subj \end{array} \right\} \rightarrow \left\{ \begin{array}{l} erg \\ subj \end{array} \right\} V + nom$

   CONDITION: if erg present, stat $\notin$ [nom]

2. $stat + V \rightarrow stat \begin{bmatrix} V \\ cop \end{bmatrix}$

The above rules differ from those presented in (xliii) in §4.9, as modified by (lxiii) in §5.7, in the addition to the SRs of rules II. i. 3. *a* (the former rule 3 becoming 3. *b*), II. i. 4 and II. i. 5, and to the DRs of rule II. ii. 1. *b* and II. ii. 2. *b*, and in the extension of rule 3 to allow for the attachment of stat to loc as well as to erg and nom. The term **stative-ergative** has accordingly been substituted for the former 'oblique' (in rules II. i. 3. *b* and II. ii. 3), since erg is no longer the only category other than nom to which stat can be added. The new rule II. i. 4 allows for the possibility of subjectivization of loc in + stative clauses, and its possible objectivization otherwise; the following rule provides (in terms of ± **stative-locative**) for the fact that in subjective non-ergative clauses stat can be attached to either loc or nom. The TRs in II. iii have also been modified in accordance with the above discussion (cf. (xvii) and (xii)). I shall return below to the phenomena of subjectivization and objectivization, when related 'directional' clauses have also been considered, since a more adequate characterization of such raises some more general considerations.

6.8 Erg on loc

Before shifting the focus of the discussion, I would like to note (incidentally, for the moment) that just as we found that erg could be added as a feature to nom, so in examples like that in (xxx):

(xxx)   His regiment contained the attack

his regiment can perhaps be regarded as representing a locative phrase in which loc is marked as erg—as in (xxxi):

(xxxi)

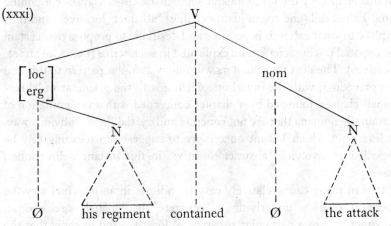

Notice that we find in such a case an imperative possibility: *Contain the attack at all costs!* Compare too the +stative equivalent in (xxxii):

(xxxii)

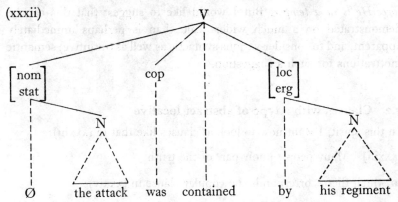

This possibility of a conjunction of the locative category with erg will assume some importance later in the discussion (in §9); I shall delay a consideration of the rules involved until then.

7   *Abstract location*

7.1   Preliminaries

In this chapter, I intend to look at some instances of clauses containing what I shall call (and try to justify calling) 'abstract' locatives, and thus explore to what extent it is possible and desirable to propose that certain non-spatial phenomena can be explicated in such terms (i.e. as 'abstract' locatives). The next two chapters will follow a similar pattern to this and the preceding, with the initial one dealing with the grammar of 'directional' clauses, followed by a chapter concerned with an examination of certain phenomena that are not concrete and spatial (in any obvious way, at least) but which I want once more to suggest can meaningfully be regarded as involving 'abstract' locative (in this instance, directional) cases.

It is in many cases relatively easy to indicate in an informal way the common relation underlying a 'concrete' or 'spatial' use and an 'abstract' use of a particular sub-type of locative, and to show that the semantic difference between them can be attributed to the content of the associated verbs and/or NPs—as in *He is in the garden/He is in the police-force/He is in a temper*. But I would like to suggest that this can be demonstrated on a much wider scale than is perhaps immediately apparent, and to consider various syntactic as well as (intuitive) semantic motivations for such a suggestion.

7.2   Clauses with a type of abstract locative

In this spirit, I want now to look at clauses like that in (xxxiii):

(xxxiii)   Many people know part of the truth

to which there corresponds the copular clause in (xxxiv):

(xxxiv)   Part of the truth is known to many people

In such clauses we have two casual phrases present. It seems reasonable to regard *part of the truth* as manifesting in both instances a nominative phrase, with absence of case-marker as object in (xxxiii) and as subject in (xxxiv). There remains the other case present in these clauses. It is clearly not ergative—no *Know part of the truth* or *He knew the language with the help of a grammar*—and rather than introduce another case category (as was done for the purposes of the discussion in Anderson, 1969*c*), it seems preferable at least to consider whether its identification as a locative can be supported. I suggest, then, that these two clauses have an underlying structure of the form represented in (xxxv):

(xxxv)

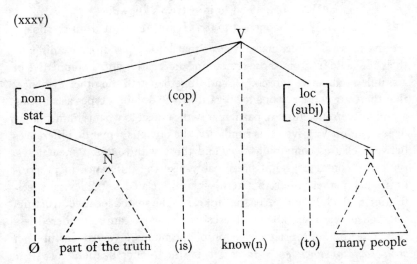

I.e. *know* is regarded as like *contain* in terms of the semantic representation governed by the V: '(knowledge of) part of the truth' is associated with ('located with respect to') 'many people'. If this is accurate, then in the case of (xxxiii) loc must be marked as subj, so that rule II. iii. 1 (as formulated in (xxix)) will operate to produce the correct sequence.

7.21 Some syntactic correlates. Various syntactic consequences should follow from such an identification as I am suggesting. Such clauses as (xxxiii) and (xxxiv) indeed share with those containing (non-ergative) *contain* and the like (as well as similarities with respect to possible sequences) the aspectual restriction exemplified in (xxxvi):

(xxxvi)   *Many people are knowing part of the truth

and this can presumably be related to the presence of stat, attached to nom, in both. We have already observed (in separate places above) that no unmarked imperative is possible with either type of verb. Consider too the anomalous nature of both sets of examples in (xxxvii):

(xxxvii)   1. *a.* What did he do? *He knew the truth.
             b. What did it do? *It contained the apples.
           2. *a.* What was done with it? *It was known.
             b. What was done with it? *It was (contained) in the box.
           3. *a.* What happened to him? *He knew the truth.
             b. What happened to it? *It contained the apples.
           4. *a.* What happened to it? *It was known.
             b. What happened to it? *It was (contained) in the box.

I think these examples make it clear that both types of clause differ in their 'behaviour' from those containing an ergative and a nominative or a simple nominative (cf. ch. 4), and (together with the other evidence) that there are some reasons for regarding the different types as showing a similarity in structure, in particular with respect to what is immediately dependent on V. Given this similarity, the obvious semantic differences between clauses containing *know* and those with *contain* ('mental' vs. typically 'concrete')—and presumably also the difference in preposi- positional marker (where not zero)—can be related to the lexical speci- fication of the NPs and verbs that appear in the shared locative structure. (Obviously, as noted above, clauses with *contain* can be rendered less 'concrete' by appropriate selection of the nouns involved—as in *That book contains some good ideas*; it is the 'concretization' of *know* that is rather more restricted.) Note too that these two kinds of case phrase are, as we would expect of subtypes of the same case (locative), mutually exclusive with respect to their occurrence in a single simple clause. If they are not both subtypes of locative, we should have to build such a restriction into the rules.

7.22   Morphological representation of dative. Together with *know* clauses, clauses containing *understand, need, hate, love, like,* etc., which show the same restrictions, can be regarded as locative. And, in general, such an account seems to be appropriate for 'affective verbs' (Vendryes, 1921: 121–5) or 'Empfindungsverben' (vs. 'Tatverben')—a distinction marked (to a certain extent) morphologically in the subject (by a 'dative' inflexion) in, for instance, Georgian.[1] Consider Georgian examples like

---

[1] See Schuchardt, 1896; Finck, 1910: 133–4; Vogt, 1938: 85–92; and cf the discussion of similar Old English phenomena below. Cf. too similar phenomena in Tamil (Vinson, 1903: §74), or the Malayalam constructions discussed in Asher, 1968: 99–

Svils deda uqvars ('The son (dat.) loves his mother (nom.)'—Chanidze, 1963: 20–1). Compare here Latin *mihi placet*, etc. Many English dative verbs (such as *like* and *think*) which now take a subjectivized locative, at an earlier stage in the history of the language preserved superficially traces of their underlying origin in the form of a dative inflexion[1]—cf. Old English *lician* + dative and *þyncan* + dative (van der Gaaf, 1904: §§13 and 16, respectively). The extension of the full subjectivizing rule to such verbs appears to take place in Middle and Early Modern English (see van der Gaaf, 1904: §170)—though a controversy concerning this usage persisted among prescriptive grammarians for some time afterwards—and for a time occasional instances with verbs like *please* are found (van der Gaaf, 1904: §159). I have suggested that the case-inflexion ('dative') which in many languages is found associated with the non-nominative phrase with these verbs (and which is characteristic of certain other constructions) marks the variant of the locative which is found with such 'affective' verbs (and is typically animate). This suggestion would seem to accord with the apparent origin of the dative in Indo-European—as reconstructed in e.g. Kuryłowicz, 1964: 190–5 ('The dative is genetically nothing less than an offshoot of the loc used with personal nouns')—and the frequent occurrence of the same inflexion or preposition for both 'dative' and 'spatial' locatives. I shall try to show below with respect to certain other constructions, at least, as well as that we have been looking at, that the distribution of the 'dative' inflexion (in e.g. many Indo-European languages) is not entirely haphazard—i.e. that the 'dative' is to a considerable extent a predictable variant of the locative in their case also. (Notice too that the fact that the animate subject in clauses with such verbs is derived (in English and other languages) from an underlying locative (sometimes marked by a 'dative' inflexion) contributed to speculations on the 'passive' nature of the transitive verb.)[2]

7.23   Ergativization of dative locatives. We should note further, however, that we find *by* as the marker of what we are regarding as a

---

100—though these have (superficially at least) nominal + copula rather than V: *avaḷkku peeṭi-y-aaṇə* ('Her-to fear is'); and see further on Georgian and Tagalog, Velten, 1931.
[1] See e.g. Jespersen, 1894: §§173–80; 1928: 208–12; van der Gaaf, 1904; Mustanoja, 1960: 434–6; Visser, 1963: §§32–43; Poutsma, 1928: 151–61; Šimko, 1957: 93–107; and the works referred to in these last two.
[2] Cf. § 4.62, and see Schuchardt, 1896; Finck, 1907: particularly 210–13.

locative case in non-subjective clauses containing, for instance, *like*, and that there is also a variant with *by* available in the case of *know*. Thus (xxxviii):

(xxxviii)   1. The play was liked by some of the audience
            2. Part of the truth is known by many people

Parallel to the variation between *known to* and *known by*, we can cite beside (xxxviii. 1) the example in (xxxix) (allowing for 'suppletion' in the sense discussed in §2.121):[1]

(xxxix)   The play was pleasing to some of the audience

The alternation could be allowed for by a 'recategorization rule' introducing erg with respect to such case elements (a rule whose formulation I would like to postpone). The locative phrases which have undergone this rule are those which contain NPs that are compatible with erg otherwise, and are thus typically animate (cf. §4.1). (Fillmore (1968*a*: §3) regards such casual phrases as 'dative', and thus animate.) That is, the verbs which require such locative phrases are those we find permitting this type of alternation (with or without 'suppletion')—i.e. transitive affective verbs. The *by*-variant is possible with verbs that are stative but not 'adjectival' (cf. below). We can refer to this sub-type of locative by the traditional name of **dative** (typically represented in Modern English by *to*). Thus, dative locatives are associated with a certain semantic set of verbs which also require the sort of specification for the locative NP that we have noted.

7.24   Objectivization and subjectivization of datives. If we now take into account other types of clause containing *please*, like that in (xl):

(xl)   The play pleased some of the audience

it becomes clear that we also find 'abstract' (dative) objective locatives (parallel to *A statue occupies the plinth*). The clause in (xl) has the structure represented in (xxv) (and being objective rather than subjective, it does not undergo the permutation we find in *Some of the audience liked the play*). And we can extend the paradigm for such dative locative clauses even further, as in (xli):

[1] On the *like/please* partial suppletion, see too Daneš, 1968: 61; Halliday, 1968: 191–5; Anderson, 1969*c*. Cf., for examples in German and Russian, for instance, Pontoppidan–Sjövall, 1964: 89–90.

(xli) 1. *a.* Many people know some of the truth
      b. Some of the truth is known by many people
      c. Some of the truth is known/familiar to many people
      d. Many people are familiar with some of the truth
   2. *a.* Some of the audience liked the play
      b. The play was liked by some of the audience
      c. The play was pleasing to some of the audience
      d. Some of the audience were pleased with the play

The *b* and *c* examples show that only the 'non-adjectival' verb form permits the ergative recategorization rule mentioned above, and indeed some require its operation. The locatives in the *d* instances in (xli) have undergone subjectivization, and the postposed nominative is represented as elsewhere in copular clauses by *with*; they are the stative-loc counterparts of the *a* examples. Compare the non-dative clause in (xix) in §6.43, and the structure represented in (xxi. *b*).

7.25 Ergativization of nom. Since we also find, as well as (xli. 2. *d*), the example in (xlii):

(xlii) Some of the audience were pleased by the play

nom in subjective stative locative clauses would appear to be subject to an ergativization rule like that we have considered (but not developed) for loc. However, in this case, it would apply rather more widely than it does with respect to loc. Parallel to (xlii) (but not dative) is (xliii):

(xliii) The plinth is occupied by a statue

(cf. (xxiv. 1)). We shall have to reconsider this situation below, particularly in §12.

7.26 Dative clauses with sentential nom. Certain of these dative verbs (like *think*, *believe*) require (with restricted exceptions) a sentential nominative. *Pleased, perturbed, annoyed, glad* also typically take such. The nominative preposition with the stative but 'non-adjectival' verbs among these, is once more either *by* (under recategorization) or some other (typically *with*, as *pleased, disgusted*, but also others required by particular verbs, as *amazed/surprised/annoyed at*). With the 'adjectival' verbs we find, as expected, only the latter possibility (*glad of/at, grateful for*). I would like to note too, in passing, the alternation represented in (xliv):

(xliv)   1. *a.*   He was surprised at/by my behaviour
           b.   *He was surprised my behaviour
         2. *a.*   He was surprised at/by the fact that I had gone
           b.   *He was surprised the fact that I had gone
         3. *a.*   *He was surprised at/by that I had gone
           b.   He was surprised that I had gone

in which the reduced sentential nominative lacks the sort of preposition markers we associate with post-'adjectival' nominatives. A plausible account of this would not seem too difficult to formulate. Compare too the sentential nominative in dative clauses like *It seems to me that he was wrong* (as the non-subjective equivalent of *I think that he was wrong*). It may be that certain modal verb forms are derived from a sub-type of stative (dative) locative clauses with a sentential nominative,[1] as *He must be coming* (cf. *I am sure that he'll be coming, He's sure to be coming*). Again, I shall not pursue this further here.

7.27 Summary. Apart from the rules recategorizing loc as erg (whatever their form), we have found considerable parallelism between clauses containing a nominative and what I have called a dative ('abstract') locative and clauses with a nominative and phrases to which the term 'locative' is usually thought appropriate—parallelism with respect to the variety of permitted structures and with regard to further restrictions on such clauses (as exemplified in (xxxvi) and (xxxvii), particularly). This parallelism allows us to consider that to a significant extent the same set of rules for the clause is appropriate in both instances, and that they operate upon underlying structures alike in containing (in particular) the locative category and differing only in the specifications of the NPs and, more particularly, verbs characteristic of dative and non-dative locatives respectively. The notion of 'abstract' locative is thus considerably extended. The adoption of a more abstract but localistic view of the grammar enables us (for instance) to proceed some way towards resolving the problems concerning pairs like *I liked the play* and *The play pleased me* outlined by Chomsky (1965: 162–3), which (with others) he considers to be 'cases that suggest the need for an even more abstract notion of grammatical function and grammatical relation than any that have been developed so far, in any systematic way'. We shall have occasion below to return to others of his problematic pairs.

[1] Cf. Ross, 1967: §§1.8–1.10; Anderson, 1969*b*.

7.3 Possessive and existential clauses

7.31 Possession and location. However, before proceeding to examine clauses of different types containing directional locatives (in §8), I would like to extend slightly the range of structures proposed as characteristic of non-directional clauses, and in so doing bring out once more the appropriateness of the term 'locative' to certain phenomena which are not obviously 'spatial'. This extension will involve us in a consideration of the derivation of clauses containing *have* as a 'main verb', the relation of the equivalents of which to locative (or 'dative') clauses has already been made clear (with respect to various languages) in a number of studies.[1] In many languages the relationship between 'possessive' (in a wide sense) and locative clauses is rather obvious, even superficially. Consider in this respect Finnish clauses like those in (xlv):

(xlv)   *a.* Kirja on Pöydällä ('The book is on the table')
        b. Minulla on kirja ('I have a book'—'A book is on me')

See too the Chinese, Russian and Turkish examples discussed by Lyons (1968a: §8.4.5). Some of the studies mentioned above (e.g. Meillet, 1924) also point out the comparative recentness of *have*-type constructions in various Indo-European languages, and the existence of earlier 'possessive' constructions more obviously parallel to 'ordinary' locative clauses; and attempts are made to relate such developments to a general tendency towards 'personal subjects' in many of these languages (cf. *like*, etc.)—see Bally, 1926. It is my intention in what follows to attempt to characterize such phenomena and to formulate such of these suggestions as I can support within the framework we have been developing.

7.32 'Copying'. Consider in the first place a clause like that in (xlvi):

(xlvi)   There is a book on the table

Here we appear to have a nominative phrase (*a book*) and two locative phrases (*there*—cf. *He lives there*—and *on the table*) one of which has been subjectivized, and has indeed little more semantic specification than

---

[1] See, for instance, Hanoteau, 1860: 85–6; Meillet, 1924; van Ginneken, 1939; Benveniste, 1960; Bendix, 1966: 37–59, 123–32; Fillmore, 1966a: 25–7; 1968a: §3.4; Lyons, 1967; 1968a: §8.4.4; 1968b; Bach, 1967; Langacker, 1968; Sedláček, 1968; Asher, 1968: 99; Christie, 1969. In many languages, the 'possessor' is locative; in others, it is the 'possessed' which is (at least superficially) locative ('comitative'). Cf. Kikuyu *Me na mĩgeka mĩingĩ*, 'They are with (*na*) many mats' = 'They have many mats' (Gecaga & Kirkaldy-Willis, 1953: 10–11, 120–1).

that it is locative. Also, the clause in (xlvi) is rather more usual than
A book is on the table, and, in a sense, (xlvi) might be regarded as a device
for avoiding an indefinite subject in such a clause: cf. Jespersen, 1924:
154–6; Kirkwood, 1969: 101–2—and see further below. We already have
a rule for subjectivizing locatives; this situation suggests that, adapting
for our present purposes Fillmore's (1968 *a*: §3.4) proposals for sentences
with 'expletive *there*', we should extend this rule to examples like (xlvi)
and derive the second locative by 'copying'. That is, we might propose
the following sketch of a derivation for such a clause. The underlying
structure is as in (xlvii):

(xlvii)

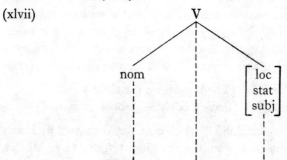

By rule II. iii. 1 (cf. (xxix)), loc is then subjectivized, exchanging places
with nom; by III. ii. 1 the two NPs are introduced. The NPs are
developed appropriately (by unspecified rules in IV) and cop is introduced after stat. The resulting structure can be abbreviated as in
(xlviii):

(xlviii)

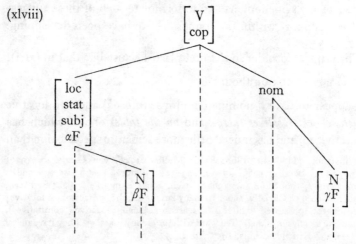

(where αF, etc. are cover symbols for whatever the appropriate specifications, including in particular referential indices (where appropriate), may
be). A late rule (which, I presume, owes its ultimate motivation to a
subcategorization rule for V) then 'copies' the locative into the neutral
locative position, and the first locative NP is 'expletivized' (its full
lexical content now being represented in the 'copy'), as in (xlix):

(xlix)

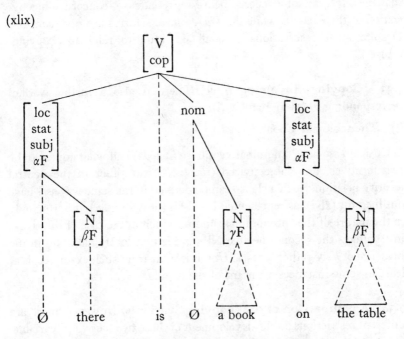

This expletive locative subjectivization is possible in types of clause
which do not otherwise permit subjectivization (which, as we have seen,
is associated with certain verbs only), as is the case with the example we
have been discussing.

7.321 *Reservations concerning 'copying'.* The details of this account
presuppose that the case categories are introduced in the order (in the
string) suggested so far; one might want to revise such an account
somewhat in view of the proposals advanced in chapter 10. I have also
not explored here the possibility that an alternative derivation, in terms
of some sort of embedding, might indeed be preferable; but this does
not affect, I think, the 'localistic' conclusions I want to draw below.
Notice however that in many varieties of Modern English—including

most formal contemporary ones?—the copula in such clauses shows number concord with the following nominative phrase (*There are some books on the table*), arguing against an interpretation of them involving a simple extension of subjectivization (in such varieties, at least)—cf. Traugott, 1969*b*[1]—unless one allows for both pre-concord and post-concord subjectivization (if such a notion as the latter is defensible), such that the *have*-variant discussed below represents pre-concord subjectivization of the locative, while the *There is/are*...forms are post-concord. Despite such reservations, I shall continue to refer to 'copying' clauses.

7.33 'Copying' involving *have*. There is also a further variant corresponding to (xlvi), namely (l):

(l)   The table has a book on it

Once again we have a nominative phrase (*a book*) and what appear to be two locatives, one subjectivized (*the table*), the other in the neutral locative position. Such a clause can be derived in the same way as I have outlined for (xlvi), as represented in (xlvii) through (xlix), differing only in the nature of the 'pronominalization', which in the case of the clause in (l) affects the second locative NP (and is non-locational), and in the presence of *have* rather than *be*. *Has*, it is clear from such examples, is at least in some instances a variant of the copula.[2]

7.34 A comparison of the 'copying' variants. However, there are different restrictions on the development of these two 'copying' variants. Consider the examples in (li):

(li)   1. *a.* *A table has a book on it
       b. The table has a book on it
       c. The table has the book on it
       d. *A table has the book on it
       2. *a.* ?There is a book on a table
       b. There is a book on the table
       c. There is the book on the table
       d. ?There is the book on a table

---

[1] For examples of the alternative usage, in English and other languages, see Jespersen, 1913: §§6.81 and 6.82; and on 'subject-like' features of *there*..., see Jespersen, 1949: §3.1.

[2] As was suggested, though without support, in Anderson, 1968*b*: 316. See too Lyons, 1968*a*: §8.4.4.

The *a* and *d* examples in (li), with an indefinite locative NP, are (as we might expect) less acceptable. Example (li. 2. *c*) with *there* and *be*, and a definite nominative NP, differs markedly in its interpretation from (li. 2. *b*): 2. *c* does not appear to be related to 1. *c* in anything like the way that 2. *b* is related to 1. *b*. Thus, 2. *c* would seem to require a rather different derivation (cf. Jespersen, 1924: 154–6; Lyons, 1968a: §8.4.3). I.e. both variants are associated with definite locatives, and the *there*-forms also with an indefinite nominative. Compare however the restrictions exemplified in (lii):

(lii) 1. *a.* There's a man in the garden
       b. ?The garden has a man in it
       2. *a.* ?There's a book with me
       b. I have a book with me

These last examples suggest that both varieties of pronominalization are possible (under the above conditions) when the nominative and the locative NPs agree in animacy, as in (li. 1. *b*) and (li. 2. *b*) or the clauses in (liii):

(liii) *a.* There's a friend with me
        b. I have a friend with me

If there is a discrepancy, the *have* variant normally occurs with an animate (and particularly a human) locative, the *be* variant with an inanimate. And this is in accord with the general principle favouring full animate subjects.[1] Thus, certain relations of implication (such that certain combinations are marked) hold with respect to the 'copying'-variant and the subcategorization of the governed NPs; these appear to throw further doubt on the interpretation of such clauses as involving simply subjectivization and 'copying'.

7.341 *With non-copular verbs.* The clauses in *b* and *c* in (liv) would perhaps allow the same sort of derivation as that we have been considering, except that the verb is not copular (the copula being segmented out) and is indeed 'abstract' in the 2 and 3 instances.

(liv) 1. *a.* A book was placed on the table
       b. There was a book placed on the table
       c. The table had a book placed on it

[1] See too Mathesius, 1929; Kirkwood, 1969: 98–9.

2. *a.* Something is wrong with the car
   b. There is something wrong with the car
   c. The car has something wrong with it
3. *a.* Something is wrong with John's leg
   b. There is something wrong with John's leg
   c. John's leg has something wrong with it

However, notice that the *b* and *c* examples show the nominative NP in each case preceding the verb; and this might lead us to question an interpretation of such (and of (xlvi), etc.) merely in terms of a further development (involving 'copying') of subjectivization of a locative (like that we find with verbs of the *contain* variety). This would be less of a problem in terms of the proposals made in chapters 10 and 12, but it suggests that (at least in the case of the examples in (liv)) an alternative derivation via embedding within a locative clause may well prove preferable. But I shall not pursue this possibility here, in that it involves many considerations outside our main area of discussion.

7.35 Existential clauses. 'Existential clauses' like (lv) presumably form a sub-type of such 'copying' clauses, however they are derived:[1]

(lv)   There are elephants in India

The nominative phrase in such is typically indefinite and generic. The unusualness of *Elephants are in India* is parallel to that of *A box contains two apples*. Together with (lv) we find *Elephants exist in India*, though a modified clause like *Elephants exist only in India* is more usual (if less true, in this particular case). This suggests that *exist* is merely the semantically most neutral verb of the *stand, sit,* etc. type. Further, *live* is the form of this verb we find with human (and, along with *exist*) animal nominatives.[2] Also, we can interpret the 'simple' *Giants exist* as involving deletion of an underlying locative pro-form (cf. Kahn, 1966): cf. *There are giants in existence*. On such and other 'existential predications' (including clauses with *happen, take place, cease*) see Sundén, 1916: 44–5.

---

[1] Cf. e.g. Bally, 1932: §63; Collinson, 1937: 50; Lyons, 1967; 1968*a*: §8.4.3.
[2] On *live/exist* and temporal locatives, see Lyons, 1968*a*: §8.1.10.

7.36 Possessive clauses

7.361 *'Copying' of an adnominal.* I want now to return to example (liv. 3. *c*), with respect to which it should be observed that another possible (and perhaps more usual?) variant is that in (lvi):

(lvi) John has something wrong with his leg

in which only a (adnominal) dependent part of the locative NP appears in initial position; and it is the part in the second locative NP corresponding to it (*John—his*) that has been pronominalized. This possibility seems to be restricted to the dependent term in 'inalienable' relations,[1] in particular 'body-parts' and the like. I do not intend here to elaborate upon this derivation, but merely to indicate that it may be that a similar structure to the one appropriate to the clause in (lvi) underlies clauses containing *have* which have a 'possessive' interpretation.

7.362 *A proposal for 'possessive* have'. Consider in this respect the sentence in (lvii):

(lvii) I have a compass

This is (at least) two-ways ambiguous, denoting either 'availability' or 'possession' (cf. Lyons, 1968*a*: §8.4.5); and it can be disambiguated as in (lviii):

(lviii) *a.* I have a compass with/on me
       b. I have a compass among my possessions

(lviii. *a*) has (in the relevant respects) a derivation like *The table has a book on it*, whereas (lviii. *b*) is rather like (lvi). It might be suggested that (lvii) is ambiguous because two rather different sorts of locative may be present in the structure underlying it; the ambiguity is the result of the operation of rules deleting these. Thus, the clause expressing the 'abstract' relation of possession (if we take it to have a derivation similar to (lviii. *b*) is a sub-type of locative which (once again) is rendered 'abstract' by virtue of features of its structure other than the casual relations involved as such—in particular, in this case, by virtue of the specification underlying *possessions*. We can perhaps characterize this type of abstract locative, in an informal way, by noting that the clauses

---

[1] Cf. e.g. Uhlenbeck, 1916*b*; Sapir, 1917*b*; Rosén, 1959, and the works referred to therein.

containing them differ from 'abstract' locative clauses with verbs like
know in that the nominative NP is 'located' not directly with respect to
the person involved, but rather with respect to something ('possession')
attributed to him—and is thus doubly locative, since *my possessions* (for
instance) is no doubt to be derived by nominalization of a clause containing the verb *possess/belong*, which is itself a dative locative verb (see
below). Thus, under such an interpretation, *possession* appears to be
regarded as 'inalienable', though 'possessions' are not.

It may be that it will be necessary to recognize further ambiguities for
a clause like that in (lvii). Consider, for instance, the interpretation
represented less ambiguously by *I have a compass in my possession*, which
does not necessarily imply either immediate availability or ownership.
However, I have at this time nothing to offer towards the characterization of such. And it may be that (lvii) is merely indifferent (rather than
ambiguous) with respect to such distinctions. Notice too that the derivation for 'possessive *have*' that I have suggested is obviously appropriate
only to instances of 'alienable' or 'separable' possession.

7.363 *Remarks on 'inalienable possession'.* There is a wide range of
syntactic properties associated with 'inalienables'. Some 'inalienables',
including 'affective' ones like *He has a pleasant disposition*, appear to
represent a simple 'abstract' locative relation; but 'genitive phrases'
involving relationship terms like *his mother*, etc., which are sometimes
considered along with these, perhaps involve rather different derivations
from those appropriate to phrases like *his bad temper* (cf. Anderson,
1968*b*: 311–13). Other instances of 'relational' nouns were discussed in
§2 (cf. too Fillmore, 1969: §11). Certain 'inalienables' involve a 'partitive' relation: *side of...*, *some of...*, etc. Clearly, 'genitive' constructions represent a superficial neutralization of a large range of (in some
cases quite complex) underlying relations, and if there is a basic (non-
derived) 'genitive' relation as such, it is presumably partitive (though
this may be a sub-type of locative). Sub-groups of 'inalienable' nouns,
e.g. those denoting 'body-parts', which in many languages are grouped
in terms of superficial morphology (as overt inalienables) with 'terms of
relationship',[1] show various distinctive syntactic possibilities. In
particular, they appear in clauses which seem to involve the sort of
copying we found in (lvi)—i.e. of an adnominal constituent of the

---

[1] See once more Uhlenbeck, 1917*b*; Sapir, 1917*b*; also Manessy, 1964—and cf.
Fillmore, 1968*a*: §5.1.4.

locative NP—but which are non-stative and include a particular subset of verbs. Consider the clauses in (lix):

(lix) *a.* I broke my leg
     b. I hurt my side
     c. I burned my fingers

In one interpretation, *I* in such clauses represents an underlying ergative phrase; but there is another interpretation with respect to which *I* perhaps (like the subject in (lvi)) be regarded as a subjectivization of the ('inalienable') adnominal within the locative phrase. At any rate, two rather different semantic representations are involved. In comparison, *I hurt his foot* is unambiguous, and corresponds to the former interpretation of the instances in (lix). On this topic, see Fillmore, 1968*a*: §5,[1] where 'inalienable possession' is discussed much more fully—though the account he proposes is perhaps inappropriate to terms of relationship,[2] and may in fact yield more generally to a more 'abstract' derivation. See also the discussion by Visser (1963: §320) of earlier constructions like *Him brekeþ þe sweore* ('He breaks his neck'). Notice too that *lack*, for instance, seems to be a (lexicalized-negative) verb which (in 'active' clauses) takes a subjectivized locative whose relationship to the object nominative is typically (though not exclusively) 'inalienable'. Compare the early history of *want*, as discussed in Bertschinger, 1941: particularly 6–48.

7.364 *Other verbs of possession.* Returning to 'alienable possession', we can observe that *possess* itself is apparently in many respects a straightforward dative verb,[3] one which requires the locative to be subject, and to which there corresponds the non-subjective verb *belong*. Compare the examples in (lx):

(lx) *a.* I possess a compass
     b. The compass belongs to me

It may indeed be that *possess* is the semantically least marked dative verb (notice, for instance, how one can be said to 'possess' or 'have' 'knowledge'). With *possess* and *belong*, also, it is the case that only definite nominative NPs are eligible as subjects (**A compass belongs to me*); and

---

[1] And, of course, many earlier studies, including de la Grasserie, 1896: particularly 91–3; Frei, 1939.
[2] Anderson, 1968*b*: 311–13; de la Grasserie, 1890: 165–74.
[3] Cf. once again, on Georgian, Chanidze, 1963: 20–1.

this also applies to clauses with *mine*, etc. (**A compass is mine*), in which the verb has been copularized (no segmentalization has taken place) and its semantic content is 'carried' by the locative NP (which has a distinctive 'shape').

7.365 *An alternative proposal for 'possessive* have'. Notice too that just as *I possess the compass* is somewhat unusual, so *I have the compass* suggests availability rather than ownership. An alternative possible derivation for 'possessive *have*' now becomes apparent; just as *possess* is the form of the verb also underlying *belong* that we find with indefinite nominatives, so we might consider a similar relationship to hold between the clauses in (lxi) (cf. Lyons, 1968*a*: §8.4.4):

(lxi)   *a.* I have a compass
         b. The compass is mine

The difference between an 'availability' and an 'ownership' interpretation of (lxi. *a*) would then be associated with the character of the copular verb (rather than the deleted locative, as under the earlier proposal), simply locative in the one instance, in the other having the specification associated with *possess/belong*. The latter would also be that we find in (lxi. *b*) (as we have observed). In view of the greater simplicity of the deletions required with respect to this second proposal for 'possessive *have*', it would appear to be preferable (in the absence of other evidence). Thus, the distinction between 'possessive' and 'non-possessive' *have* might be said to reside simply in whether the locative is dative or not, the verb being respectively the semantically least marked dative or locative verb.

7.366 *The structure of possessive clauses.* We also find with 'possessive verbs' the ergativized locative variant we associate with datives, as in (lxii. *b*):

(lxii) *a.* That company owns many stores
         b. Many stores are owned by that company

If we adopt the second interpretation of the derivation of 'possessive *have*', then the structure underlying all the clauses in (lx) to (lxii) can be represented as in (lxiii):

(lxiii)

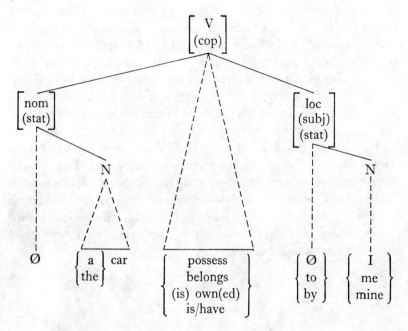

Stat is attached to loc in the case of *belong* (to explain the absence of copula); otherwise it is added to nom. In accord with such a derivation, all of the verbs reject 'progressive aspect':

(lxiv)   *a.*   *I am possessing a car
         b.   *The car is belonging to me
         c.   *I am owning a car
         d.   *The car is being owned by me

7.4 Summary

I want now to move on to 'directional locatives' (in §8); but before doing so, let me try to summarize. A further case element, locative, has been proposed in chapter 6. Its occurrence is dependent upon the selection of −ergative or +causative, but we find both stative and non-stative locative clauses; and there are a number of further distinctions dependent upon +locative. In particular, in clauses which are also stative, the locative may or may not be subjectivized, and if it is, there may be in certain circumstances 'copying' of the subjectivized locative. In non-stative clauses, the locative may be objectivized. Only certain verbs (like *contain*) appear in clauses containing subjectivized locatives if no 'copying' has taken place. Subjectivization is also characteristic of clauses containing verbs like *know*, which involve relations that are not obviously spatial, but which I have tried (in the present chapter) to show can reasonably be regarded as representing a sub-type of locative clause, distinguished from more 'concrete' instances in terms of the sub-categorization of their particular NPs and verbs (which may be reflected in, for instance, the shape of the prepositional markers). Associated with this locative sub-type (dative) is the possibility of ergativization (to the characterization of which we shall return in chapter 12). Two types of copying can be distinguished, depending on whether the initial locative phrase is pronominalized (as *there*) or the copy is (as *it*, etc.)—in which case the copular verb has the shape *has*. Different interpretations for *have* as a 'main verb' ('availability', 'ownership', etc.) can be explicated with respect to such a derivation.

8 Ablative

8.1 Preliminaries

I want now to consider locative clauses that are 'directional' or 'dynamic' (in the sense of Lyons, 1968 a: §8.4.7), as exemplified in (lxv):

(lxv)   The ball rolled from Jane to Mary

This differs from the clauses containing simple ('concrete') locatives that we have been looking at (in chapter 6) in a number of respects, including the following: (1) there are two 'locational' phrases either present or implied: (2) the 'shapes' of the locational prepositions are different from those characteristic of the 'concrete' locatives in chapter 6 (and from each other); (3) the verbs which occur in clauses like (lxv) are for the most part distinct from the locative verbs we have considered so far; (4) (lxv) is notionally 'non-stative', whereas the corresponding clause allowed for in chapter 6 (e.g. *The ball lay on the floor*) is 'stative'.

8.11 'Static' and 'dynamic'. Let us consider how we might account for such phenomena, noting, before considering this in detail, some further relevant observations. For the moment, I shall refer to the category represented by *to* in (i) as **allative** and that manifested as *from* as **ablative** (ignoring once again such further contrasts as those between *from* and *out of*—ablative/elative—and *to* and *into*—allative/illative), these indicating respectively the terminal and initial location of the nominative with respect to the 'process' involved. There exists a not inconsiderable overlap in the 'prepositional' forms that manifest the allative and the 'static' locative in English (e.g. *inside*—see Sapir & Swadesh, 1932: 15–16) and other languages.[1] We should note too, in this regard, the 'implicational' relationship indicated by Lyons (1966: 229; 1968 a: §8.4.7—cf. too Traugott & Waterhouse, 1969) and represented by the 'aspectually' different pairs in (lxvi):

---

[1] E.g. French *en, à, dans*. On this last, see Condillac's discussion in Le Roy, 1947: 478b. Cf. too the Ossetic locatives discussed by Vogt (1944: 22–30); and on Indo-European, see Kuryłowicz, 1964: 189–90.

(lxvi)   1. *a.* He has come here
         b. He is here (now/already)
     2. *a.* He has gone to London
         b. He is in London (now/already)

(though of course this can be 'cancelled': *He has come here often*). In such cases, too, although superficially we find only one casual phrase apart from the nominative in the *a* examples, the other (ablative) phrase is implicit ('He has come here from somewhere else'; 'He has gone from here, or somewhere else, to London')—just as the allative is implicit in *He has come*. As well as the relationship exemplified by the *a* and *b* instances in (lxvi), we must also take account of that represented in (lxvii)—which in linking the ablative with a negative locative clause, illustrates once again (cf. §5.4) the relationship between the occurrence of *from* and a negation (cf. *be absent from/be missing from* (=*not be in/on*)):

(lxvii)   1. *a.* He has come here from London
         b. He is not in London
     2. *a.* He has gone from here to London
         b. He is not here

There would appear to be some kind of antonymic relation ($\pm$ab ?) between loc and abl. Stated in more general terms, loc and abl are $\pm$ negative with respect to the semantic dimension of direction.

8.2   A proposal for directional clauses

We can account for at least part of such phenomena, and in particular the relationship between locative and allative, in the following way. There is a subcategorization rule dependent upon (at least) + locative— let us call it $\pm$ dynamic—the effect of choosing the positive of which is to introduce (via a dependency rule) the category abl(ative) before loc. The 'allative' is to be interpreted as no more than the variety of loc we find when abl is also present (in the same clause). Some prepositions are found representing loc only when abl is absent (*at*), others only when abl is present (*to*—unless loc is dative) and yet others occur (as we have noted) indifferently (in this respect). Verbs are classified as to whether they require abl or reject it (i.e. as + dynamic or − dynamic); the verbs underlying the *a* and *b* instances of (lxvi) and (lxvii) differ only in this respect (cf. Lyons, 1966: 229). And presumably we are to regard the selection of +dynamic as overruling the 'stative' character of non-ergative locative clauses: thus (lxv) is notionally 'non-stative', whereas *The ball lay on the floor* is the reverse. This, then, would in principle allow for all the features we noted with respect to the clause in (lxv) (though questions remain in the case of the ablative/negative-locative relationship). Under such an interpretation, we could suggest for (lxv) the (relevant) underlying structure in (lxviii):

(lxviii)

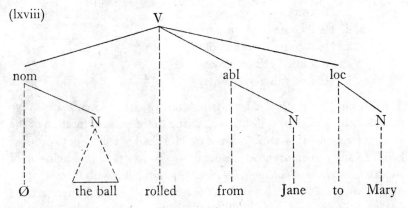

A similar structure to that represented in (lxviii) underlies the *a* example in (lxvi) and (lxvii), except that in their case nom is marked as erg (and the verb is of course causative)—and also, in the examples in (lxvi. *a*), the ablative phrases have been deleted. Equivalent clauses containing *bring*, *take* and *send* (for instance) are like (lxvi. *a*) and (lxvii. *a*), except that, in particular, erg occurs (with them) as a separate category (and not as a feature attached to nom). They are also causative.[1] Consider, too, in this connexion a verb like *move*, which occurs in clauses of all three types, non-ergative, causative reflexive and causative non-reflexive, as represented in (lxix. *a*), (lxix. *b*), and (lxix. *c*), respectively:

(lxix)   *a.* The rock moved
         b. John moved
         c. John moved the rock

(with which both locational phrases may be deleted—as indeed in these examples).

---

[1] Compare the Aleut examples discussed by Jochelson (1927). Here too there is a discussion of the distinction between 'bring' and 'take' on the one hand, and 'send' on the other—which topic is also touched on in Anderson, 1968*b*: 310. See also Sapir & Swadesh, 1932: 32–4.

8.21 Remarks on *come* and *go*. In many clauses, at least, *come* and *go* (and *bring* and *take*) do not represent independent lexical selections (for the verb), but the occurrence of one rather than the other is dependent on the (deictic) specification of the co-occurrent locative NP. The difference in lexical content is derived (in the sense of §2.121). Consider the examples in (lxx):

(lxx) 1. *a.* He comes here often
         b. He comes there often
     2. *a.* He'll come here tomorrow
         b. He'll come there tomorrow
     3. *a.* He came here yesterday
         b. He came there yesterday

The *a* examples in (lxx) all contain *here*, which represents a locative phrase with a deictic specification referring to the present location of the speaker ('*ego*-deixis'—an account of which I shall not attempt to propose here). In such an environment, *come* normally occurs to the exclusion of *go*: thus, no **He goes/will go/went here.*[1] The situation with *there* is rather more complex. Clearly, parallel to the *b* examples in (lxx), there are the following instances:

(lxxi) 1. He goes there often
      2. He'll go there tomorrow
      3. He went there yesterday

But the deictic specification underlying *there* in such cases is different from that associated with the *there* in the *b* examples in (lxx), and it is this difference that is reflected ultimately in the difference in phonological shape of the verb. I want to suggest that the set of specifications for *there* which requires *come* and the set which requires *go* are mutually exclusive. The precise division of the specifications between *come*-clauses and *go*-clauses appears to vary with different varieties of English, but one common situation is as follows. The *there* in (lxx. 3. *b*) refers either to the present location of the addressee or to the past (co-temporal with when 'he came') location of the speaker or addressee: *there* in

---

[1] Though we should note the possibility of sentences like *Go here!* when, for instance, directions on a map are being indicated (cf. Householder, 1966: 238). However, in such circumstances the deictic specification of the locative is obviously rather different. Observe that in Sora (Ramamurti, 1931: 27) and Pareng (Bhattacharya, 1954: §21), for instance, something like the distinction between 'come' and 'go' is marked by the presence or absence of a suffix: cf. Pareng *i-* ('go') vs. *i-ai* ('come').

(lxx. 2. *b*) refers either to the present location of the addressee or the future (co-temporal with when 'he will come') location of the speaker or addressee; and in (lxx. 1. *b*), *there* refers to the present location of the addressee (and perhaps, in some varieties of English, the future or past location of the speaker or addressee). The occurrences of *there* in (lxxi) on the other hand, represent underlying specifications other than those underlying *here* or *there* in the corresponding examples in (lxx). Part of the ambiguity here derives from the absence in Modern English (of most varieties) of 'second person' demonstrative ('*tu*-deixis') forms.

However, we also find instances like those in (lxxii):

(lxxii) 1. He comes to London quite often
  2. He'll come to London tomorrow
  3. He came to London yesterday

which contain a lexically full locative NP, but which allow the same deictic interpretations as I have outlined for (a combination of) the *a* and *b* examples in (lxx). Unless we are to propose that in instances like those in (lxxii) there is an independent (deictic) lexical choice between *come* and *go*, we must suppose that the locatives in (lxxii) can be specified in a similar fashion to those in (lxx)—presumably in terms of speaker/addressee referential indices. The latter proposal has the advantage of restricting the specification of deixis to a single type of element. And an extension of this type of explanation will also account for the alternation between *come* and *go* in sentences like *He had come/gone to Carthage the previous year*. I shall not develop here a characterization of the notion of deixis, but I think it is possible to envisage, in the light of the above, an account of the syntax of *come* and *go* in which the selection of one rather than the other is determined by deictic elements in the locative phrase in the same clause. What I have outlined in this informal manner owes much to Fillmore's (1966*b*) proposals, but unlike them the account envisaged here is not interpretative, and it does not attribute semantic distinctions directly to the verb, but regards the verbal differences as a lexicalization of distinctions originating elsewhere. It thus illustrates two principles which recur throughout our discussion.

8.3 Stative directional clauses

Fillmore also suggests (1966*b*: footnote 12) that the distinction between locative phrases like those in *I am at the shop* and *I have come to the shop*, respectively, is merely a reflexion of the distinction between 'motional' and 'non-motional' verbs (on this, cf. Vasiliu, 1968). Lyons, too, has suggested such a dependency (1966: 229). It might be worth considering too whether it could be interpreted as holding rather in the reverse direction. Both distinctions could also perhaps be regarded as in some sense superficial markers of an underlying opposition at a 'higher rank' (cf. Lyons, 1968a: §8.4.7). The discussion of 'directional' clauses conducted above accords with the last of these suggestions, with the 'directional' case abl introduced with respect to a verb opposition (± dynamic). But a simple account in terms of ± dynamic (or ± motional) fails to account for the fact that we find clauses which are 'directional' but nevertheless 'stative' ('non-motional'), as exemplified in (lxxiii):

(lxxiii)   *a.* The road goes from London to Brighton
          b. The fog stretched from London to Brighton

That is, in such examples we have the *from* and *to* (etc.) prepositions we associate with the selection of + dynamic (which introduces abl), but these differ from the dynamic clauses we have been looking at so far in that they are also 'stative', as illustrated in (lxxiv):

(lxxiv)   1. *The road is going from London to Brighton
          2. He is going from London to Brighton

(unless perhaps 'the road' in (lxxiv. 1) is still being built!). In §6.45 we associated 'stativeness' primarily with the selection of + stative. If we propose that this is also the case with respect to examples like those in (lxxiii), then stat in their case must not be attached to nom—otherwise, we would expect a copula to be present. Such a structure, with stat attached to nom, underlies rather a clause like that in (lxxv):

(lxxv)   It is stretched from wall to wall

(which is 'stative' in the absence of an underlying ergative category). Let us suppose then that it is added to loc in the case of clauses like (lxxiii). We can allow for this by an extension of the rule involving ± stative-locative to clauses that are + dynamic (as in II. i. 5 in (lxxvii) below). Thus, both (lxxiii) and (lxxv) differ from (lxv) in being + stative rather than its opposite and differ from each other in the distribution of the stative element within the clause. 'Dynamic' clauses are merely the non-stative sub-type of what I shall now refer to as **directional** clauses.[1] Thus (lxxiii) have the structure represented in (lxxvi. *a*) and (lxxv) that represented in (lxxvi. *b*):

(lxxvi) *a.*

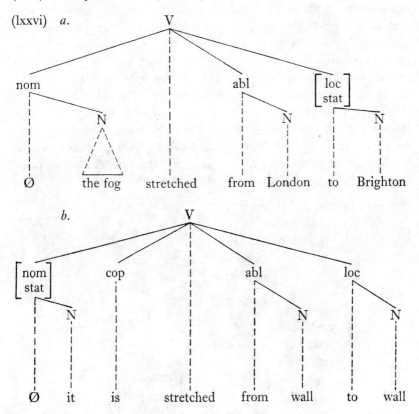

b.

8.4 **Fragment of grammar, 4**

Let us try to gather these various proposals together by formulating a revised set of rules for the clause to supersede that suggested in the previous chapter. These will also allow without modification for directional clauses with an objectivized locative, as exemplified in (lxxvii):

(lxxvii) *a.* They reached Canada (on Tuesday)
          b. He entered the room

1 Clauses like *The picture hangs from a hook* and *The grill projects from the wall* are a sub-type of stative directional clause in which the lexical content of the locative phrase ('downwards', 'outwards') has been 'transferred' to the verb (by a verbalizing rule (cf. §9.5)) with subsequent deletion of the locative phrase.

and for subjective clauses like *London was reached on Tuesday*. It is doubtful whether there are directional clauses which are +subjective but −stative-locative—i.e. which correspond to non-directional *The box contains two apples*. Perhaps a clause like *The Rhine receives the waters of the Mosel* is an example of such. The possibility is catered for by the rules proposed below. But, for the moment, I shall not attempt to provide for objective ablatives like that in *They left Canada (on Tuesday)* or for subjective ablatives (if any there be—*Canada was soon left (behind)*?); I shall return to such when we have taken into account some 'abstract' directional clauses. But it is perhaps worth noting here that once more (cf. §6.5) such subjectivizings and objectivizings (of loc and abl) are not semantically empty. I shall use the extended set of rules presented in (lxxviii) as a basis for the following discussion:

(lxxviii)   *Fragment of grammar, 4*

II. i. 1. $V \rightarrow \begin{bmatrix} \pm \text{ergative} \\ \pm \text{stative} \end{bmatrix}$

       2. $+ \text{ergative} \rightarrow \begin{bmatrix} \pm \text{causative} \\ \pm \text{reflexive} \end{bmatrix}$

       3. *a.* $\left\{ \begin{array}{l} - \text{ergative} \\ + \text{causative} \end{array} \right\} \rightarrow \pm \text{locative}$

          b. $\begin{bmatrix} - \text{causative} \\ + \text{stative} \\ - \text{reflexive} \end{bmatrix} \rightarrow \pm \text{stative-ergative}$

       4. $+ \text{locative} \rightarrow \begin{bmatrix} \left\{ \begin{array}{l} \pm \text{subjective} \;/\; \left[\overline{+ \text{stative}} \right] \\ \pm \text{objective} \\ \pm \text{directional} \end{array} \right\} \end{bmatrix}$

       5. $\begin{bmatrix} + \text{stative} \\ - \text{ergative} \end{bmatrix} \rightarrow \pm \text{stative-locative} \;/\; \begin{bmatrix} \overline{\left\{ \begin{array}{l} + \text{subjective} \\ + \text{directional} \end{array} \right\}} \end{bmatrix}$

   ii.   The rules are as in §6.7 (xxix) with the addition of the following, and the consequent re-ordering of the rules under 2. *a* to 3, 3 to 4:

          2. *a.* $+ \text{directional} \rightarrow \text{abl}//V$—

   iii.   As in §6.7

Rule II. i. 4 has an additional sub-part to those proposed in §6.7 (xxix), and, together with II. ii. 2. *a*, it allows for what I have decided to call 'directional clauses'—which, for the reasons discussed above, seems to be preferable as a term to the former 'dynamic'. Otherwise, the rules are unmodified, except for II. i. 5, which now allows for stat to be added to loc not only when it is subjective (as in *The ground was strewn with litter*) but also in clauses that also contain abl (i.e. are directional) as exemplified by (lxxiii) above. However, as I have already indicated, we shall have to return below to the characterization of the subjectivization and objectivization of locatives. I am also not proposing here any rules allowing for different sequences of post-verbal casual phrases (when more than one is present). I assume that these (together with the rules preposing such phrases, when 'thematic'—Halliday, 1967: particularly §5) are rather superficial, though some at least derive their motivation from the semantic representation. The sequence allowed for in the above rules is to this extent arbitrary.

9 *Abstract direction*

9.1 Preliminaries

Examples of (different types of) rather obvious non-spatial directional clauses are not difficult to find. The examples in (lxxix) form an interesting sub-type of these:

(lxxix) *a.* His mood changed from indifference to anger
        b. Her interests range from philately to epistemology
        c. They changed him from a shy youth (in)to a dangerous psychopath

(Cf. the non-directional *He was in a temper, She is interested in a range of subjects, He was a dangerous psychopath* (?—see §11.62).) Again it seems reasonable to suggest that such examples differ from their spatial equivalents with respect to the specification of the nouns and verbs rather than the casual relations involved. With regard to the particular examples in (lxxix) there are obvious restrictions to be drawn in connexion with the compatibility of the ablative and locative NPs, and both of these and the nominative NP; and once more (cf. §5.9) difficult problems of co-reference are involved. Such clauses express 'change (or scope) of class or state' rather than 'change (or scope) of place'. However, rather than pursue at this point the analysis of clauses like these (though clearly this is not without interest, and I shall indeed return to them in §11.62), I want to try to provide rather stronger evidence for the localist hypothesis by considering certain phenomena less obviously parallel to the 'spatial' directional locatives we have been looking at. Also, the type of clause I am going to look at now can be shown to be related to some of the 'abstract' non-directional locative clauses we were concerned with in §7. In this case, their analysis as locative should be mutually reinforcing; and this, I hope, will emerge from the following discussion.

9.2   A type of abstract directional clause

9.21   A proposal. Consider then the familiar clauses in (lxxx):

(lxxx)   1. *a.* John sold the book to Mary
       b. Mary bought the book from John
    2. *a.* The book was sold by John to Mary
       b. The book was bought from John by Mary

In each of these we have three NPs present. One of them, *the book*, which is the object in the (non-copular) 1 examples and the subject in those in 2 (which are +stative), it seems reasonable to regard as in all cases representing an underlying nominative. Compare the examples in (lxxxi):

(lxxxi)   What happened to the book? $\begin{cases} a. \text{ John sold it} \\ b. \text{ Mary bought it} \end{cases}$

where *the book* (and its substitute) 'behaves' as we would expect of a nominative dependent on a causative verb. In the *b* examples in (lxxx) *John* is preceded by the *from* preposition we have associated (among others) with the ablative category; but in (lxxx. 1. *a*), as subject, it lacks a prepositional marker, and in 2. *a* it is preceded by the *by* we have found as a characteristic marker of the ergative. *Mary*, on the other hand, shows these latter characteristics in 1. *b* and 2. *b* respectively, while in the *a* examples this NP is preceded by *to* (a typically locative marker). Notice too that we also find imperative forms like those in (lxxxii):

(lxxxii)   *a.* Sell the book!
       b. Buy the book!

suggesting that the subjects in (lxxx. 1) have an ergative source—thus reinforcing the evidence of the *by* in (lxxx. 2). The sentences in (lxxx) are all rather similar in meaning, but the *a* examples differ from the *b* with respect to whether the relevant 'agency' in the transaction is imputed to *John* (*a*) or *Mary* (*b*), the agent appearing as subject (in the non-stative instances) or as *by*-phrases (where the clause is +stative). In view of these various observations, I want to propose that all of the clauses in (lxxx) are basically directional ('from John to Mary'), with a superimposed system of agency, such that either locative phrase can be marked as ergative. Compare Greimas' (1966: 130) comments on *Ève donne une pomme à Adam*: 'Le sujet *Ève* est le point de départ d'une double relation: la première s'établit entre Ève et pomme, et la seconde

entre Ève et Adam, Ève étant à la fois actant-sujet et actant-destinateur.'
Compare too de la Grasserie's (1890: 42) characterization of such *to*-phrases as those in (lxxx. *a*) as representing an 'allatif idéalisé'.

9.22 The structure of 'buying' and 'selling'. Let us now consider
the kind of structures which we might suggest as a characterization of
these proposals. Those for the 2 examples in (lxxx) can be represented
as in (lxxxiii).

(lxxxiii)   *a.*

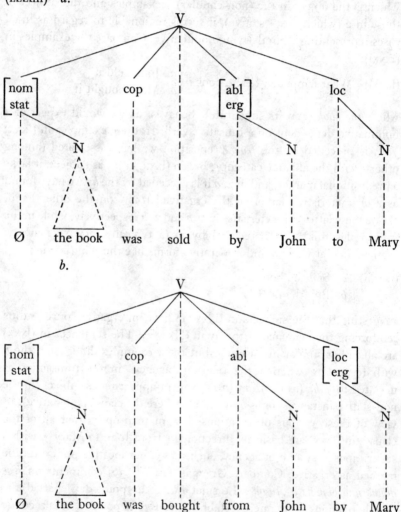

b.

The examples in (lxxx. 1) differ in that nom is not marked as stat, and therefore no copula is introduced, and also rule II. iii. 1 will operate to permute the nominative phrase and the particular locative phrase marked as erg (the ablative in 1. *a*, the locative in 1. *b*). Rule II. iii. 1 will thus have to be modified to allow for the fact that the ablative phrase comes between the elements to be permuted in instances like 1. *b*; it might be reformulated as in (lxxxiv):

(lxxxiv) II. iii. 1. nom + V (abl) $\begin{Bmatrix} \text{erg} \\ \text{subj} \end{Bmatrix} \to \begin{Bmatrix} \text{erg} \\ \text{subj} \end{Bmatrix}$ V + nom (abl)

CONDITION: if erg present, stat $\notin$ [nom]

These structures (in (lxxxiii)) account for the distribution of *by*, *to* and *from* in the examples in (lxxx), in that abl and loc have their normal markers, *from* and *to*, except when erg is attached, the presence of which requires a *by* if the phrase is post-verbal. They also allow for the various sequences we find there (in terms of rule II. iii. 1, as reformulated in (lxxxiv)). In order to generate such structures we shall have to modify the rules of subcategorization and dependency to provide for the distribution of erg as a feature on abl and loc (with causative verbs). We have already noted (in §6.8) that the syntax of *contain* requires some such modification (though we did not implement this at that point). Thus, I am proposing that underlying all of these is a common structure that we can represent as in (lxxxv):

(lxxxv)

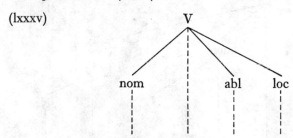

i.e. a simple directional clause. The *a* examples in (lxxx) differ from the corresponding *b* only with respect to the distribution of erg with regard to the locative cases in this structure, and the different sequences are allowed for by this (i.e. the placing of erg) in conjunction with rule II. iii. 1.

9.23   Objectivization and subjectivization of loc. Without essential modification, the rules also provide for variants like those in (lxxxvi):

(lxxxvi)   *a.* Mary was sold the book by John
         b. John sold Mary the book

in which the locative phrase is respectively subjectivized (in the +stative clause) and objectivized (in the −stative clause). The structure underlying (lxxxvi. *a*) and (lxxxvi. *b*) can be represented as in (lxxxvii. *a*) and (lxxxvii. *b*) respectively:

(lxxxvii)   *a.*

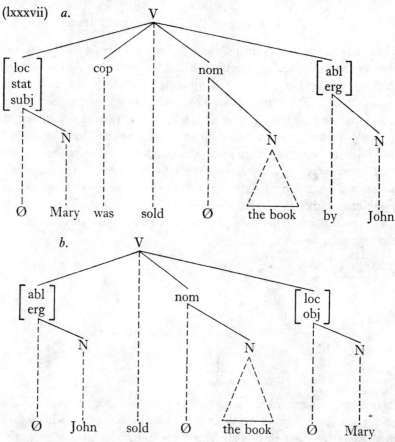

Thus, both 'primary' and 'secondary' passivization (cf. e.g. Kirchner, 1962: §293), as well as the two kinds of object ('direct' and 'indirect') are allowed for in this way. Obviously, we need a further rule placing the objectivized element directly after the V (a rule which in many instances will operate vacuously).[1] Compare with (lxxxvi. *a*) German *Mir ist ein Buch gegeben worden*, wherein the form *Mir* reflects the locative origin of this phrase. Chomsky (1969 *b*) notes differences in the presuppositions associated with an 'objectivized' variant like (lxxxvi. *b*) and its 'non-objectivized' equivalent, and adduces this as evidence of semantic distinctions not determined by deep structure differences. However, in terms of the present account, we can once again relate this distinction to the presence or absence of obj, and a similar position can be adopted with respect to other of Chomsky's arguments involving so-called 'stylistic' transformations (cf. Halliday, 1967: particularly §§4–7).

The example in (lxxxvi. *a*) is both + subjective and + stative-locative; a + objective and − stative-locative example would be *The book was sold me by a dealer*—in my variety of English, examples with other than a pronoun locative seem much less acceptable, and such a possibility (even with a pronominal locative) appears to be excluded in certain varieties of English. In examples of this kind (though this is also true for other parts of the *sell* paradigm) the co-occurrence of subject nominative and object locative can lead to the kind of ambiguity noted by Fries (1952: 180–2). However, although both Fillmore (1965: 13–14) and Kuroda (1968: 375) find such clauses acceptable (though the examples they cite contain only pronominal locatives), they do exclude *I was bought a hat* and *A hat was bought me*, which (under the interpretation discussed below) are unexceptionable in my English. Likewise, many of the passive possibilities described by Poutsma (1928: ch. 3, §44) as 'hardly possible' or excluded by him, I find quite acceptable; Poutsma (1926: ch. 47, §35(*a*)) also describes as 'either awkward or quite impossible' *The boy was given the money*. Compare with sentences like those we have been considering, examples with *send*, in which one finds objectivization and subjectivization of a (animate) locative in clauses in which erg appears as a separate category from abl—as in *He sent Mary a book (from Chile)/Mary was sent a book/A book was sent her*. (It is worth noting once again that subjectivization and objectivization apply much more widely to animate phrases than non-animate.) No + subjective and − stative-locative (or, of course, + objective and + stative-locative) variant seems possible— i.e. there is nothing corresponding to *That box contains two apples*. We have already noted above that it is doubtful whether we should allow for

---

[1] With regard to English, Jespersen (1928: 301–11) discusses a large number of such clauses, and points to similar phenomena in Danish. See too, on their history in English, Jespersen, 1894: §§181–3; Curme, 1913: 97–101.

such a possibility with respect to directional clauses in general; the rules in (lxxviii) would require some additional modification in order to accommodate such a restriction. But I want to extend the discussion somewhat before considering necessary revisions to the rules.

9.24 ...and of abl. We did not allow (in terms of the rules in (lxxviii)) for the objectivization of ablatives—though I referred in passing to examples like (lxxxviii):

(lxxxviii)   They left Canada (on Tuesday)

Notionally, the effect of objectivization of the ablative is to emphasize that the goal (the locative) is not necessarily reached; and this is marked in the locative preposition—as in *They left Delhi for Colombo*. However, there is some doubt about there being a subjective possibility (cf. above); and such variants also seem to be excluded in the case of verbs of the type of *buy*. We do not find examples of subjectivization of the non-ergative ablative corresponding to (lxxx. 2. *b*) in §9.21, nor does there appear to be a subjectivized ablative clause parallel to (lxxx. 1. *b*). As I have noted, clauses like those in (lxxxix) are quite acceptable:

(lxxxix)   *a.* Mary bought John the book
              b. John was bought the book by Mary

but these are related to (xc) rather than (lxxx. 1. *b*) and (lxxx. 2. *b*):

(xc)   *a.* Mary bought the book for John
          b. The book was bought by Mary for John

Compare the set in (xci):

(xci)   1. *a.* Mary brought the book for John
             b. Mary brought John the book
          2. *a.* The book was brought for John by Mary
             b. John was brought the book by Mary

The examples in (xci) show respectively objectivization and subjectivization of what appears to be a sub-type of locative (whose derivation need not concern us here—but see §11.43) in a clause where erg appears not as a feature on loc but as a separate category (cf. *Mary brought John the book from Canada*, with an ergative, a locative and an ablative phrase all expressed superficially). The clauses in (lxxxix) are presumably similar (cf. too *Mary bought John the book from that shop*). Thus, *buy* can appear both in clauses with erg attached to loc and in clauses in which erg is found as a separate category (in which case loc is marked by *for* or is objectivized/subjectivized); in the latter instance, it takes the second kind of 'indirect object' recognized by, for example, Fillmore (1965).

However, we do find clauses containing an ergative locative and an objectivized ablative with verbs other than those we have been considering. Compare *John robbed Mary of the book* (with objectivized ablative) and *John stole the book from Mary* (without such). Note too the subjective *Mary was robbed of the book*. (Cf. Fillmore, 1968*b*: 376.) Also: *I asked a favour of him/ I asked him a favour*.

9.25   Summary. A small part of such an account of sentences like these I have outlined elsewhere (in Anderson, 1968*b*: 313–15—see too Lyons, 1968*b*: 500), and opposed once again (cf. the discussion of *come* and *go* above) to an explanation relying on the elaboration of an interpretative semantic apparatus of some sort.[1] The account I have offered suggests that the selection of *buy* as against *sell* is dependent on a single distinction—a verb subcategorization rule that determines whether erg is added to loc rather than abl; they are thus perhaps intrinsically suppletive in the sense of §4.32.

9.26   Further examples. The occurrence of other pairs with a similar syntax is illustrated in (xcii):

(xcii)   A. 1. *a.* John lent the book to Mary
                b. Mary borrowed the book from John
          2. *a.* The book was lent to Mary by John
                b. The book was borrowed from John by Mary
          3.   John lent Mary the book
          4.   Mary was lent the book by John
       B. 1. *a.* John taught that subject to Mary
                b. Mary learnt that subject from John
          2. *a.* That subject was taught to Mary by John
                b. That subject was learnt from John by Mary
          3.   John taught Mary that subject
          4.   Mary was taught that subject by John

---

[1] Katz, 1967: particularly 171–3; Staal, 1967*a*—see too Katz, 1966: particularly 167–70; Bierwisch, 1969: §2.4. It seems probable to me that devices of this nature will prove in general unnecessary with respect to such relations, at least, given a sufficiently abstract view of transformational relations (or their equivalent) and an essentially semantic interpretation of the base (cf. §2.12).

Cf. too *give* and *obtain/get/take*:

(xciii)   1. *a.* Jɔhn gave the book to Mary
              b. Mary obtained the book from John
          2. *a.* The book was given to Mary by John
              b. The book was obtained by Mary from John
          3.   John gave Mary the book
          4.   Mary was given the book by John

Cf. too *The book was given me by my uncle*, with nominative subject and objectivized (pronominal) locative. Notice too that *That subject was taught me by John* and *The book was lent me by John* are quite acceptable with a pronominal locative. Observe however that *take* appears to be distinguished from *obtain* as implying the absence of a 'giver' or 'offerer' (though cf. the 'accept' use noted below in §9.6) whereas *obtain* is neutral in this respect (just as *give* does not pre-suppose 'acceptance'). This use of *take* differs from the one in contrast with *bring* in that erg and loc appear in the same CS. The examples in 3 and 4 in (xcii) in each case correspond to the *a* instances in 1 and 2; once again, the absence of *b* clauses in 3 and 4 is related to the non-susceptibility of ablatives (with such verbs) to subjectivization and objectivization. Beside the *b* forms in B, there are also ablative phrases like *from a/the book* to which there are no *a* instances corresponding (since *book* is normally excluded as an ergative ablative—though cf. *That book taught me a lot*). Also, we should note that the sentences in A and B respectively, though similar in structure, nevertheless have in certain respects rather different implications. For instance, *John has lent Mary the book* implies that John no longer has the book, whereas *John has taught Mary French* does not imply that John no longer knows French (cf. T. R. Anderson, 1968). This is presumably related to the characterization of the individual verb. For a discussion of other such sentences within the framework of a case grammar of the kind proposed by Fillmore (1966*a*, 1968*a*, 1968*b*), see Corder, 1968, though in such an account both (what I have described as) animate locatives and animate ablatives are grouped together (rather misleadingly, it seems to me) as 'datives'.

9.27   Some lexical identities. An account like the preceding would explain the absence in many languages of distinct verb-forms corresponding to *lend/borrow*, etc., since such pairs (as intrinsically suppletive) differ only in the character of their 'arguments'. Compare the Icelandic pair in (xciv):

(xciv)   *a.* Hann fekk mér bókina ('He gave me the book')
         b. Ég fekk bókina frá honum ('I got the book from him')

Cf. too Serbian *pozajmiti* or Faroese *læna* ('lend'/'borrow') or the
dialects of English in which *learn* is equivalent to both 'teach' and
'learn'. In Modern English we find such a situation with verbs like *hire*
and *rent* (*from/to*).

**9.28 The relationship between objectivization and subjectiviza-
tion.** One generalization that has been implicit in our discussion of these
various directional clauses can be formulated in a preliminary way at this
point. The possibility of objectivization of the locative in such clauses is
restricted to verbs which also permit subjectivization (in stative clauses)
—cf. Curme, 1913: 110. Thus, though we find both *John mentioned the
book to Mary* and *The book was mentioned to Mary by John*, neither **John
mentioned Mary the book* nor **Mary was mentioned the book by John* is
acceptable. We shall return to this relationship between subjectivization
and objectivization below (in chapter 10), in connexion with its relation
to the ± stative opposition, and pursue there the implications of this
relationship.

9.3 Locative and directional relationships

Once again, such a localistic interpretation goes some way towards
resolving the difficulties concerning one of the problem pairs discussed
by Chomsky (1965: 162–3)—see too Fillmore, 1966a: 28–9. It is indeed
not surprising that there should be a connexion between the resolution
of this problem and that involving *please* and *like* considered in §7.2.
It is clear that the relationship between *John is here* and *John has come*—
or rather, perhaps, *The book is here* and *John has brought the book from the
library*—is paralleled by the pair in (xcv):

(xcv)   *a.* Mary knows Greek
        b. Mary has learnt Greek from that book

In all three cases, it seems reasonable to consider the former clause
(apart from differing aspectually) to be the (stative) non-directional
equivalent of the latter. Further, sentences with *know* and *teach* will
show a similar, though obviously distinct relationship. If this is just,
then it also provides further evidence for the identity of allative and
locative. Consider the instances in (xcvi):

(xcvi) *a.* Mary knows Greek
        b. John has taught Mary Greek
        c. Mary has learnt Greek from John

Under the proposed interpretation, *Mary* represents an underlying locative in all three. Such an identity also underlies the distribution of dative inflexions in languages like Latin (*Mihi est liber/Mihi áedit librum*), which, in this respect at least, is thus less 'random' than has sometimes been suggested. Compare 'the identical modes of expression for possession and indirect object' in Abaza, Kabardian and Ubykh alluded to by Allen (1964: 342). Thus, just as the choice between *teach* and *learn* is dependent upon which locative category (ablative or simple locative) is ergative, so the difference between them and *know* is related not so much (in this case) to whether abl is present or not (we do find *I know from John that...*) but rather to whether one of the locative categories is marked as ergative or not. In some significant sense, *know*, *teach* and *learn* in such sentences (elsewhere (with different kinds of nominative) *know* is associated with *tell* and *learn*) come close to being 'the same verb'—they are intrinsically suppletive, except that *teach* and *learn* are +causative. In the light of the relationship between the clauses in (xxxi), forms for 'know' originating in 'perfects', like Greek οἶδα (Sanskrit *véda*, Gothic *wait*—see e.g. Meillet & Vendryes, 1924: 203–5, 294), should not surprise us. Notice too that *know* can co-occur with a temporal like *already* normally associated with the perfect, whereas *have known* tends to reject it. *Contain* (cf. causative *put in*) and *have* and *own* show a similar potentiality. This principle also presumably underlies in part the development of *have* as 'perfect auxiliary' in English.[1]

Related in the same way as the clauses in (xcvi) with *teach* and *know* are the clauses in (xcvii):

(xcvii) *a.* Mary understands the theorem
         b. John has explained the theorem to Mary

Cf. too *remember/remind* (with once again no forms equivalent to (xcvi. *c*)). *Buy*, *sell* and *possess* (*own*, *belong*) show the same range as in (xcvi):

(xcviii) *a.* The book belongs to Mary
          b. John has sold the book to Mary
          c. Mary has bought the book from John

---

[1] However, *since* normally requires (as elsewhere) the perfect form—thus no **I know that since Tuesday*. In Fulani, such verbs 'are used with the preterite ending to translate English present tenses' (Taylor, 1953: 78).

and in this set *belong* (*possess*, *own*) is strictly non-directional (not merely non-directional), as opposed to the directional *sell/buy*. Compare with the examples in (xcviii) the following:

(xcix) *a.* Mary has the book
        b. John has lent the book to Mary
        c. Mary has borrowed the book from John

which groups *lend/borrow* and 'non-possessive *have*' (cf. §7.362). If we now consider parallel examples with *give* and *obtain* (or *get*) then it seems clear that either (xcviii. *a*) or (xcix. *a*) could be related to such clauses as those in (c):

(c) *a.* John has given the book to Mary
     b. Mary has obtained the book from John

These verbs are thus indifferent to the distinction separating the sets in (xcviii) from those in (xcix). It must be marked otherwise: *I gave you it to keep/as a loan*.

The naturalness of these pairings which result from our localistic interpretations of verbs like *know* on the one hand and like *learn* and *teach* on the other, which have their independent motivations, lends additional support to the individual proposals. And as further confirmation, we should note that we also find variants showing 'copying' (cf. §7.32) of subjectivized versions of either locative category, as in (ci):

(ci) *a.* Mary had a book stolen (from her (library))
      b. Mary had a rotten peach sold (to) her

(where the (*to*) *her* in *b* is not deletable). We have already remarked (in §5.4) on the ambiguity of sentences like those in (ci) when discussing the derivation associated with the other (causative) interpretation.

9.4 Some non-causative directional clauses

9.41 With receive. *Get* is like *obtain* (cf. (xciii) in §9.26), except that clauses like that in (cii):

(cii) Mary got the book from John

are ambiguous between an interpretation with an ergative locative as subject and one where the locative is not ergative. That is, the first interpretation is like that for (xciii. 1. *b*); the second is rather more like that associated with a sentence like that in (ciii), containing *receive*:[1]

(ciii)   Mary received the book from John

This latter is, of course, the classic counter-example (together with *suffer* and a few others—see e.g. Buyssens, 1950: 40) to accounts of transitivity conducted in terms of 'actor–action–patient' and the like. Its syntax can be readily accommodated by extension of the set of rules proposed in §8.4, as the directional non-stative equivalent of verbs like *contain*. Thus, the structure of (ciii) can perhaps be represented as in (civ):

(civ)

Abl is not erg—cf. *I received a letter from Jugoslavia yesterday*. *Learn* appears to be ambiguous in the same way as *get*; it appears in structures like that in (civ) as well as those containing an ergative locative discussed above. Consider a clause like *I learned from John that she had left*, which is like *I heard from John*... in having a non-ergative locative subject.

9.42   With *owe/due*. Like *receive*, etc., but stative (and consistently 'non-concrete'), is the verb *owe/due*—which however also allows non-ergative ablative subjects. We find the following range of structures:

---

[1] On a number of such verbs in the history of English, see Sundén, 1916: 61–2. In some varieties of English, *obtain* appears to be ambivalent like *get*. Such verbs appear to permit examples of subjectivization of loc in a −stative clause, which we have not allowed for so far. We shall return to this question in §11.44.

(cv) *a.*

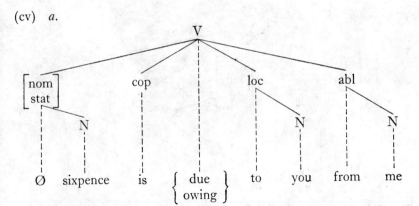

b.

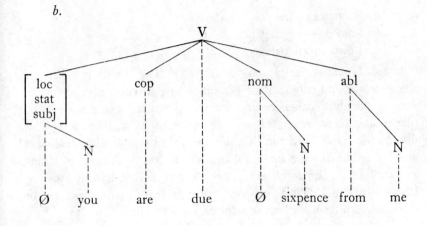

c.

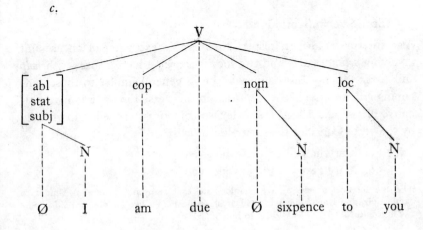

d.

Corresponding to *a*, *c* and *d* are the forms in (cvi) with objective locative:

(cvi) *a.* Sixpence is due you from me
   b. I am due you sixpence
   c. I owe you sixpence

(Cf. too Kirchner, 1937: 99–100; 1940.)[1] The distribution of the elements stat and subj (and obj) in different positions provides for the various possible sequences and for the presence or absence of cop (depending on whether the verb is preceded by stat or not). This distribution is allowed for by the rules in §8.4 plus additional ones generating the conjunction of abl and stat (in (cv. *c*)). There appears to be lacking a variant with subjective locative and stative nominative. Presumably, such restrictions on particular sets of paradigms can be formulated in terms of lexical redundancy rules (but cf. p. 133).

9.5 Some verbalizations

Also interpretable with respect to a simple extension of an account involving a nominative and two locatives are perhaps clauses with *help* and *thank*. Such clauses appear to be in general similar to those containing *give* and the like, except that in their case the underlying nominative phrase is deleted, and its lexical content is 'carried' superficially by the verb. Consider the examples in (cvii):

(cvii) *a.* Mary helped anyone who asked
   b. Mary gave help to anyone who asked

[1] With reference to (cvi. *b*), we should note that Hansen (1949: 200) alludes to objectivization after 'adjectives' in Danish even in cases like *Hun er ham huld* ('She is him faithful' = 'She is faithful to him').

I am suggesting that *a* and *b* are variants of a common underlying structure which includes in particular two locative phrases and a nominative—except that in 'reduced' clauses like *a* the locative is necessarily objective:

(cviii)

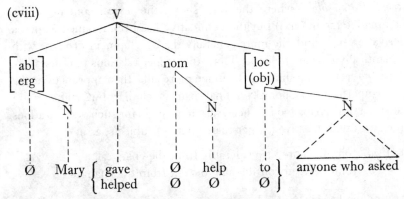

The lexical content that separates *helped* from *gave* is derived from the associated nominative NP. In Old English such verbs were constructed with a 'dative personal object' (cf. van der Gaaf, 1929: 3–6), and even when it becomes possible for them to appear in passive clauses with the locative in subject position, the locative NP sometimes remains in an oblique form (van der Gaaf, 1929: 7).[1] Cf. too German *Ich helfe der Mutter*. In the history of a number of languages, one finds that such verbs 'oscillate' between the one superficial construction ('transitive': *I help my mother*) and the other ('intransitive': *Ich helfe der Mutter*)— see e.g. Vendryes, 1921: 125–6. Cf. Basque *Obeditzen du aitari* ('He obeys his father'), in which the verb is 'transitive in form' but *aitari* ('his father') is 'dative', alongside which we find such sentences with *aita* in the nominative. It seems plausible to regard the distinction as minimal—i.e. a question of the presence or absence of verbalization. I am proposing, then, that both constructions can be derived from an underlying structure containing a locative, an ablative and a (deleted) nominative whose content is re-lexicalized (copied) in the verb.

Other verbs of this type are *advise, assure, guide* (cf. *give advice to*, etc.). And another of Chomsky's (1965: 162) problem pairs, viz. that in (cix):

(cix) *a.* John struck Bill
       b. Bill received a blow at the hands of John

[1] Many such Old English verbs are listed by Quirk & Wrenn (1955: 65), though some in their list are non-directional—i.e. take simple dative locatives.

would seem to be at least in part explicable in these terms, if we consider *strike* to be a verb of the kind we have been considering, with an ergative ablative as subject and a locative as object and in the underlying specification a nominative which is deleted superficially. Compare *John struck Bill a blow*, where the verb shows the lexical content of the nominative (as in (cix)) but the nominative has been retained. (Such a derivation may underlie more generally the development of verbs with semantically cognate objects.) Thus, the deeper relations in clauses like those in (cix) can be shown to be much more alike than appears to be the case superficially. Chomsky's final pair is similar but stative (and 'abstract'). Perhaps too it is necessary to provide for such verbalizations in clauses with locative (rather than ablative) subjects, as in (cx. *a*):

(cx)   *a.* John benefited considerably from the changes
       b. John derived considerable benefit from the changes

And no doubt we should also allow for verbalization in the case of non-directional locative causatives: cf. *Everyone put the blame for the accident on Fred* and *Everyone blamed the accident on Fred*, or, with objectivized loc, *Everyone blamed Fred for the accident.*[1] Consider too *I am afraid of Mary, I fear Mary, Mary frightens me*—all perhaps with a deleted nominative, the first with a (stative) subjective locative, the second with a subjective locative and objective ablative and the third with a subjective ablative and objective locative—and compare French *avoir peur de.*[2] However this may be, it seems likely that, in a number of cases, nominatives in the kind of directional (and simply locative) clause we have been looking at provide another source for the (derived) lexical content of different verbs (cf. §2.121).

9.51   *Speak, say* and *tell.* There is some evidence that *speak* is a verb like *help*, except that in its instance there is no objectivization of the locative, as in the example in (cxi):

(cxi)   John spoke to Mary

It is like *strike* in that it does permit superficially an undeleted cognate object: *He spoke a few words*. We do find certain other kinds of object (*He spoke French, He spoke the truth*), but these may be derived either

---

[1] Incidentally, notice that the *for* in the last of these has presumably the same source as the *for* in the first—i.e. in the adnominal case within nom.
[2] It may be that in this case too the ablative is of adnominal origin.

from elements subordinate to the underlying nominative (cf. *He spoke a few words of French*) or from some other source altogether than the nominative phrase (cf. *He spoke in French, He spoke truthfully*). *Talk* seems to reject the cognate objects we find with *speak*, though it permits names of languages and something like *He talked nonsense*. Once again these superficial objects admit the same sort of interpretations (of their derivation) as were appropriate in the case of *speak*. *Utter*, on the other hand, does not take language names, and we do find *He uttered a few words*.[1] Notice further the following restriction:

(cxii)   *a.* I spoke a few words about that to John
        b. I spoke about that to John
        c. *I spoke something about that to John

I.e. *speak* rejects the non-cognate object (in (cxii. *c*)); and we can explain the occurrence of (cxii. *b*) in terms of the deletion of a cognate nominative noun to which the *about*-phrase is subordinate. Compare with the use of *speak* and *talk* clauses like those in (cxiii):

(cxiii)   *a.* He gave a speech to the association
        b. He gave a talk to the association

which differ primarily in the degree of formality implied (clauses with the verbs *speak* and *talk* being unmarked in this respect).

Semantically similar verbs like *say* and *tell* are rather different in their superficial syntax. Thus while *speak* can appear without a superficial object, this is not possible in their case:

(cxiv)   *a.*   John spoke
        b. *John said
        c. *John told

((cxiv. *c*) is perhaps acceptable under the rather different interpretation 'John informed on someone'.) On the other hand, *say* and *tell* do permit the sort of objects excluded by *speak*:

(cxv)   *a.* I said something about that to John
        b. I told John something about that

Cf. too (cxvi):

(cxvi)   *a.* *I spoke to John that I would come
        b.   I said to John that I would come
        c.   I told John that I would come

---

[1] As compared with the other two, it is also aspectually restricted: *He spoke for two hours, He talked for two hours, *He uttered for two hours.*

The range of underlying nominatives possible with *say* and *tell* suggests that they do not derive their lexical content from an underlying (usually deleted) nominative, as seemed quite probable in the case of *speak*, *talk* and *utter*.[1] This serves to characterize *say* and *tell* as compared with *speak*, etc. But *say* and *tell* differ with respect to whether the locative can be objectivized (and subjectivized) or not (*I told John that I would come*, **I said John that I would come*) and with respect to what can be deleted—the locative (in the case of *say*) or the nominative (in the case of *tell*):

(cxvii)　1. *a.*　I said that I would come
　　　　　　 b.　*I told that I would come
　　　　　2. *a.*　*I said to John
　　　　　　 b.　I told John

Objectivization (or subjectivization) of the locative with *tell* is obligatory if the nominative is deleted or is sentential (cf. *I told that to John*). *Tell* also permits a wider range of nominatives than does *say*, whose objects are typically sentential (as in (1. *a*)) or cognate (*say a few words*) or pro-formal (*say something*). Such restrictions will form part of the specification for these verbs, in the way suggested by Corder (1968) with respect to a much larger set of 'double object' verbs. Note too that such differences cannot be dismissed as semantically irrelevant in that they coincide with the different ways in which we interpret *say* and *tell*—and, for that matter, *speak*—however difficult it may be to formulate the distinction. Thus, *tell* is 'oriented' towards the animate locative (which is not deletable), *say* towards the (embedded) 'content' of the (non-deletable) nominative phrase, and *speak* towards neither (but perhaps towards the act of speaking itself).

9.6　Remarks on some 'performative' verbs

Say and *tell* (but not *speak*, etc.) have a 'performative' use.[2] Such is also the case with *accept* and *offer*:

(cxviii)　*a.*　I (hereby) accept the proposals
　　　　　 b.　I (hereby) offer my services

[1] This does not mean that their lexical content is necessarily inherent; it may be derived via some other process of lexicalization, such as from a manner or instrumental adverbial—cf. *communicate verbally/by means of words*.

[2] On 'performatives', see Ross, 1969, Boyd & Thorne, 1969, Householder, forthcoming, and the works by Austin referred to by them.

Accept and *offer* appear to be like *obtain* and *give*, respectively, in the case configurations they require, but they differ from them in certain interesting ways which seem to be connected with their performative potentiality. As we observed above, *obtain* (or *get*) can take a non-animate ablative (*I obtained/got it from the University Library*), and it does not necessarily presuppose a complementary 'giving'. *Accept*, on the other hand, presupposes an 'offer' of some sort (cf. *buy/sell*—see Lyons, 1963: 72–3), though not a completed transaction. As well as being used in the ways discussed earlier (in §9.26), *take* is sometimes equivalent to *accept*; a clause like *John took the book from Mary* is ambiguous and can be disambiguated as in (cxix), wherein the *a* instance also permits *accept* in place of take:

(cxix)   *a.* John took the book from Mary when she offered it
　　　　b. John took the book away from Mary

Cf. too *Does the hotel take/accept cheques? Offer* similarly differs from *give* in implication, in that in its case, in contrast with *give*, the occurrence of the 'exchange' may not take place. Notice further that we also find *offer* with a sentential nominative:

(cxx)   *a.* John offered to come
　　　　b. John offered to give the book to Mary

It may be that we should relate *John offered Mary the book* and the like to a structure such as underlies (cxx. *b*)—which would enable us to avoid having to suggest two rather different kinds of underlying structure for clauses containing *offer*. In a similar way, *accept* typically has a nominalization as nominative NP—as in (cxviii. *a*). In many such instances we could substitute *agree to*. However, corresponding to the *a* instance with *accept* in (cxxi), we have rather a clause with *agree* like (cxxi. *b*):

(cxxi)   *a.* Mary accepted the book
　　　　b. Mary agreed to have the book

It is tempting to propose that the same relation holds here as that we have suggested with respect to *John offered the book* and *John offered to give the book*: i.e. the *a* instance in (cxxi) represents a reduced form of the *b*. This proposal with respect to *accept* and *agree* is supported by the fact that corresponding to them both we have the single antonymous verb *refuse*:

(cxxii)   *a.* Mary refused the book
          b. Mary refused to have the book

Offer, then, expresses an enquiry concerning willingness to have (or be given); *accept* expresses a response indicating willingness to have. Clearly, an adequate account of such relationships will depend upon the formulation of a general theory of 'speech acts' of the kind proposed by Boyd & Thorne (1969), and the establishment of the place of such a theory within the grammar as a whole.[1] This lies without the scope of our present enquiry, and I shall not pursue the matter further here. However, it seemed worthwhile at this point to indicate another sort of complexity in the relations underlying 'simple' items (cf. §2.12) related to the group we have been mainly concerned with in what immediately precedes.

9.7   Verbs of sensation

'Verbs of sensation' would seem to form an interesting sub-type of locative construction, the precise interpretation of which raises a number of problems. Although I have no very firm proposals to make here, I would like to survey the phenomena concerned and indicate the nature of some of the problems.

9.71   *Smell.* Consider a verb like *smell*, and in particular the variant in (cxxiii):

(cxxiii)   The rose smells nice

Smell also occurs as a noun in clauses like those in (cxxiv):

(cxxiv)   *a.* The rose has a nice smell
          b. The rose gives off a nice smell

It seems natural to regard *the rose* in (cxxiv. *a*) (as elsewhere in clauses with *have*) as deriving from an underlying locative, with *a nice smell* as a nominative. In (cxxiv. *b*) *a nice smell* is also nominative, but *the rose* apparently derives from an ablative, *off* representing the locative. Now it would clearly be desirable to relate (cxxiii) to one of the clauses in (cxxiv), with the verb 'carrying' the content of the underlying (now

---

[1] Similar considerations appear to be relevant to a further analysis of clauses containing *owe*, etc. in terms of a superordinate modal clause (cf. *ought to give*). This possibility suggests that it may be unnecessary to allow directly for subjectivization and objectivization of the abl in its case.

deleted) nominative. But, if these latter are as distinct as they seem, to which one is it to be related? In a sentence like *It smells nice to me, it* is presumably ablative and *to me* locative. It seems advantageous to extend this to (cxxiii) also, with a deleted pro-form locative (cf. *It would smell nice to anyone*). If we follow out such an interpretation, in the clause in (cxxv):

(cxxv)   He smelled the rose

He is apparently locative (ergative or non-ergative) and *the rose* ablative. (Cf. *He got a whiff of it*.) Such a verb at an earlier period was constructed with a 'genitive object' or an 'object' preceded by *of* (cf. Visser, 1963: §375). However, the decision is not clearcut; and we are still in a position in which *the rose* in (cxxiv. *a*) and (cxxiv. *b*) appears in two rather different case phrases with the same verb. This may not constitute a problem if we can show a closer relationship between abl and loc (cf. §12.1). But it may be that a resolution lies in re-interpreting (cxxiv. *a*) as involving subjectivization not of a clausal locative but of an adnominal phrase within a nominative—i.e. as being related to *The rose's smell is nice* (cf. *The smell from the rose is nice*).[1]

9.72   *See* and *hear*. Similar to *smell* in many ways are *taste* and *feel* (though for instance, there is no precise parallel to (cxxiv. *b*)). The situation with the 'verbs of perception' *see/look/look at* and *hear/sound/ listen to* is, however, rather more complicated, and there is indeed some evidence (though the issue does not seem to me settled) that in their case the 'directionality' I have suggested for *smell* (with locative subject in active clauses like (cxxv)) is in fact reversed (the object is locative)—see Gruber, 1967. To complete this rather inconclusive paragraph, I shall note that there are suggestions also that *please/like* may appear in directional clauses in certain instances, rather than simple locative clauses. The directional possibility is perhaps associated with non-stative 'particular instance' occurrences (*I liked his performance*—cf. *His performance gave me great pleasure*), whereas the non-directional is more obviously stative (*I like him*). *Pleased (with)* is similarly ambivalent, while *fond (of)* (if it belongs to this paradigm) is only non-directional.

---

[1] Perhaps, similarly, the subject in *It weighs two kilos*, etc. has an adnominal source.

9.8 Summary and prospect

We have, I think, reached a point where it might be convenient and (hopefully) illuminating to consider in detail the nature of the modifications to the rules presented in §8.4 which are necessitated by our subsequent discussion. The main burden of this discussion has been to reveal evidence for a localistic interpretation of some further phenomena, involving in this instance directional clauses in many of which one of the locative phrases is also ergative. As with the 'abstract' locatives discussed in chapter 7, these are intended merely as examples of the way in which non-spatial phenomena can be given a localistic interpretation; they obviously do not constitute an exhaustive survey of such, though, as I remarked above, I do not anticipate an extension of the set of clause case categories that we have surveyed. With respect to the grammar of §8.4, the coverage of the rules must be extended: to allow for subjectivization and objectivization of ablatives (cf. *We left Canada*, etc.) and for the occurrence of stat as a feature on abl (*I am due you a pound*); to distribute erg as a feature on abl or loc, in addition to nom (*He gave me the book/I got the book from him/They contained the enemy*); and to relate such a distribution for erg to the subjectivization and objectivization possibilities for loc and abl. There remains too to be considered the fact that the rules in §8.4 provide for the co-selection of +subjective and −stative-locative, a possibility whose realization is rather doubtful. However, the formulation of the required modifications entails a considerable complication of, in particular, the rules of subcategorization; and there are reasons for thinking that at least part of that complication points to a need to reconsider a number of assumptions embodied in the rules as conceived of up to this point. There are in particular two questions that I want to raise in relation to phenomena we have already surveyed. The first of them is concerned with the status of the notions of 'subjectivization' and 'objectivization', and raises important considerations concerning the nature of the underlying structural descriptions. The second concerns particularly the concept 'causative', and is connected with the further pursuit of our localistic goal. These two, in part familiar, areas will occupy our attention anew in (respectively) the following two parts.

Part IV

INTERLUDE

10 *Sequencing*

In this brief digression from our main theme, as indicated at the end of chapter 9, the first of two main outstanding topics will require our attention; both of them involve a reconsideration of things already discussed in previous chapters. At this point, I want to review certain of the phenomena we looked at in Part III, in particular. I am going to suggest that an attempt to formulate a more adequate account of these phenomena has important consequences with regard to a question I have in the main avoided (or rather assumed an answer to) up to now—viz. whether or not the categories of the base are initially introduced in a significant linear order. I shall then conclude in Part V with a discussion of possible extensions of the localistic hypothesis explored in the preceding two chapters to the kind of phenomena surveyed (from a nonlocalist point-of-view) in Part II.

10.1 'Concatenation-system' vs. 'set-system'

Various scholars in the past, and particularly more recently, have proposed formulating a 'theory of grammatical structure in terms of a non-catenating system of rules which generated not strings of elements, but unordered sets' (Lyons, 1968a: 210). Interpretable to a certain extent (at least) in this way are the proposals made by Pāṇini (cf. Whitney, 1893; Laroche, 1964; Staal, 1967b: particularly 26–45), by Tesnière (1959), by Curry (1961), by Worth (1964), by Šaumjan (1965), by Fillmore (1966a; 1968a) and by Staal (1967b).[1] Chomsky (1965: ch. 2, §4.4) is critical of such suggestions (and specifically those of Curry and Šaumjan) with respect both to English in particular and to universal grammar; and Staal (1967b), while proposing a 'set-system' for universal

---

[1] See too Lyons' own suggestions (1968a: ch. 8), and the discussion in Theban, 1968 and 1969, and Theban & Theban, 1969; and compare the characterization of 'functional' elements proposed by Pike, Halliday and their associates (cf. e.g. Longacre, 1964: 15–23, etc., Halliday, 1966: 57–9). On the relevance of historical considerations (exemplified from English), which might be used to supplement the argument developed below, see Traugott, 1969a: 5–6.

grammar (on the evidence of a language like Sanskrit), allows that English represents a linguistic sub-type to which the properties of such a system are largely inappropriate.

Clearly, the empirical motivations for advocating a 'set-system' for the 'base' are of a very restricted kind. Discrepancies between the superficial sequence of elements in different languages obviously fail to constitute sufficient evidence, given the sort of arguments we are familiar with, for favouring one underlying order rather than the others (or some abstract order not identical to any surface sequence). Further, although they might seem to be the most obvious source of evidence, the existence of discrepancies between the underlying orders that can be shown to be appropriate (by virtue of evidence internal to each language) to different languages is not crucial. On the one hand, it could be argued that one should discriminate between 'majority' and 'minority' orders and in some way treat the latter as a special case (though I would not want to defend this position myself). On the other hand, it would still be possible, without resorting to such a device, to maintain a slightly weaker version of the 'concatenation-system' position: namely that what is universal is the principle of concatenation rather than any particular order. That is, in terms of the instances discussed by Chomsky (1965: 124), one could allow the base for different languages to generate either NP⌢V or V⌢NP (as constituents of VP), the claim then being that from the evidence internal to each language one of these orders can be shown to be appropriate for that language (cf. e.g. Ross, 1967: §2). Within any language, the underlying order is determinate; there is a set of relevant criteria that is uniform in this respect. The argument for a 'set-system' is required to show that in some respect or respects this claim cannot be met, i.e. in particular that it is after all not possible to motivate the selection of one particular underlying order. As we have noted, Staal (1967b) argues (within the framework of a grammar like that outlined in Chomsky, 1965) that such is the position in Sanskrit. It seems to me that certain of the phenomena we have discussed above can be interpreted as providing evidence (within the framework of a case grammar like that developed in the preceding chapters) for such an argument with respect even to English, and that accordingly such languages need not be regarded as an exception to Staal's generalization. The interpretation obviously must be plausible on other grounds—and as our understanding of these deepens, so our particular interpretation may be modified, perhaps even destroying—though I consider it unlikely—its value as this sort of evidence.

But I think it worth elaborating at this juncture, as one piece of evidence, within the framework developed here, for the appropriacy of a 'set-system' to a particular part of the grammar—especially since I anticipate that deepened understanding will not involve the revelation of new kinds of evidence for a 'concatenation-system'.

10.2 Objectivization and subjectivization as nominativization
10.21 In ergative clauses. In Part III subjectivization and objectivization of the locative categories were treated as distinct 'processes' involving a pair of subcategorization rules (e.g. in II. i. 4 in (lxxviii) in §8.4), as reproduced in (i):

$$\text{(i)} \quad \text{II. i. 4.} \quad +\text{locative} \rightarrow \left\{ \begin{array}{l} \pm \text{subjective } / \left[\overline{\quad +\text{stative}\quad} \right] \\ \pm \text{objective} \end{array} \right\}$$

Thus, to take directional examples, (ii. 1) are +subjective and (ii. 2) +objective:

(ii) 1. *a.* London was reached (on Tuesday)
      b. Mary was given the prize
    2. *a.* They reached London (on Tuesday)
      b. They gave Mary the prize

Loc in 1 is marked as subj, in 2 as obj. Notice that by the rule in (i) ±subjective is limited to +stative clauses; ±objective is operative in other—i.e. −stative—locative clauses. The two selections are mutually exclusive: loc can be subjectivized only in +stative clauses and objectivized only in −stative. Further, the ergative verbs that permit such subjectivization are the same as those which allow objectivization. This suggests that some generalization involving both subjectivization and objectivization is being missed. Moreover, appearance as subject in +stative clauses and object in −stative clauses is the normal distribution of nom in 'verbal' clauses containing erg as a category. Compare with, for instance, (ii) the examples in (iii):

(iii) 1. *a.* Egbert was dismissed (on Tuesday)
      b. The prize was given to Mary
    2. *a.* They dismissed Egbert (on Tuesday)
      b. They gave the prize to Mary

In the +stative clauses (i.e. (iii. 1)) nom is subject; in the −stative, it is object. To capture this parallelism and unify the treatment of subjectivization and objectivization, I propose that we regard loc in examples like (ii) as being nominativized, such that in all of them nom has been added to loc by a DR dependent on the selection of the positive term in the rule in (iv):

(iv)   II. i. 4.   + locative → ± nominative

which replaces II. i. 4 in (i). If nom is added to loc in a + stative clause, then it appears as subject; if the nominativized loc is in a − stative clause it becomes the object.

Thus, the structures underlying the *a* examples in (ii), after the operation of the objectivizing and subjectivizing rules, can be represented as in (v. *a*) and (v. *b*) respectively:

(v)   *a.*

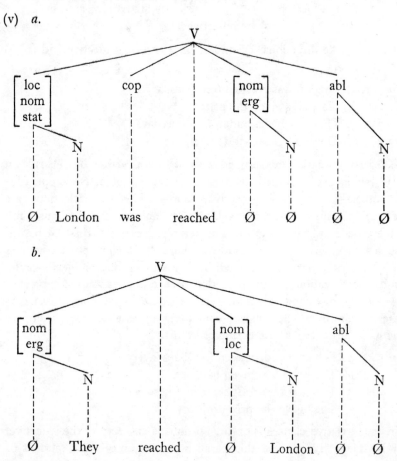

Notice too however that (ii. 1. *a*) must also be + stative-locative in order for cop to be introduced (after stat). Similarly, loc in (ii. 1. *b*) must also be marked as both nom and stat, just as nom (in iii. 1) is marked as stat. There are also clauses in which stat is attached to nom and nom (but not stat) to loc, namely (vi):

(vi)   The prize was given her

If neither loc nor nom is marked as stat and loc has nom attached, then we find a clause with two post-verbal noms—two objects (an 'indirect' and a 'direct'), as in (ii. 2. *b*). Thus, it was not entirely true to say that loc is subjectivized only in + stative clauses: it is subjectivized (in the ergative clauses we have been looking at) only in + stative-locative clauses—i.e. when it is itself marked as stat. If the obligatory nom has stat added to it and nom is added to loc, then, as in (vi), the nominative loc will become object and nom will be subjectivized. (Rule II. i. 4 in (i) would have had to be modified anyway, since it was originally formulated (in (xxix) in §6.7) before such a possibility as is represented by (vi) was envisaged.)

We have, then, in clauses of the type exemplified, the following possible combinations of nom, loc and stat:

(vii)   *a.*   nom $\begin{bmatrix} \text{loc} \\ \text{(stat)} \end{bmatrix}$ e.g. (iii. 2. *b*)

    b.   nom $\begin{bmatrix} \text{loc} \\ \text{nom} \end{bmatrix}$ e.g. (ii. 2. *b*)

    c. $\begin{bmatrix} \text{nom} \\ \text{stat} \end{bmatrix}$ loc   e.g. (iii. 1. *b*)

    d. $\begin{bmatrix} \text{nom} \\ \text{stat} \end{bmatrix}$ $\begin{bmatrix} \text{loc} \\ \text{nom} \end{bmatrix}$ e.g. (vi)

    e.   nom $\begin{bmatrix} \text{loc} \\ \text{nom} \\ \text{stat} \end{bmatrix}$ e.g. (ii. 1. *b*)

Observe that even if stat is added to loc (as allowed in (vii. *a*)), it must also have nom attached if it is to be subjectivized: thus, in (one interpretation of) *It stretches to the edge* stat is attached to loc (cf. §8.3). However, with respect to the distribution tabulated in (vii), we should note also that in terms of rule II. i. 5 in (lxxviii) in §8.4, we have allowed for ± stative-locative only in clauses which are − ergative; clearly, this rule, or our interpretation of causatives, will have to be revised. Further, it would appear that there are no examples corresponding to the +reflexive clauses in (ii. *a*) (and (v))—or equivalent non-directional clauses—in which stat is attached to nom.

10.22   In non-ergative clauses. Notice too that if we extend such an interpretation to clauses without erg, then (with respect to the proposals in chapter 6) the distribution of nom and loc can in general be straight-forwardly allowed for—if we assume that nom (obligatory or attached to loc (or abl)) is pre-posed if stat occurs in the same CS. Thus, the examples in (viii) are such:

(viii) *a.* Papers are strewn over the floor
      b. The floor is strewn with papers

$\left(a \text{ having stat attached to (obligatory) nom, } b \text{ to } \begin{bmatrix} \text{loc} \\ \text{nom} \end{bmatrix} \right)$ and in them $\begin{bmatrix} \text{nom} \\ \text{stat} \end{bmatrix}$ is subject; otherwise, the obligatory nom must be subject:

(ix)   *a.* The tower stands on a hill
     b. The tower occupies a hill
     c. Bill died/is dead

10.3   The scope of ± subjective

But this fails to account for the sequence of (x):

(x)   *a.* Mary knows the truth
     b. Mary received a prize
     c. Mary owes me sixpence

in which, though in *a* and *c* nom is marked as stat, loc (or abl) has been subjectivized. I propose that we retain for the moment the ± subjective distinction with regard to such clauses: in these examples in (x) loc (or abl) is marked as subj, and this overrides the presence of $\begin{bmatrix} \text{nom} \\ \text{stat} \end{bmatrix}$. The examples in (xi) are −subjective:

(xi)   *a.* The truth is known to Mary
     b. Sixpence is $\left\{ \begin{matrix} \text{owed} \\ \text{due} \end{matrix} \right\}$ to me

10.4 Implications of nominativization

The expression of the generalization embodied in the notion of 'nominativization' presents certain problems for a 'concatenation-system'. Notice, for instance, that the clauses containing erg, if interpreted in the way I have suggested, introduce an interesting dilemma for such—which is as follows. If we account for the distribution of loc as subject and object in +ergative clauses in terms of its subcategorization as nom, with the selection of the subject or object position for it being dependent on whether it is marked as stat or not—i.e. dependent on the same consideration as determines the position of the obligatory nom in clauses in which erg is present as a category—then it should be possible to accommodate this in terms of some natural extension of rule II. ii. I (cf. (xlii) in §4.9), re-stated here:

(xii)   II. iii. I.   nom + V + erg → erg + V + nom
    CONDITION: stat ∉ [nom]

But, clearly, on the assumption that a post-verbal position is the neutral one for loc (as occurrences of non-nominativized loc suggest), a rule distributing nominativized loc appropriately will have to be rather different from II. iii. I, in that loc requires to be shifted to a pre-verbal position in circumstances when (obligatory) nom is already so placed by the DR that introduces it. But II. iii. I (as in (xii)) allows for the distribution of nom in an obvious manner, given the normal pre-verbal position of nom in clauses without the category erg. The 'unmarked' distributions for loc and nom conflict with respect to the formulation of such a rule. Thus, it would be difficult to express the generalization concerning the distribution of nominativized loc and nom in a natural way. And I suggest that this derives from the requirement (associated with the 'concatenation-system') that nom and loc be introduced by the DRs (i.e. from the first) in their respective 'neutral positions'.[1] If this requirement (and the associated assumption of determinacy of 'neutral positions') is dropped, and we choose (say) to introduce nom and loc arbitrarily in one of the orders which permit an extension of the equivalent of the rule in (xii) to nominativized loc, then the initial ordering

---

[1] We did, in fact, observe difficulties with respect to the formulation of the original rule (in §4.41), attributable, I would suggest, to similar considerations, and resolvable once again with regard to the proposal made in what follows. See too p. 165, n. I.

is clearly vacuous. If it is retained, then (as I have tried to show) the criteria for the 'neutral positions' conflict.

10.5   Sequencing rules

One alternative which avoids this problem is to introduce the categories simply as members of an unordered set rather than as elements ordered in a string. The various different sequences of elements can then be allowed for by **sequencing** rules,[1] which (in any particular instance) determine the appropriate order in accordance with which combination of categories and features is present. For instance, if erg is present and neither nom nor (nominativized) loc nor abl (if any or all of them are present and separate from erg) is marked as stat, then erg is placed by the sequencing rules in subject position. Let us try to formulate such rules more precisely. We shall assume that DRs introduce categories as members of a set—i.e. that all right-hand side environments of the form 'cat$_i$—' or '—cat$_i$' have been eliminated. DRs which introduce features (rather than categories) in effect form subsets within this set, and we must thus continue to specify the environment for such.

10.51   For ergative clauses. Let us consider first of all the clauses containing erg as category that we have been most concerned with in the preceding argument. We shall add then what rules are necessary for clauses lacking such an erg. Of the clauses containing erg, those in which a CS including nom also includes stat have a rather different sequence from those in which stat is either attached to erg or is lacking. Accordingly, the first two sequencing rules might be formulated (in a preliminary fashion) as in (xiii), replacing II. iii. 1 in (xii):

(xiii)   II. iii. 1. $\begin{cases} \begin{bmatrix} \text{nom} \\ \text{stat} \end{bmatrix} & V & (\text{nom}) & (\text{abl}) & (\text{loc}) & \text{erg} \\ \text{erg} & V & (\text{nom}) & (\text{nom}) & (\text{abl}) & (\text{loc}) \end{cases}$

The first part of the disjunction states that, given the presence in the set of cases of $\begin{bmatrix} \text{nom} \\ \text{stat} \end{bmatrix}$, erg and optionally nom, loc, abl, the appropriate sequence is as represented there. The second part is to be similarly interpreted. The ordering of the two parts reflects a 'sequencing hierarchy' among the cases, such that, in this instance in particular, the

---

[1] Forming part of Chafe's (1967) process of 'linearization'.

presence of $\begin{bmatrix} \text{nom} \\ \text{stat} \end{bmatrix}$ 'over-rules' the pre-posing of erg. There is no simple clause which contains all the categories listed, but in terms of this full set of obligatory and optional elements we provide for the full range of clauses containing at least erg and a CS which has in it both nom and stat.

The first part of the rule allows for the sequence of case phrases in each of the examples in (xiv):

(xiv)　*a.* Mary was sent the book (from Australia) (by John)
　　　b. The book was sent her (from Australia) (by John)
　　　c. The book was sent to Mary (from Australia) (by John)
　　　d. Mary was sold the book (by John)
　　　e. The book was sold her (by John)
　　　f. The book was sold to Mary (by John)
　　　g. Mary was robbed of the book (by John)
　　　h. The book was stolen from Mary (by John)
　　　i. The country was occupied (by his troops)
　　　j. London was reached
　　　k. (?) Canada was left
　　　l. The book was destroyed (by John)

which all involve subjectivization of an original nom or a nominativized loc or abl. Similarly, the second part of the disjunction accounts for the corresponding clauses in which stat, if it is present, is not attached to a CS containing nom:

(xv)　*a.* John sent Mary the book from Australia
　　　b. John sent the book to Mary from Australia
　　　c. John sold Mary the book
　　　d. John sold the book to Mary
　　　e. John robbed Mary of the book
　　　f. John stole the book from Mary
　　　g. His troops occupied the country
　　　h. John sat on the floor
　　　i. John reached London
　　　j. John went to London
　　　k. John left Canada
　　　l. John went away from Canada
　　　m. John destroyed the book

Notice too that part two will also allow for (xvi):

(xvi)   *a.* John was careful with the vase

in which stat is attached to erg. It also will provide the sequence of (xvii):

(xvii)   *a.* John worked
         b. John was cautious

since this is not accounted for by the first part of the rule as formulated in (xiii), which requires that nom and erg be present as separate categories. As it stands, part two of the rule permits a certain indeterminacy, in that the relative sequence of two post-verbal noms (typically, the 'direct' and 'indirect' objects) is not specified. This could perhaps be remedied by adding loc or abl where necessary to the appropriate nom, or by framing sequencing constraints in terms of complexity of the CS containing nom, such that with non-pronominal NPs in non-statives a CS containing nom and another case will normally precede a simple nom. Note however that we do find both sequences superficially in the case of (in particular) a pronominal nominativized locative phrase (*I gave her it/I gave it her*). It may be that the resolution of the indeterminacy should be left until later in the grammar.[1] Other post-verbal sequences show surface variation (*The book was sold to Mary by John/The book was sold by John to Mary*), but I suspect this too is rather more superficial, involving 'secondary word-order factors' (cf. Uhlířová, 1966). The sequencing rules envisaged here account for 'primary word-order' (principally subjectivization and objectivization). It is possible that such part combinations also should not be concatenated at this point but remain unordered until later.

10.52   For non-ergative clauses. We must now add to the disjunction in (xiii) further parts to allow for sequences not containing erg. I propose that the three sub-parts in (xviii) be added to II. iii. 1 after those in (xiii) and in the order represented as follows:

[1] Particularly in view of the relation between order and the character of the governed N (cf. §9.23). See further, however, §§11.39 and 11.44. The restriction associated with pronominal objectivized locatives (*I gave the woman the book/(?)I gave the woman it*) and the grammaticality of *I gave it him* (as well as *I gave him it*) but not **I gave the book the woman* (or **I gave the book him*) can perhaps be accounted for with reference to a language-general principle favouring incorporation (as affix, proclitic or enclitic) into the verb of pronouns susceptible to subjectivization and objectivization.

(xviii) $\left\{ \begin{array}{c} \text{subj} \\ \begin{bmatrix} \text{nom} \\ \text{stat} \end{bmatrix} \\ \text{nom} \end{array} \right\}$ V (nom) (nom) (abl) (loc)

The feature subj is, as we have noted, required to account for *John knows the truth, John owes sixpence*, etc. in which a $\begin{bmatrix} \text{nom} \\ \text{stat} \end{bmatrix}$ element is postposed. In addition to the variations allowed for which were noted above ((viii) to (xi)), these permit the following, with nominative locative in a directional clause:

(xix) *a.* I am due a pound from you
      b. A pound is due me from you

or with nominative (*a*) or subjective (*b*) abl (if it is necessary to derive such in this way):

(xx) *a.* I am due a pound to you
      b. I owe a pound to you

or with subjectivized abl and objectivized loc:

(xxi) *a.* I am due you a pound
      b. I owe you a pound

or with $\begin{bmatrix} \text{nom} \\ \text{stat} \end{bmatrix}$ (in a clause from the same paradigm):

(xxii) A pound is due from me to you

10.6 Sequencing hierarchies

One further convention required for the operation of such rules is an order of precedence among the cases, such that if a CS contains, say, both erg and abl and is thus 'ambivalent' with respect to the sequencing operation, then it will occupy the position stated for erg rather than that for abl. Thus, in (xv. *c*) and (xv. *d*) *John* takes the erg position (as subject) rather than that for abl. Nom, erg and subj would appear to have precedence (in this sense) over loc and abl. Accordingly, in addition to the sequencing hierarchy embodied in the disjunctive ordering in (xiii) and (xviii) (or as revised in (xxiii) below), there exists a further hierarchical relationship between the cases with respect to the operation of these rules. This 'precedence' is perhaps better formulated, however, as a preference for 'grammaticalization'—i.e. for subject (pre-verbal) or object (immediately post-verbal) position rather than any other (where there is ambivalence); such would indeed provide for almost all the ambivalent instances I have noted, since CSs containing loc and abl are enabled to become subject or object only by also containing erg or nom or subj.[1] I am suggesting then that we substitute this set of sequencing rules ((xiii) followed by (xviii)) for rule II. iii. I as formulated in (xii).[2]

10.7　The sequencing rules revised

Before leaving (for the moment) the sequencing rules, let us consider a possible simplification. The similarity between the first part-rule in (xiii) and the second in (xviii) suggests that an amalgamation should be performed, provided that the first rule in (xviii) precedes the amalgamated rule:

$$\text{(xxiii)}\quad \text{II. iii. I.}\quad \left\{ \begin{array}{l} \text{subj} \\ \begin{bmatrix} \text{nom} \\ \text{stat} \end{bmatrix} \\ \text{erg} \\ \text{nom} \end{array} \right\}\ V\ \text{(nom)}\ \text{(nom)}\ \text{(abl)}\ \text{(loc)}\ \text{(erg)}$$

Obviously, the introduction of such sequencing rules entails changes in II. ii, changes involving in particular the dropping of various specifications of right-hand side environments, since one of the main consequences of the new, rather more elaborate rule II. iii. I is to remove the necessity for such when categories (rather than features) are being introduced. I shall however not discuss these changes (or the modification to II. i required to allow for the distribution of nom and subj) at this point: they are fairly straightforward, and I intend anyway to consider now certain other modifications to these (and the rules in II. i)— modifications which will in their turn have consequences for our ultimate (for the moment) formulation of the sequencing rules. They are indeed

---

[1] However, this would not account for the sequence of *The castle occupies the hill.* I shall be proposing below (in §11.44) a further modification which eliminates subj, and this makes the subjectivization and objectivization of loc and abl entirely dependent on their being marked as nom or erg.

[2] It may be too that we should allow for such rules elsewhere in the grammar: note, in particular, that the relative sequence of N and some modifiers shows a variation associated with different transformational operations (*the man with the beard/the bearded man*).

such that (if these modifications are accepted) the precise character of the arguments I have advanced in the preceding would have to be altered somewhat: however, the conclusion, I think, remains valid.[1]

[1] Many of the sequences we have attributed in the present chapter to nominativization will be accounted for with respect to ergativization in terms of the proposals made in §11.4. Thus, these at least would not fall any longer within the scope of the argument advanced above, and in particular would not pose the problem I have associated with rule (xii). But observe that (as we indeed noted above—§§4.41) this rule is in itself problematical—even if we discount the nominativization of locatives. Just as there is a conflict between the 'neutral positions' for nom and loc and the formulation of a natural rule for nominativization, so we find analogous problems in determining the underlying relative sequence of the categories nom and erg.

Part V

'LOCAL' AND 'NON-LOCAL'

II *Ablative and ergative, locative and nominative*

The modifications to II. i and II. ii anticipated at the conclusion of the preceding chapter—which will indeed form the main topic of the present chapter—derive from various considerations connected with the further development of the primary, localistic theme of our discussion. I am going to propose in what follows the adoption of an account which will show a more intimate relationship between the 'non-local' (nom and erg) and the 'local' cases (loc and abl). Thus, I intend to delineate (albeit very tentatively) the underlying notions (and some syntactic consequences) shared by the 'local' and the 'non-local' and to indicate how a localistic account of such also relates to certain unresolved questions raised (in particular) in Part II—concerning among other things 'causativity'. But, as a preliminary to such a comparison of the cases, we must now extend slightly the 'local' possibilities allowed for.

II.I 'Reflexive' directional clauses

Consider in this regard the clauses in (i):

(i)   *a.* He walked along the street
      b. He walked across the room
      c. He walked around the park
      d. He walked through the valley

The second (post-verbal) case phrase in each of these is clearly (semantically) 'locational' and indeed 'directional' (and the term 'prolative' suggests itself); the verb is one that elsewhere occurs in clauses containing such. But in (i) there is only one 'locational' category present (cf., with regard to *a*, *He walked from one end of the street to the other*), which situation we have associated specifically with non-directional clauses (*He sat in the garden*). We appear to have here then the anomaly of a directional clause containing only one 'locational' element. Observe also that the preposition, which is typically distinct from those we have associated with loc or abl, though 'directional' in some sense, does not indicate merely the initial or the final point of the movement involved, but rather both. Hjelmslev (1937: 4) characterizes the prosecutive in Avar as 'désignant "par, à travers", et par conséquent à la fois éloignement et rapprochement'. However, these facets of such clauses can be quite naturally accounted for (and the anomaly avoided) if we allow abl, as well as being introduced as a separate category, to be added (as a feature) to loc, as in (ii):

(ii)

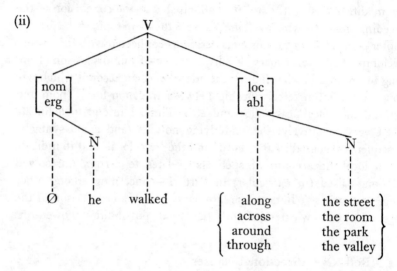

(Clauses like *He walked for four miles* perhaps represent a sub-type of such directional clauses.) Thus abl can be 'reflexive' with regard to loc as erg is to nom. Notionally, such a characterization relates to the fact that the initial and terminal locations of the nominative N are included within a single referent. We find objectivized and subjectivized locatives in the case of this type of clause also: *They crossed the river, The river was crossed.* (Cf. *He covered four miles/Four miles were covered.*) Notice too the +stative-locative *The bridge spans the river.* There would indeed appear to be no unexpected restrictions; and the incorporation of rules permitting such a possibility for directional clauses should prove quite straightforward.

11.11   An 'instrumental' sub-type. A further type of locative category is perhaps that exemplified by the last case phrase in (iii):

(iii) John travelled (from Edinburgh) (to Glasgow) $\left\{ \begin{matrix} \text{via} \\ \text{by way of} \end{matrix} \right\}$
   Stirling

However, it seems possible to account for the distinctness of such a phrase in terms of a derivation involving a complex sentence in which this phrase originates in a different clause from the others. That is, (iii) is perhaps related to the clause in (iv) (though the suggestion of 'purpose' in (iv) is perhaps stronger):

(iv)   John went through Stirling (in order) to travel from Edinburgh to Glasgow

which preserves the underlying two-clause structure in which the case phrase containing *Stirling* is an ordinary $\begin{bmatrix} \text{loc} \\ \text{abl} \end{bmatrix}$. A further variant is perhaps (v):

(v) John travelled from Edinburgh to Glasgow by going through Stirling

Compare the 'instrumental' set:

(vi)   *a.* John stabbed Seymour with a knife
   b. John used a knife to stab Seymour
   c. John stabbed Seymour by using a knife

(and cf. Lakoff, 1968). It seems quite likely that the relationship between (iii), (iv) and (v) is similar to that between the clauses in (vi) (whatever that might be), and that in neither case is it necessary to allow for a distinct underlying kind of 'locational' or 'instrumental' case-type. Though it may be that a *with*-phrase is present in the 'subordinate' clause in (vi. *b*) (cf. Chomsky, 1969*b*), its 'instrumental' (rather than merely locative ('comitative')) character is perhaps derived from the presence of the 'superordinate' clause—cf. *John laid the tiles out on the table/John used the table to lay the tiles out on.* However, Chomsky notes that the *c* variant may be closer to the underlying representation.

11.111   '*Instrumental*' *syncretisms.* Such a similarity in paradigm variations might (together with the notional parallel) explain the frequent syncretism found with respect to the representation of the instrumental and that corresponding to the preposition in phrases like *via Stirling*—and $\begin{bmatrix} \text{loc} \\ \text{abl} \end{bmatrix}$ in general—cf. Kuryłowicz, 1964: 189. Compare too *durch* in German, *þurh* in Old English,[1] and consider the examples in (vii):

(vii) *a.* They travelled by way of Stirling
       b. They travelled by car
       c. They travelled in a car

where the *b* and *c* examples would appear to be in some sense 'instrumental', but *b* shares the use of *by* with the complex directional in *a* and *c* has the 'locative' preposition *in*. *By* has, as well as the 'instrumental' and 'directional' uses illustrated in (vii), an agentive use (as marker of the category erg). This again correlates with the relation I have been drawing, and suggests further (cf. the quotations in Murray, 1888: 1227–33) that the agentive use may be the result of a 'promotion' from 'marker of instrument' to 'marker of autonomous agent' (cf. French *par*?). *With* is itself a 'marker of the agent' in Middle English (see Green, 1914: 522); and such a process of 'promotion' is proposed as an explanation for this by Green (1914: 524–5).[2] As noted above, 'markers of the instrumental' (like *with*) also often have a simple comitative (sociative) function (as in *Bill was with John/Bill came with John*), which represents clearly in non-directional clauses a sub-type of locative. *By* too has a simple (non-directional) use, as in *He lay by the roadside*. And I would also suggest that the directional instances of comitative *with* are perhaps derived from a conjunction of a directional and a non-directional (sociative) locative (*John came and Bill was with him*). However, to do justice to these various relations that I have tried to indicate (in a very informal way) would divert us somewhat from our primary aim. It has merely been my intention to point to some directions by which various, apparently distinct, case uses might be reduced to combinations of those we established in the preceding chapters, and one sort of evidence that would be relevant. I shall now leave this area (though we shall return to 'locative' *with* below) to return to the confrontation of nom and erg with loc and abl.

[1] Bosworth & Toller, 1898: 1077–8; Green, 1914: 519–20, 547–8.
[2] Green also suggests (1914: 528–31, 548–50) an explanation for the use of certain other originally 'local' prepositions to mark the agent. See too on Indo-European, Uhlenbeck, 1916*a*: 213.

11.2   Transitivity and direction

11.21   The parallel in distribution. The starting-point of the preceding excursus (the structure represented in (ii)) is however very
relevant to this topic. Both the case categories in (ii) have a further case
element attached to them, a case element which can appear elsewhere as
a separate category. Further, the case categories in (ii) can appear without
their respective further element being present, either as category or
feature. If we abstract the instances in which the 'local' and the 'non-
local' case elements appear in the same CS, then there is a quite striking
parallelism between the co-occurrence possibilities for the 'non-local'
and 'local' cases, respectively: the distribution of abl with respect to loc
is analogous to that for erg in relation to nom. The possible combinations
of erg and nom and abl and loc are represented schematically in (respectively) (viii. 1) and (viii. 2):

(viii)   1. *a.* nom   *b.* nom erg   *c.* $\begin{bmatrix} \text{nom} \\ \text{erg} \end{bmatrix}$

      2. *a.* loc   *b.* loc abl   *c.* $\begin{bmatrix} \text{loc} \\ \text{abl} \end{bmatrix}$

That is, nom and loc either appear alone (as in *a*) or together with erg
and abl either as a separate category (as in *b*) or as a feature in the CS
initiated by nom or loc (as in *c*). 'Transitivity' and 'direction' show the
same range of possibilities. They are also, I contend, semantically
parallel. Thus, I am going to suggest that it would be advantageous if
we could incorporate such a generalization into our rules. In particular,
we should be able to show that the rules in II. i involving ± ergative and
± directional are in some significant sense instances of the same rule, the
latter merely being dependent on the selection of +locative; the
distinction is one between locative and non-locative 'direction' or
'transitivity'. Similarly the difference between the *b* and *c* combinations
in (viii) could in both instances be related (as anticipated above—§11.1)
to the operation of a rule involving 'reflexive'.

11.22   Syncretisms and the semantic parallel. Notice that a
parallelism between erg and abl is reflected within various languages in
the fact that the two categories can be represented superficially in the
same way: consider *a*(*b*) in Latin (*a quo loco, caedetur ab aliquo*) or *fram*
and *of* in Old English (Green, 1914: 520–1) or *hača* in Avestan (Green,

1914: 517–18) or German *von* (Schuchardt, 1922: 244–6; Green, 1914: 537–9) or $\gamma\tilde{o}/g\tilde{o}$ in the Amdowa dialect of Tibetan (Roerich, 1958: 31–3) or Gothic *us* (Green, 1914: 544–5), etc. Compare too Uhlenbeck's suggestions (1916*a*: 196–7) concerning the Indo-European nominative and ablative. And one can discern that there is a 'semantic element' in common: if we try to formulate this in a rough way, we can say that the addition of erg and abl to nom and loc (respectively) introduces 'directionality',[1] with erg and abl indicating initial points and nom and loc terminal. Erg and abl are 'sources'—abl commonly spatial (or temporal); erg causal with causatives, and in general 'the source of the action'. Nom and loc in the presence of erg and abl (respectively) indicate 'goals' (of an 'action' or a 'movement'). Thus, with respect to these latter 'goal' cases, it is not surprising that in some languages (as we noted in chapter 1) we find a case-inflexion which can mark (superficially) both the object 'goal' of a transitive verb and the 'goal' of a movement; cf. the Latin accusatives in *Hostem occidit* and *Romam eo*.[2] It might be that such is merely a reflexion of the nominativization of loc discussed above (in chapter 10)—though the particular susceptibility of loc to this is perhaps in itself significant. The nominative and locative are in the absence of erg and abl (respectively) non-'directional' (cf. Hjelmslev, 1935). It might be argued that the distinction between nom and loc themselves has to do with the obligatory character of nom (cf. Jakobson's (1936) distinction between 'marginal' ('Randkasus') and 'non-marginal' cases). However, before pursuing this relationship further, I want to consider in more detail how we might incorporate the generalization concerning 'transitivity' and 'direction' into our grammar.

11.23   A restriction on the distribution of loc and abl. With regard to this, a restriction which we have observed (in Part III) with regard to the distribution of loc (and of predicative nom—cf. §5.9) is very pertinent. We noted in these places that loc (and predicative nom) co-

---

[1] Cf. Hjelmslev's (1935: 128) first dimension of 'direction'; the term 'transitive' itself involves a spatial metaphor. Markers associated with abl also often introduce non-animate (and particularly 'abstract') 'causes' even where abl and erg have quite distinct realizations—cf. English *He died from exhaustion*.

[2] See Meillet & Vendryes, 1924: 500–4; Kuryłowicz, 1964: 182. For references to a number of discussions of such phenomena with respect to the Indo-European languages, particularly Sanskrit, see Gonda 1957; compare too Schuchardt, 1922: 244–6. This inflexion is also often found in such languages representing $\begin{bmatrix} \text{loc} \\ \text{abl} \end{bmatrix}$— 'accusative of extent' (Meillet & Vendryes, 1924: 504–5; Kuryłowicz, 1964: 82).

occurs (in the same clause) with erg only if the clause is causative. Thus, we find (to take directional examples) either (ix. *a*) (non-ergative) or (ix. *b*) (causative):

(ix)   *a.* The ball rolled across the floor
       b. Egbert rolled the ball across the floor

If it were not for the causative examples, we could formulate a generalization that erg and loc were mutually exclusive. Such a generalization becomes possible if we consider causatives to involve superordination: in this case, the ergative would appear in the superordinate clause, the locative in the subordinate. Thus, clauses containing loc could not also include erg as an element.

11.24 A proposal concerning transitivity and direction. Now, consider this restriction in the distribution of erg in relation to the affinity I have suggested for abl and erg. In terms of such an account as is suggested in §11.23, not only loc but also and more particularly abl will not appear in the same clause as erg. I propose that we provide for the erg/abl relation and for the restriction on the co-occurrence of erg and locative cases by, in the first place, adopting the superordination account of causatives, and secondly, regarding erg as being equal to abl in the absence of loc. That is, instead of regarding ±directional (a positive selection of which introduces abl) as dependent on +locative, I suggest that ±locative and ±directional be made simultaneous, and that ±ergative be eliminated—the former erg being interpreted as abl in a clause which does not also contain loc:

$$(\text{x}) \quad \text{II. i. I.} \quad V \rightarrow \begin{bmatrix} \pm \text{locative} \\ \pm \text{directional} \\ \pm \text{stative} \end{bmatrix}$$

(Let us ignore ±stative for the moment.) If $\begin{bmatrix} +\text{locative} \\ -\text{directional} \end{bmatrix}$ is selected, then a clause like *A statue stands on the plinth* is the result. The selection of $\begin{bmatrix} +\text{locative} \\ +\text{directional} \end{bmatrix}$ is associated with a clause like (ix. *a*) in §11.23. A clause like *John read the book* (which under our previous interpretation involves the selection of +ergative) is now derived via the co-selection of +directional and −locative: the former +ergative corresponds to the selection of +directional when +locative is not simultaneously chosen. *Egbert sneezed* is straightforwardly $\begin{bmatrix} -\text{locative} \\ -\text{directional} \end{bmatrix}$. Causative sentences can then be interpreted as involving the subordination of one of these types of clause to a clause of the $\begin{bmatrix} -\text{locative} \\ +\text{directional} \end{bmatrix}$ ('ergative') type. Thus, the structures underlying (ix. *a*) and (ix. *b*) might be represented (as a first approximation) as in (xi. *a*) and (xi. *b*) respectively:

(xi)   *a.*

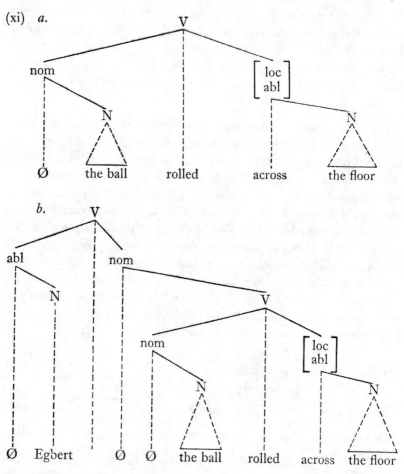

A representation for (ix. *b*) closer to the surface is derived via a rule which **conflates** the specifications for the two Vs, with the subordinate V adopting the sequence of the upper source V, and one which 'prunes' the superordinate nom (as a case governing only cases). This derived representation corresponds with the initial representation for causatives we have assumed up to this point.

11.25 Revised rules for transitivity and direction. The following set of SRs appear to be necessary to allow for the range of structures envisaged. (I ignore for the moment rules not directly relevant to this particular area):

(xii) II. i. 1. $V \rightarrow \begin{bmatrix} \pm \text{locative} \\ \pm \text{directional} \end{bmatrix}$

2. $+ \text{directional} \rightarrow \pm \text{reflexive}$

3. $\begin{bmatrix} -\text{locative} \\ -\text{reflexive} \end{bmatrix} \rightarrow \pm \text{causative}$

I assume that +locative and +directional (respectively) introduce (by DRs) loc and abl; and that the selection of +reflexive results in abl being added to nom (if loc is absent) or to loc (if present). II. i. 3 represents the fact that only clauses lacking loc and in which abl appears as a separate category can be causative. Associated with the selection of +causative is a DR of the form:

(xiii) II. i. $+ \text{causative} \rightarrow \text{eff(ect)} \ // \begin{bmatrix} \text{nom} \\ \underline{} \end{bmatrix}$

The effect of eff is to introduce V rather than N after nom, as in (xi. *b*). Rule III. ii. 1 (cf. ch. 3 (iii)) is thus modified as in (xiv) (assuming that, for English, sequence is relevant here initially).[1]

(xiv) III. ii. 1. $\text{case} \rightarrow \begin{Bmatrix} a. \ V \\ b. \ N \end{Bmatrix} \ // \ \text{case}-$

CONDITION FOR *a*: eff $\in$ [case]

Accordingly, eff should be added to the superordinate nom in (xi. *b*). All causatives, under such a proposal, involve embedding in a clause which is $\begin{bmatrix} -\text{locative} \\ -\text{reflexive} \\ +\text{causative} \end{bmatrix}$. I want now to consider how adequate such an

---

[1] I ignore here completely the relation of this sort of embedding to others or to possibilities for coordination, as well as, of course, the numerous problems connected with the nature of embedding in general. Notice, however, that since it has been assumed that (e.g.) tense originates in structures generated by rules (whatever form they may take) in I (i.e. outside the structures governed by the Vs we have considered), the embedded V (in particular) is tenseless.

A less radical proposal for accommodating the parallel between transitivity and direction would consist of merely once more conflating ±ergative and ±directional as ±directional, but allowing +directional to introduce erg in −locative clauses and abl in clauses containing loc. However, this is perhaps not an entirely satisfactory explanation of the detailed morphological similarities between erg and abl (though this could be provided for in terms of the proposal made in §12.3).

interpretation is for the range of causative clauses we have surveyed in previous chapters.

11.26   The 'stativeness' hierarchy. Before considering causatives in more detail, I would like to interpolate a further general observation in support of a proposal for deriving causatives in this way. The suggestion that erg is merely abl in a clause which lacks loc enables us to formulate in a natural way the semantic hierarchy alluded to in note 1, p. 48. Observe that in terms of the rules in (xii) above, we have allowed for four distributional possibilities within the clause for loc and abl: both absent, loc only present, abl only present, both present. If both are absent, then the 'stativeness' of the clause is simply determined by the presence or absence of stat (*John is nice* vs. *John fell*). If only loc is present, then even in the absence of stat (*The statue stands on a plinth*), the clause is notionally 'stative', in the sense of §6.45. On the other hand, if only abl is present in a clause (i.e. we have an instance of 'erg'), then even if stat is also present, its 'stativeness' is 'over-ruled' (*John is careful with the vases*). Finally, if both are present, the divergent characters (with respect to 'stativeness') of loc and abl are 'neutralized', and once more the presence or absence of stat is crucial for the 'stativeness' of the clause (*The fog stretched from London to Brighton* vs. *The ball rolled from here to there*). It is not my concern to attempt here to formulate this in a precise way. However, it would appear that we can consider loc and abl to be inherently respectively 'stative' and 'non-stative'; and this, as well as ± stative, can affect the strength of 'stativeness' of the clause. Clauses containing abl but not loc are 'non-stative'; clauses containing stat (and not abl without loc) are strongly 'stative' (in forbidding 'progressive' aspect); clauses containing loc but not abl or stat are weakly 'stative' (in allowing 'progressive aspect' but forbidding certain adverbials (like *slowly*) which are also incompatible with stat).

11.3   Causatives as superordinate

11.31   With subordinate loc. We have already considered an example ((xi. *b*)) with a subordinate loc and abl. With a simple loc, we have clauses like *He stood it on the table*, which differ from (xi. *b*) only in lacking abl in the subordinate clause. To allow for reflexive causatives, we must have structures like (xi. *b*) but in which the subordinate nom

NP is referentially identical to the superordinate abl: so *He walked across the room*, and—without subordinate abl—*He stood on the chair*. Compare the examples with *stand*:

(xv)

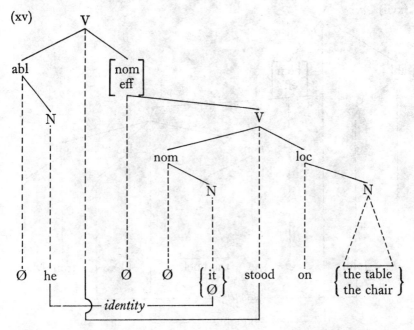

Where there is identity between the (superordinate) ablative N and the (subordinate) nominative N, then these two case phrases are also conflated (with once more the adoption of the sequential position of the upper category):

(xvi)

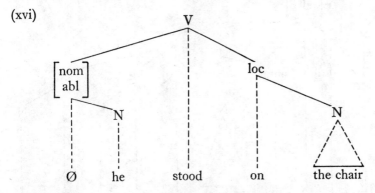

with the upper case becoming a feature on the lower.

11.311 *'Buying' and 'selling' again.* Clearly, we must also allow for instances in which the subordinate locative or ablative is identical to the superordinate abl, as in (xvii):

(xvii) *a.*

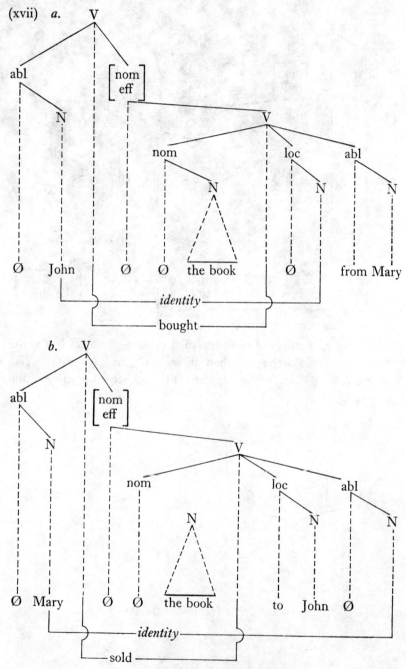

Compare with (xvii. *a*) a clause like *John bought the book for Egbert* in which the subordinate loc is not identical to the superordinate abl. Perhaps similarly different from (xvii. *b*) would be something like *Mary sold the book for/on behalf of Seymour*. However, it may be that there are some verbs (*teach/learn?*) which normally require such identity. Once more, to derive more superficial structures in instances where identity holds, the identical case phrases are conflated, with the lower case element becoming the category and the upper a feature on it. With regard to (xvii. *a*), $\begin{bmatrix} \text{loc} \\ \text{abl} \end{bmatrix}$ is the result; with (xvii. *b*), $\begin{bmatrix} \text{abl} \\ \text{abl} \end{bmatrix}$.

11.32   **With simple subordinate nom.** A subordinate clause with a simple nominative is illustrated in (xviii):

(xviii)

though *die* (like its euphemistic equivalents—*pass away*, etc.) may in fact be a directional verb (just as *live* is locative—cf. too *come alive, come into the world*).[1] This clause illustrates once again that when the two Vs are conflated, it is the sequence of the higher V (with regard to the case elements) that is adopted:

---

[1] Cf. too *go to sleep, be asleep, be awake.*

(xix)

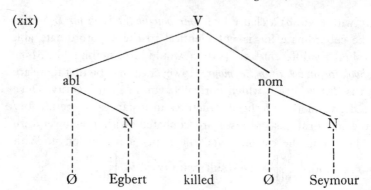

11.33   With superficial 'sentential' nom. The clauses containing 'causative verbs with sentential nom' that were discussed in §5.4 represent causative structures in which conflation has not taken place.

The operation of conflation will depend on the development of a specification for which there is available a single item corresponding to the conflated Vs. Where there is such, we may get (with some semantic difference) either a conflated or a non-conflated variant. This is true of both 'verbal' and 'adjectival' forms (cf. *make slack(er)/slacken*).[1] We can associate whatever semantic difference there may be (between the conflated and non-conflated variants) with the presence vs. the absence of the feature that 'triggers off' conflation.

It would seem that in non-conflated forms there is raising of the sub-ordinate subject—cf. *Egbert made him leave* (in which the pronoun is inflected as if it were the object of *make*) and *He was made to leave* (compare Kiparsky & Staal, 1969: §11), with the subordinate subject becoming subject in a passivized superordinate:

(xx)

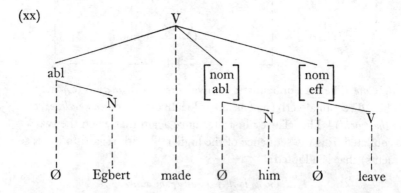

[1] Observe that the subordinate clause must apparently be either non-stative or 'ergative' in both conflated and non-conflated forms: *I made him be careful/fall/*be dead. (I made it slack(er)* involves an 'inchoative'.) We shall return to this below.

This suggests that sequencing applies separately to the superordinate
and subordinate clause, and that sequencing of the latter precedes that
for the former (see further §11.39). Raising (and conflation?) would also
appear to have taken place in examples like *We appointed him treasurer*
(derived from an embedding of a nominal clause within a causative),
since, for instance, the obligatory nom from the subordinate clause is
once more inflected as if it were the object of appoint, and can also
appear as subject in a 'passive' (*He was appointed treasurer*). This is
another way of deriving (superficial) double-object constructions.
Presumably, there is also raising in conflated forms, but the effect of this
is wiped out by conflation, in that this eliminates the distinction between
superordinate and subordinate, except in passives. (See further §11.38.)

11.34 With subordinate 'erg'. Examples like *He worked them hard*
represent conflation of an embedding of an (reflexive) 'ergative' clause
in a causative (cf. Lyons, 1968 a: §8.2.12). And *He marched the prisoners
round the yard* presumably is derived via a double causativization:

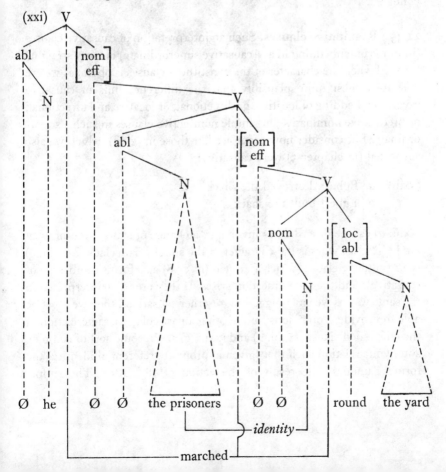

(in which the intermediate abl NP is identical to the nominative NP).
After (double) conflation, we find:

(xxii)

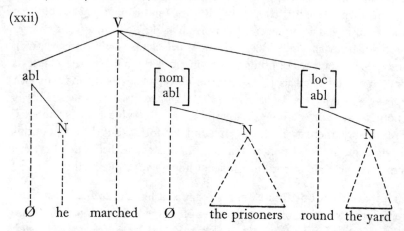

where the identical case phrases, as well as the verbs, have been
conflated.

11.35 Resultative clauses. Such an interpretation of causative clauses
(in terms of embedding in a + causative superordinate) is fairly straightforward when the character of the constituent clauses is obvious: we are
able to suggest quite plausibly that the different kinds of causative
involve embedding of locative, or directional, or locative and directional,
or predicative nominative, or simple nominative clauses in such a superordinate. But consider now examples like those in (xxiii), which we also
suggested (in chapter 5) were causative:

(xxiii)   *a.* Egbert destroyed the shack
          b. Egbert built the shack

(xxiii. *a*) can be described as involving 'a change of state'—but of what
kind? That is, what is the character of the subordinate clause? (xxiii. *b*)
is a resultative clause (which I argued (in §5.8) also forms a sub-type of
causative); and the same question arises. If they are to be interpreted in
the same way as we have suggested for other causatives, then we must be
able to provide motivations for adopting a particular characterization of
the embedded clause. (xxiii. *a*) and (xxiii. *b*) are in some sort of complex
antonymic relation such that (given appropriate referential identity) the
former 'undoes' the result of the action of the latter. The simple

negative corresponding to *a* expresses a failure to undo this result; the negative of *b* denotes that the action producing the result did not take place. If such clauses involve embedding, then the occurrence of a negative is associated with negation of the superordinate causative clause. The *build/destroy* antonymy has to do with the character of the process denoted by the subordinate verb (positive or negative). Now, the result of the action of *b* which *a* undoes is the 'existence' of the shack; and the result of *a* is to 'put the shack out of existence'. Thus, I suggest (cf. Bally, 1932: 54; Anderson, forthcoming *b*) that the embedded clause in the case of (xxiii) is 'existential'—i.e. a sub-type of locative (cf. §7.35), and presumably directional (cf. *bring into existence*):

(xxiv)

```
                        V
        _____/|
       /             /  |
      abl         [ nom ]
     /  \           eff
    /    N          |  _____V
    |    |          |        _____/ | _____
    |    |          |       /          /  |           \
    |    |          |     nom        loc  abl
    |    |          |    /  \         |     |
    |    |          |   /    N        N     N
    |    |          |  /    /|\       |     |
    |    |          | /    / | \      |     |
    |    |          |/    /__|__\     |     |
    Ø  Egbert  Ø   Ø    the shack   Ø  Ø  Ø  Ø
                    |_____  _____|
                          { built    }
                          { destroyed }
```

In the case of (xxiii. *a*) the subordinate is 'negative' (note *unmake*, *undo*), in (xxiii. *b*) 'positive' (compare *prevent/cause*).[1] If such an analysis is adopted, then we can relate all the different kinds of causative clauses—

---

[1] It would appear further that ...*bring it about that*... involves embedding of a sentence into an existential causative of this kind ('...bring V into existence'). Notice that the use of the terms 'negative' and 'positive' in relation to *build* and *destroy* is perhaps a little misleading. The distinction seems rather to have to do with the direction of the 'existential movement' ('into' or 'out of existence').

and, in particular, the distinction between resultative and non-resultative—to the character of the embedded clause (and not to inherent
differences in the (superordinate) verb, say).

11.36   Restrictions on the subordinate clause. At this point there
are various restrictions (involving particularly +stative—which was not
included in the rules in (xii)) to be accounted for. The clause subordinate
to a causative can only be +stative if it is also 'ergative':

(xxv)   1. *a.* He had/made them be careful (with the vase)
       b. He had them killed
    2.   *He had/made them (be) dead

The subordinate clause is notionally 'non-stative'. Even in *He rubbed it
smooth/He smoothed it (by rubbing)* the subordinate V is 'inchoative': the
±stative ('adjective' vs. 'inchoative verb') opposition is neutralized.
There is also no 'passive' possibility (for the higher clause) with superordinate *have*; thus there is nothing corresponding to (xxv. 1. *b*) in which
both the superordinate and the subordinate clause are 'passive'—**They
were had/made (to be) killed*—unless one accepts *They were made/com-
pelled to be examined by a doctor* as a simple example of such. (This may
be a universally marked possibility: cf. Tesnière, 1959: ch. 109.) But
They were made to be careful appears to be quite acceptable. This is
associated with the apparent requirement imposed by *make* on the
structure of the subordinate clause, that the 'ergative' CS, if present, be
subjectivized.

Note too that, in conflated structures, if the superordinate clause is
'passive', the case elements deriving from the subordinate clause show
the sort of distributional possibilities we would associate with the
selection of +stative for it:

(xxvi)   *a.* Mary was sold the books
       b. The books were sold to Mary

The originally subordinate case elements 'behave' as if they belonged
to the same clause as contains the +stative causative verb, and we must
provide for this within our account of raising.

11.37   Fragment of grammar, 5. If we ignore for the moment such
restrictions, the requisite subcategorization and dependency rules could
be formulated as in (xxvii):

(xxvii)   *Fragment of grammar, 5*

$$\text{II. i. 1}\quad V \rightarrow \begin{bmatrix} \pm \text{directional} \\ \pm \text{locative} \\ \pm \text{stative} \end{bmatrix}$$

2. *a.* $+ \text{locative} \rightarrow \pm \text{nominative}$
   b. $+ \text{directional} \rightarrow \pm \text{reflexive}$

3. *a.* $\begin{bmatrix} - \text{reflexive} \\ - \text{locative} \end{bmatrix} \rightarrow \pm \text{causative}$

   b. $\begin{bmatrix} - \text{nominative} \\ + \text{stative} \end{bmatrix} \rightarrow \pm \text{subjective}$

4. $\begin{bmatrix} + \text{stative} \\ \left\{\begin{array}{l} + \text{nominative} \\ \begin{bmatrix} + \text{directional} \\ + \text{locative} \\ - \text{causative} \end{bmatrix} \end{array}\right\} \end{bmatrix} \rightarrow \pm \text{oblique}$

ii. 1. *a.* $V \rightarrow \text{nom}$
    b. $+ \text{locative} \rightarrow \text{loc}$

2. *a.* $+ \text{directional} \rightarrow \text{abl} \;//\; \left\{\begin{bmatrix} \text{loc} \\ - \end{bmatrix} \\ \begin{bmatrix} \text{nom} \\ - \end{bmatrix}\right\} \;/\; \begin{bmatrix} \underline{} \\ + \text{reflexive} \end{bmatrix}$

   b. $+ \text{causative} \rightarrow \text{eff} \;//\; \begin{bmatrix} \text{nom} \\ - \end{bmatrix}$

3. *a.* $\left\{\begin{array}{l} + \text{nominative} \rightarrow \text{nom} \\ + \text{subjective} \;\rightarrow \text{subj} \end{array}\right\} \;//\; \begin{bmatrix} \text{loc} \\ - \end{bmatrix}$

   b. $+ \text{stative} \rightarrow \text{stat} \;//\; \left\{\begin{array}{l} \left\{\begin{bmatrix} \text{loc} \\ - \end{bmatrix} \\ \begin{bmatrix} \text{abl} \\ - \end{bmatrix}\right\} \;/\; \begin{bmatrix} \underline{} \\ + \text{oblique} \end{bmatrix} \\ \begin{bmatrix} \text{nom} \\ - \end{bmatrix} \end{array}\right\}$

The SRs are self-explanatory. Note, however, that since loc and erg no longer co-occur in a single clause, 'stative-locative' and 'stative-ergative' can be dispensed with in favour of 'oblique'. In a +oblique clause stat is added to the case category other than nom. (Rule ii. 3. *b* does not allow for clauses in which loc and abl co-occur.) The DRs each introduce an element, either as one of the set of categories dependent on V (as in ii. 1—no environments now being necessary) or as a feature on a category or categories (as with 3. *b*, whereby stat is added either to loc or abl (if the V is marked as + oblique) or to nom). Some elements appear either as features or categories: abl, if the condition $/ \left[\begin{array}{c} \overline{} \\ + \text{reflexive} \end{array} \right]$ is not met, is introduced as a category; if the condition is met, then abl is added to loc, if present, or nom (if loc is absent). The present set of rules does not allow for subjectivization or nominativization of abl; if such are desired, the necessary extensions are fairly clear. A set of rules which does allow for such is proposed in the final chapter.

11.38 More on restrictions on the subordinate. To account for the 'non-stative' restriction in clauses embedded in a causative, it might seem to be necessary to introduce a modification such that ±stative is dependent upon '+ergative' when the clause is governed by $\left[\begin{array}{c} \text{nom} \\ \text{eff} \end{array} \right]$. However, we can perhaps relate this restriction to a sub-type of causative, since there are 'causatives' which show a ±stative opposition in the 'non-ergative' clauses subordinate to them: *He requires that his assistants be/become qualified.* The causative Vs associated with obligatory raising belong to the sub-class of 'true causatives' requiring the ±stative restriction; the restriction can then be stated as one on the occurrence of such verbs rather than a restriction imposed by them—and thus need not be incorporated in the particular rules we have been considering. That is, operation of the SRs in a clause dependent on $\left[\begin{array}{c} \text{nom} \\ \text{eff} \end{array} \right]$ need not be restricted in the way I have indicated. 'Quasi-causatives' like *require* are associated with both 'stative' and 'non-stative' dependent clauses; 'true causatives' are restricted to the government of 'non-stative' clauses.

On the other hand, to provide for examples like those involving *sell*, etc. mentioned immediately above (in (xxvi)), it seems to be necessary to distribute the stat associated with a + stative selection in the superordinate with respect to cases from the subordinate clause. This could be allowed for by introducing a rule copying a + stative specification in the superordinate clause on to the V in the subordinate in those instances when no independent + stative selection is possible. This would allow subsequent rules (though we must exclude + subjective—and this is problematic) for the (subordinate) clause involving prior selection of + stative to be operative, and thus provide for the alternatives dependent on the distribution of stat noted above with respect to examples (like (xxvi)) involving verbs like *sell, rob*, etc.

However, given that the sequencing rules apply separately to the superordinate and subordinate clauses (see immediately below), it is probably preferable to allow for such possibilities with respect to the $\pm$ subjective distinction (in the subordinate clause), such that $\begin{bmatrix} \text{loc} \\ \text{subj} \end{bmatrix}$ is subjectivized in the subordinate clause, or nom if loc is not so marked. The element stat, if attached to $\begin{bmatrix} \text{nom} \\ \text{eff} \end{bmatrix}$ in the superordinate clause, is transferred to the subject of the subordinate (replacing subj in the subject case CS), which, when it is raised, is then subjectivized by the operation of the sequencing rules with respect to the superordinate clause. The operation of these sequencing rules demands that the raised subject also have the nom of $\begin{bmatrix} \text{nom} \\ \text{eff} \end{bmatrix}$ copied on to it. The raising and nom-copying (and stat-transference) rule might be formulated roughly as follows:

$$(\text{xxviii}) \quad \begin{bmatrix} \text{nom} \\ \text{eff} \\ (\text{stat}) \end{bmatrix} \begin{bmatrix} \text{case} \\ (\text{subj}) \end{bmatrix} \rightarrow \begin{bmatrix} \text{case} \\ \text{nom} \\ (\text{stat}) \end{bmatrix} \text{eff}$$

However, it is to be noted that such an interpretation involving $\pm$ subjective in the subordinate clause requires that it be not restricted to +stative clauses in this instance: we shall find further motivations for this modification below.

Observe also, as a further restriction, that if *They were made to be examined by a doctor*, etc. are rejected as examples of causativization of an underlying stative clause with non-'ergative' subject, then the selection of +oblique (cf. rule II. i. 3. *c* in (xxvii)) would have to be made obligatory for such clauses.

11.39   Sequencing revised. If we assumed that the sequencing rules were ordered after the rules of conflation and pruning and are therefore late (after at least the semantic rules in III rather than in II. iii), then they could be retained for conflated clauses as formulated in (xxiv) in chapter 10, except for clauses with *march*, etc. ((xxi), (xxii)), provided we maintain 'erg' as a cover symbol (for abl introduced in a clause which does not also contain (before conflation) loc). But this formulation will not account for the sequence of examples with *make*, etc. (or with *march* and the like); nor is it compatible with the notion of raising formulated above. This suggests rather that the sequencing rules apply separately to the superordinate and subordinate clauses before conflation. Let us suppose (in accordance with the interpretation of raising in §11.38) that the sequencing rules apply first to the subordinate clause. They will develop subjects, objects, etc. in accord with the particular combination of elements present. In terms of the proposals made in §11.38, I suggest that a further rule then raises and marks as nom the subject of the subordinate clause, and this phrase then takes part in the sequencing rules for the superordinate clause.

11.391 *Sequencing with raising and conflation.* Consider the following sample 'derivation' (for *Mary was sold a hat*):

(xxix)   *a. by the sequencing rules for the subordinate clause*

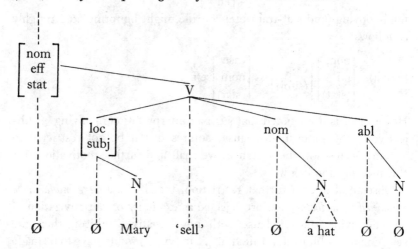

b. *by raising, nom-copying, sequencing of the superordinate and cop introduction*

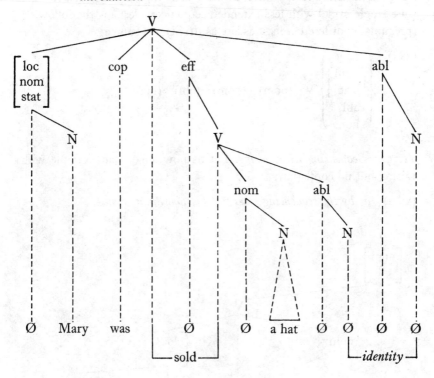

c. *by conflation and pruning*

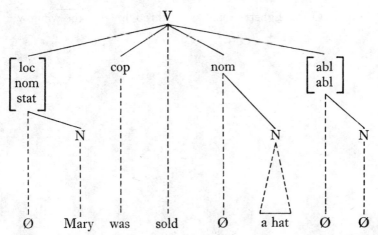

The sequencing rules required can obviously be somewhat reduced (cf. (xxiv) in chapter 10) since, in particular, they are required to cope (in a single cycle) with less extended sequences. Perhaps the following (presumably ordered at least as late as III. iii) will suffice:

(xxx) $\left\{ \begin{array}{l} \text{subj} \\ \left[\begin{array}{l} \text{nom} \\ \text{stat} \end{array} \right] \\ \text{abl} \\ \text{nom} \end{array} \right\}$ V (nom) (nom) (abl) (loc)

11.392 *Sequencing with raising.* Let us now look at an example with raising but no conflation:

(xxxi)   *a. by the sequencing rules for the subordinate clause*

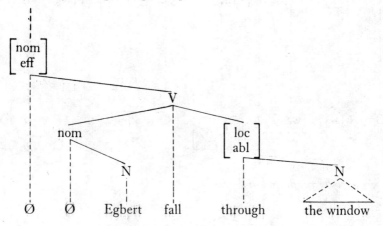

b. by raising, nom-copying and sequencing of the superordinate

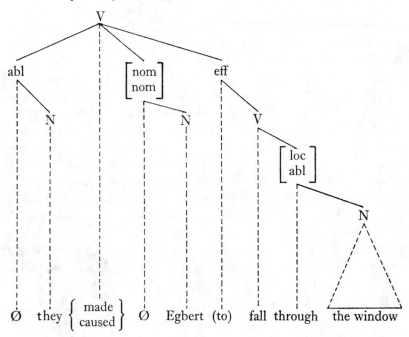

11.4   An alternative interpretation for causatives

However, there is one particular modification to our interpretation which, because it will enable us to avoid the complexities of a rule like (xxviii), I would like to consider now. In all of the sentences involving (true) causatives we have had to allow (via (xxviii)) for the raising and recategorization of the subject of the embedded clause. Suppose instead that the subject is not raised but rather it is required to be identical with the nominative N in the superordinate. Now, in terms of our previous account, there is no such nominative N, but by a rule like that in (xiv) V is introduced after $\begin{bmatrix} \text{nom} \\ \text{eff} \end{bmatrix}$ (i.e. the nom in +causative clauses). I propose instead, then, that the DR dependent on +causative introduces a new V directly rather than indirectly after eff:

(xxxii)   +causative → V

(Cf. 11. ii. 2. *b* in (xxvii).) The (*a*) part of the rule for cases in (xiv) can be eliminated, and nom in causative clauses, as elsewhere, will introduce a

N. It is with this N that the subject of the embedded clause (dependent on the V introduced by (xxxii)) must be identical.

I do not consider here the further possibility that the subordinate V is governed not immediately by the causative V but rather by a locational case dependent on the latter. This would be loc in the case of (e.g.) *He compelled me to leave*, with *to* as its marker, but abl in *He prevented me from leaving*, abl (*from*) being the 'negative' of loc (cf. the suggestion made finally in §12.3). A causative clause could then be defined as one which contains an erg and a locational case (which combination is not possible otherwise). I am not clear how much support such a modification could be given; obviously, it would require a considerable revision of the framework we have been developing in the discussion so far (though this would be lessened in terms of the proposal put forward in §12.3). Observe, however, that such a suggestion allows for the appearance of abl in a clause that does not contain loc. It may be that we should provide for this possibility anyway with respect to sentences like *Arnold was absent from the meeting*. Abl is then not merely ablative but 'ablocative', in the sense that 'locative' includes 'allative'. We shall return to this briefly in §12.3.

11.41   ...exemplified

11.411   *With verb conflation.* Consider once again *Mary was sold a hat*. The sequencing rules for the subordinate clause can still operate to result in the sequence in (xxviii. *a*), but under the new proposal there is no raising (etc.) of the subject phrase. After the operation of the sequencing rules (and the introduction of cop), the relevant structure can rather be represented as in (xxxiii):

(xxxiii)

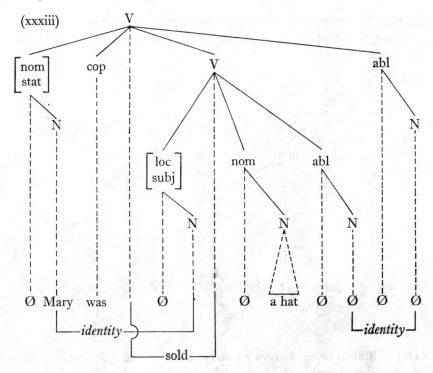

After conflation—notice that no 'pruning' rule is required—we find
the structure represented in (xxxiv). Now both the identical abl phrases
and the identical phrases which are the nom in the superordinate and the
subject of the subordinate are (respectively) conflated.

(xxxiv)

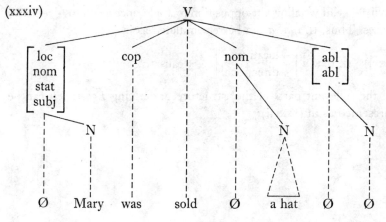

11.412   *...and without.* Similarly, the structure underlying *They made/ caused Egbert (to) fall through the window* (cf. (xxi)) can be represented as in (xxxv):

(xxxv)

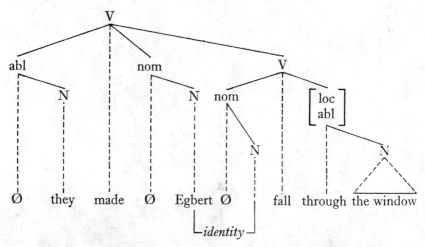

11.42 **Reflexive causatives reinterpreted.** Notice, however, that if the rules are simply modified as I have proposed, then underlying a clause like *Egbert left* there will be a structure containing three co-referential Ns: the superordinate ablative and nominative and the subordinate subject. This consequence can be avoided if we make $\pm$ causative dependent on $\begin{bmatrix} -\text{locative} \\ +\text{directional} \end{bmatrix}$ simply (cf. 11. i. 3. *a* in (xxvii))—i.e. if we allow the opposition to apply once again to + reflexive clauses. Thus, 11. i. 3. *a* can be reformulated as in (xxxvi):

(xxxvi)   11. i. 3. *a* $\begin{bmatrix} -\text{locative} \\ +\text{directional} \end{bmatrix} \rightarrow \pm \text{causative}$

and the (relevant parts of the) structure underlying *Egbert left* can be represented as in (xxxvii):

(xxxvii)

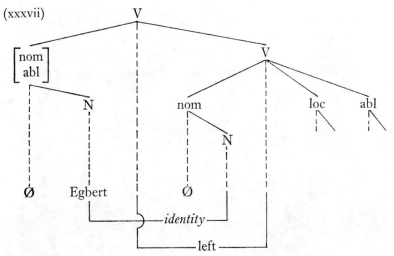

11.43   Elimination of N-identity requirements. Now, if the rules of sequencing and conflation for both the governing and dependent Vs precede the rule introducing N—i.e. are located after all in II. iii—then the various N-identity requirements we have found necessary can be dispensed with. These rules will operate with regard to structures lacking Ns. The difference between the clauses in (xxxviii)

(xxxviii)   *a.* John bought her a hat
            b. John bought a hat

will reside in the degree of conflation: in (xxxviii. *b*) the abl of the super-ordinate and the loc of the subordinate have been conflated (and thus only one N is introduced for the conflated case CS), whereas in the (xxxviii. *a*) instance, there is no such conflation, and two Ns are intro-duced—one with respect to loc (*her*) and one for abl (*John*). Thus, in a sense, 'identity' is dependent on conflation rather than (as was suggested above) vice versa, though, of course, non-conflated Ns can still show identity: *John bought himself a hat.* Underlying both of these clauses in (xxxviii) will be the structure represented in (xxxix):

(xxxix)

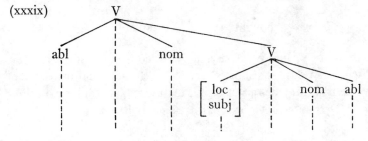

They differ in that whereas with (xxxviii. *a*) only the superordinate nom and the subordinate loc (and of course the two Vs with each other) are conflated, in the case of (xxxviii. *b*) the conflation also involves the abl of the superordinate. So (after conflation and the introduction of the Ns):

(xl) *a.*

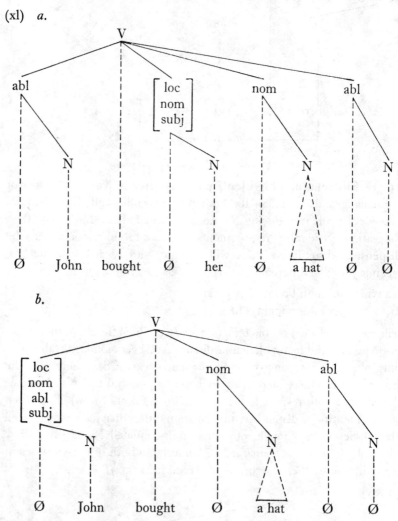

      b.

Thus, the nom in causative clauses is regarded as an abstract 'place-holder' with respect to the subject case of the clause subordinate to the causative verb; it provides a slot for raising the subject. Subject-raising is accordingly re-interpreted as a sub-type of conflation.

It is likely that occurrence of conflation of e.g. Vs depends on the selection of some feature additional to those we have considered. But it may be that conflation of Vs occurs later in the grammar than the case conflations (perhaps even post-lexically); apart from being more restricted in their application, there do not seem to be the same motivations for their early placement as there are with the conflations involving cases. However, I shall not pursue this topic further here (and conflation schemata only will be proposed in the rules in chapter 12). Clearly too, there are limitations on the 'depth' of conflation involving Vs. As was observed above, I shall not attempt to examine the relationship between causative embedding and other sources for complex structures—even those which also result in 'accusative and infinitive' constructions (van Ek, 1967). However, it may be that complex structures governed by verbs of perception constitute a non-causative equivalent of the construction we have been investigating.

11.44 Sequencing revised again: ergative for subjective. The sequencing rules, as proposed in (xxix), must also be modified to include a dependent V. And before leaving the sequencing rules, I would like to consider a further possible reduction in their number. In §7.23 I suggested that the alternation between *by* and *to* after *know* and the like, as in (xli):

(xli)   The plan is known by/to lots of people

can be attributed to the presence *vs.* the absence of 'recategorization' of the loc as erg. We observed that, with dative verbs, such clauses alternate with one containing a subjectivized loc:

(xlii)   Lots of people know the plan

in which the subjectivization of loc is associated with the addition of subj to the CS initiated by loc. But the alternation between subject position and post-verbal position with *by* as a surface marker is what we have associated with the element erg (abl in clauses lacking loc). This suggests that we might substitute ±ergative for ±subjective in 11. i. 3. *b* in (xxvii), erg being added to loc as a result of the selection of +ergative. The sequence of the *by* variant in (xxxviii) will then be allowed for, as before, by the second part of (xxiv) in ch. 10. And we associate subjectivization of the loc in (xlii) with the presence of erg—but only if nom is not marked as stat. That is rule 11. i. 3. *b* would have to be modified by

eliminating the $\left[\overline{\phantom{+ \text{stative}}}\atop +\text{stative}\right]$ requirement: (xli) is +stative, but (xlii) is
not. We have already noted above (§11.38) a motivation for such a
modification with regard to the subordinate clause in sentences like those
in (xxvi): it is necessary to allow for loc to be subjectivized in clauses
subordinate to a causative verb, and therefore −stative. The specification
on the left-hand side of 11. i. 3. *b* can also be simplified to −nominative.
It is then possible to eliminate the first part of (xxiv) and reformulate the
rest as in (xliii):

(xliii) $\left\{\begin{array}{l}\left[\begin{array}{l}\text{nom}\\ \text{stat}\end{array}\right]\\ \text{erg}\\ \text{nom}\end{array}\right\}$ V (nom) (nom) (V) (abl) (loc)

where erg represents either the ergativization feature introduced as we
have been discussing, or is a cover symbol for abl in a clause lacking loc
(a convention which I anticipate will be useful elsewhere). This is
intended to capture the generalization that loc in such a clause 'behaves'
as if it were erg. Such an account might also be extended to the 'ergativization' of nom noted in §7.25—in examples like *He was pleased by the
book* (as opposed to *He was pleased with the book*) and *The book pleased
him* (as opposed to, say, *He occupies this position*, in which the nom is
subjectivized not as a result of being marked as erg, but rather simply by
the last part of the sequencing rule). In such clauses, nom would be
ergativized and loc nominativized! Ergativization of nom would depend
on nominativization of loc. This observation can be allowed for by
making ±ergative and ±nominative simultaneously dependent on
+locative. If both +ergative and +nominative are selected erg is added
to nom and nom to loc; if +ergative and −nominative, erg is added to
loc; if −ergative and +nominative, nom is added to loc.[1]

11.441 *Some reservations.* However, such a modification has certain
apparent drawbacks. In chapter 6 we associated the restriction on the
distribution of 'progressive aspect' with the presence of stat (and
absence of erg) in the clause. Under the proposed modification, a clause
like (xlii) would no longer contain stat, and we would have to associate

---

[1] Rule 11.i.4 can consequently be re-ordered to 3.*b*. Modifications in 11.ii are also
obviously required as a result of such a proposal: see the grammar proposed in the
final chapter.

the 'progressive aspect' restriction with either +stative or ergativization. Further, we find the ...*by*... form only with 'dative' verbs—cf. (xliv):

(xliv)   Two teachers are (included) in the committee

to which there corresponds no sentence with *by*, though there is one with subjectivized loc:

(xlv)   The committee includes two teachers

If we associate the occurrence of (xlv) with ergativization of loc, then either this occurs only in the −stative instance ((xlv)) or it has no superficial marker in the case of the +stative ((xliv)). A reason for this lack of superficial indication of ergativization might be found in the fact that *by* is preempted by the corresponding causative:

(xlvi)   Two teachers were included (in the party) by the committee

One might wonder too whether the distinction between the form (in (xliv)) with segmented copula and that without such segmentation has anything to do with a difference between non-ergativization and ergativization. But apparently one must reckon either with the retention of +subjective with respect to examples like (xlv) or with a restriction of full ergativization to dative verbs. However, it may rather be that (xlv) and the like involve nominativization simply, the nominative CS that is also locative being preposed by some extension of the sequencing constraint for clauses containing more than one CS including nom discussed in §10.51, whereby the more complex CS has first position. Such an extension would be in conflict with the sequencing constraint that subjectivizes the obligatory (i.e. simple, non-locational) nom when two are present and neither is marked with stat—as in *The statue occupies a plinth*. Perhaps the syntactic difference between clauses with *contain*, etc. and *occupy*, etc. might be formulated in terms of which constraint is applicable.

Observe too a verb like *receive*, which we associated in §9.41 with subjectivized locative subjects. It shows once more that the ±subjective (or ±ergative) opposition should be applicable in −stative as well as +stative clauses. But, if we do also associate the subjectivization of the locative category in such clauses with the attachment of erg to loc (i.e. with ergativization) rather than, say, nom to loc, then we must modify our formulation of the constraint on 'progressive aspect', to exclude it from $+$ stative and $\begin{bmatrix} -\text{directional} \\ +\text{ergative} \end{bmatrix}$ (not all $+$ ergative) clauses. How-

ever, the grammar suggested in chapter 12 substitutes $\pm$ ergative for $\pm$ subjective (and various subsequent rules depend on this), just as it incorporates the account of causatives involving 'direct' introduction of

V rather than via $\begin{bmatrix} \text{nom} \\ \text{eff} \end{bmatrix}$.

11.5   Causatives by a subcategorization cycle

11.51   The causative cycle. The nature of the restrictions required by true causative clauses of clauses subordinated to them (if the restriction is formulated in this direction—cf. §11.38) might raise another more general query with respect to the account of this aspect of the grammar offered in the present chapter. In particular, the restriction of $\pm$ stative to clauses that are '$+$ ergative' $\left(\text{i.e.} \begin{bmatrix} +\text{directional} \\ -\text{locative} \end{bmatrix} \right)$ might be accommo-

dated (not by having $+$ causative effect the introduction of a further V with respect to which the restrictions must be formulated, but) by allowing the selection of $+$ causative to initiate a re-cycling through the rules. Thus:

(xlvii)   II. i. I. $\left\{ \begin{matrix} V \\ +\text{causative} \end{matrix} \right\} \rightarrow \begin{bmatrix} \pm\text{directional} \\ \pm\text{locative} \end{bmatrix}$

The availability of $\pm$ stative on the second cycle would be dependent on the selection of $\begin{bmatrix} +\text{directional} \\ -\text{locative} \end{bmatrix}$. The forms containing (superficially)

two verbs (the non-conflated forms under the other interpretation) could be derived by segmenting out (from V) $+$ causative (realized as *make*, etc.). This too would avoid having to introduce a rule like (xxviii) to copy nom (and stat) on to the subject of a subordinate clause to account for the syntax of examples like those in (xxvi). Such a modification, which would result in underlying specifications intermediate in complexity between those proposed in earlier chapters and those suggested immediately above, thus has some attractiveness.

11.52   Counter-arguments. However, it is not certain that the statement of the restriction on $+$ stative will be dealt with much more neatly; and there are certain apparent drawbacks which are not found with an account involving embedding of V. In the first place, it would not be possible to simplify the sequencing rules in some of the ways I have suggested. Moreover, special rules would be required to allow for sequences like *They were forced to be careful*, with (superficially) two 'main verbs' and two copulas. Consider too the problems associated with providing (within such a framework) for sequences of causatives like *John forced her to make them allow Mary to stay*, or (with 'passives') *She was allowed to force them to make John go*, or (with negations) *She wasn't allowed to make him not leave*, etc. These difficulties are particular to an account in which the surface verbs in such sentences are not present in the underlying representation. Moreover, such an account will obviously not allow for sentences involving *require*, etc., which would have to be derived in another way (presumably via embedding). (However, it might just be that an account involving some combination of embedding (for 'non-conflated' structures) and 're-cycling' (for 'conflated' structures) will eventually prove preferable.)

11.6 The relationship between loc and nom

11.61 Some considerations. We must now consider whether it is plausible to posit a common source for loc and nom, in something like the way that we have been able to subsume erg and abl as alternative manifestations of a single category. The situation is obviously somewhat different in the present instance. We were able to regard erg and abl as 'suppletive' because they are mutually exclusive within a single clause (if we accept the interpretation of causatives involving embedding— they are exclusive with regard to a single cycle, on the re-cycling view). The occurrence (in a particular clause) of loc does not exclude nom (from that clause), or vice versa. But loc and nom differ in that nom is an obligatory dependent of each V while loc requires the selection of +locative. Might we then interpret nom as being no other than the obligatory loc, a loc which is in all instances marked as nom—nom then being a feature (like erg) relevant to the more superficial distribution of any loc, in permitting it to be either subject or object (depending on other circumstances)? We can then relate the difference between, for instance, (xlviii. *a*) and (xlviii. *b*), containing a sub-type of location:

(xlviii)   *a.* John is with Mary
           b. Mary is with John

(which express a 'logically symmetrical' relation), to the choice of one 'locative' phrase (rather than the other) as 'obligatory' (and so also marked as nom)—the one represented by *John* in *a*, by *Mary* in *b*. Compare too (xlix. *a*) and (xlix. *b*):

(xlix) *a.* A bright flash accompanied the explosion
       b. An explosion accompanied the bright flash

in which the 'non-obligatory' loc is also marked as nom. The difference has to do in both instances with the 'information structure' (in Halliday's (1967–8) terms) of the clause (cf. Huddleston, 1969: 9). We can consider nom and erg, as features on the basic case categories loc and abl (if the proposals I have just made are accepted), to be concerned with the primary stage of this ('information structure'), as opposed to the 'experiential' (or 'cognitive') structure represented in terms of the clause categories (V, loc, abl).

However, it may be that *with* represents a 'complex preposition'—i.e. one including an underlying nominal, and thus derived by casualization (§2.121). Other symmetrical prepositions would appear to be such, with a structure (at some stage) like that in (l):

(l)

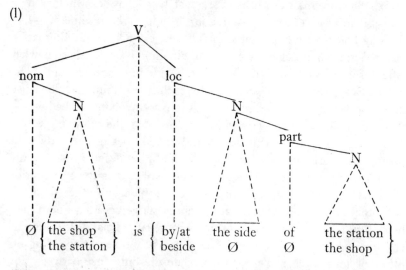

(I have nothing here to say about the relation of the adnominal case, part(itive), to the other cases, though it is quite likely that it is merely an adnominal locative.) The same holds for 'converse' prepositions like *behind* ((*in*) *back of*) and *in front of* (*before*). Yet, a derivation of this sort for *with* presents a number of problems. It may rather be that an underlying conjunction is ultimately involved ('Both John and Mary are in a certain place'), here and elsewhere, with the examples in (xlviii) differing in which member of the conjoined pair is (subsequently) subjoined to the locative N ('John/Mary is in the same place as Mary/ John'), which would presumably once again be a matter of 'information structure'. However this may be, the pairs like that in (xlviii) do nct constitute firm evidence, of themselves, for the identity of nom and loc.

We have, nevertheless, already noted above a notional parallelism between nom and loc (and erg and abl). Also apparent is a number of shared characteristics like the possibility of reflexivization (addition of abl) and ergativization (addition of erg) as well as nominativization (though this last may be appropriate to abl also). However, as we find in the case of the *with* clauses, it is difficult to discern what unambiguous surface syntactic consequences of such a proposal (for the underlying identity of nom and loc) are available as a source of (dis-)confirmation. The incorporation of an identification of nom and loc into the grammar presents indeed a number of problems, and would appear, in particular, to necessitate an extension of the use of cover-symbols, such that it is necessary to regard nom as a cover symbol for obligatory loc, as well as a feature on loc or abl. Notice however that such an identification, as well as perhaps underlying the 'symmetry' of (xlviii. *a*) and (xlviii. *b*), might explain the occurrence of *to* in *What happened to Seymour?* etc. (and *What did Egbert do to Seymour?* etc.), which contains a dummy subject (*what*) and in which nom is represented by a 'locative' preposition. Compare too the French causative construction involving *faire* + V + *à quelqu'un* (Tesnière, 1959: ch. 108), or the 'objects' with English 'adjectives', in which the underlying nominative once more is marked with a locative preposition.

For the present, perhaps the furthest that one can argue is that the case we have been terming 'nom' is the 'unmarked' case which is obligatorily nominativized. That is, if loc and abl are, respectively, the 'positive' and 'negative' locational cases, this other case merely does not take part in this antonymy—or perhaps is neutral, or complex (in Hjelmslev's (1935) terms). And, further, say that, nevertheless, we continue to regard the elements nom and erg as relevant to 'information structure' rather than 'cognitional structure'—i.e., in particular they are crucial for the primary sequencing rules (as formulated in §11.44): then, whereas the locational cases are nominativized only optionally, the unmarked case has as its primary characteristic the role which it plays in 'information structure', deriving from the fact that it is always nominative.

11.62 Predicative nom. But there are more obvious signs of both a notional and a syntactic affinity between (at least some instances of) the predicative nominative and the locative. A clause like *He's a policeman* expresses membership of a class; it locates someone in a class ('He is in the class of policemen'), and thus in some instances has a paraphrase with an overt locative (*He's in the police*). In some languages (like Welsh) the presence of a locative marker with the predicative is quite normal; and a locative origin for the essive in e.g. Finnish has been proposed (cf. Eliot, 1890: 157). Thus, the head predicative noun may start off as dependent on a partitive case governed by a locative N specified in the same way as *class*. Corresponding inchoatives and causatives are found with a 'directional' locative: beside *Fred has become a monster* we find (li):

(li) Fred has turned into a monster

Consider also the causatives *They turned/made Fred into a monster*; and, corresponding to *He's in the police, He has gone into the police*.[1] Thus, the predicative NP in such 'nominal' sentences can (superficially at least) be marked in the same way as a locative. We also find in 'non-stative' nominal clauses prepositions associated with both kinds of locative case: *They made it into butter, They made it out of milk, They changed it from a mansion to a slum*. 'Change of class' is represented superficially in a fashion which suggests a locative source for the 'class' NPs. Predicative nom, like loc, as was observed in §5.9, does not co-occur with erg within a single clause, unless it is +causative; and we have proposed immediately above an account which would explain this restriction with respect to loc. If predicative nom were a sub-type of loc, then we could account for the restriction in the same (not just a parallel) way. Notice that certain other restrictions are shared by locative and 'nominal' clauses, as instanced in (lii):

(lii) 1. *a.* Fred is a monster
       b. ?A monster is Fred
       2. *a.* The apple is in a box
       b. ?A box contains the apple

---

[1] Compare the Swahili examples cited by Christie (1969); and notice once more the local origin of the translative in Finnish (Eliot, 1890: 158). See too Anderson, forthcoming *b*.

However, such a simple parallelism exists between locatives and 'intensive' (in Halliday's (1967–8) sense) predicative nominatives only—see particularly Halliday, 1967: 67–71. An 'extensive' instance like *John is the policeman* seems to me to involve a rather different derivation (or rather derivations), perhaps similar to constructions involving *same* or *equal*. I shall assume in terms of the rules that follow (in §12.1) that 'predicative nom' is a sub-type of locative.

11.63 Further speculations. Clauses containing certain kinds (at least) of adjectives might permit such a (locative) derivation (cf. *He is exhausted/He is in a state of exhaustion*). Compare once more Welsh, and see too, on Swahili, Christie, 1969. Notice too that the inchoative verbs used with such adjectives are in English, for instance, typically directional: *go mad, turn nasty, grow tall, become old*. The (historically locative) translative in Finnish is used with both nouns and adjectives after such verbs. The notional and representational similarities between location, classification and attribution of a (non-inherent) state (and changes in location, classification and state) suggest a localistic interpretation like that I have outlined, such that the predicative noun or adjective of state originates as a dependent of an abstract locative.

It may indeed be that all (or most) sentences (including perhaps even 'passives') containing the copula involve (at some stage in their derivation) a superordinate locative clause in which the 'verb'/'adjective'/'noun' predicate is embedded. The accommodation of this would, of course, require considerable modification of the grammar so far elaborated here; and an adequate discussion would necessarily involve us in a closer scrutiny than has been possible above of factors (like those observed by Darrigol (1829) and by Garnett (1846–7; 1848–50)) to do with tense and aspect (a topic which I propose to discuss elsewhere). I shall therefore not strain the reader's patience and imagination further in this direction, for the moment.

One consideration seems nevertheless worthy of mention at this point. Suppose that there were (at least) these two different sources for 'adjectives', one involving subordination to a (copular) locative clause ('X is in a state of...'), the other something like the account outlined above, with segmentation of the copula as a dependent of the (adjectival) V. The two sources are markedly different, in terms of such a derivation for the copula, and the rules for collapsing them as a single type of surface representation would prove rather complex. This (and various other considerations) suggests that we should adopt for simple (non-subordinate) adjectives (if such there be) a derivation rather like that proposed by Tesnière (1959: chs. 67 and 74). In terms of such an account, the copula is segmented out not as a dependent but as a governor. Thus, rather than proposing (after cop-segmentation) for *Mice are small* a structure like (liii. *a*), I suggest that (liii. *b*) might be more adequate.

(liii)   *a.*

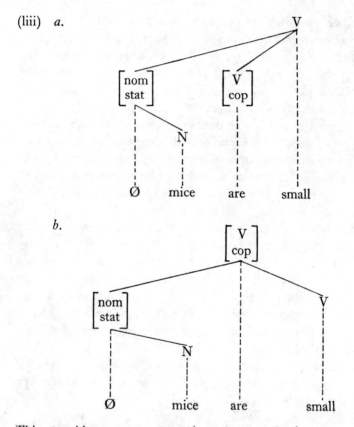

b.

This provides a more natural more superficial representation for adjectival clauses derived via a superordinate locative clause. So too perhaps for *The house is situated in the country* (cf. (xii. *b*) in §6.33):

(liv)

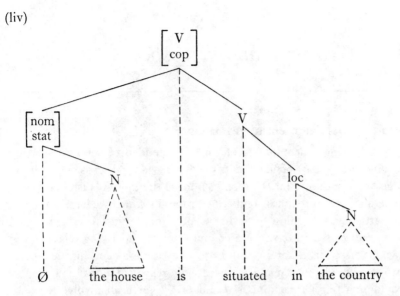

Observe too that this makes it easier to regard forms like *mine* as verbalizations of a dative (cf. §7.366) rather than as a strange sort of locative.

I shall not pursue such questions further here. However, rather than trying to provide some pretence at firm conclusion(s) for a discussion that has been in many places very inconclusive, I should like to conclude with a brief summary and some final speculations. In the present state of our (or at least my) knowledge, the fragment of grammar suggested in §12.1 represents as much of a conclusion as it seems possible or decorous to advance.

12   *Prospect and retrospect*

12.1   A final fragment of grammar

The following schematic set of rules is intended to summarize a not inconsiderable part of the results of the preceding discussion. It draws together what seem (at the moment) to be the more plausible or more general of the sometimes conflicting proposals which we have surveyed. In particular, they allow for clauses containing, for instance, *contain* and *know* and *possess* in terms of a common set of underlying relations—as was discussed in chapter 7. Similarly, they are intended (in the respect proposed in chapters 9 and 11) to provide representations for sentences containing (e.g.) *move* and *send* and *teach* which all involve the subordination of a directional clause to a causative. In terms of such representations, the notional relationship between clauses containing, for example, *buy*, *sell* and *possess* can also be characterized. These are proposed merely as a sample of the range of clauses involving 'abstract' relations that can (I would argue, plausibly) be given a localist interpretation. There is synchronic and diachronic, semantic, syntactic and morphological evidence that even the notion of transitivity, involving the 'most syntactic', 'least concrete' of relations, is directional in nature. And this can be in part accommodated, as was suggested in chapter 11, in terms of the identification of erg with abl and the interpretation of causatives as involving superordination. I have not attempted in what follows to identify nom (except predicative nom) and loc, the relationship between which remains somewhat uncertain.

Included in the rules are SRs and DRs in 11, the rule introducing N, and relevant TRs—which appear to be ordered after at least the semantic rules in 11. Of these latter, the sequencing rule applies like the others to each clause separately. As was suggested in §2.4, the 'rules' in 11.i which follow should be regarded as statements of well-formedness conditions on semantic representations. Similarly, the 'partial derivation' in §12.2 can be taken to represent a demonstration that the structures underlying the sentence concerned are in conformity with these constraints.

II. i. 1. $V \rightarrow \begin{bmatrix} \pm \text{locative} \\ \pm \text{directional} \\ \pm \text{stative} \end{bmatrix}$

2. *a.* + locative $\rightarrow \begin{bmatrix} \pm \text{ergative} \\ \pm \text{nominative} \end{bmatrix}$

   b. + directional $\rightarrow \begin{bmatrix} \pm \text{causative} \ / \ \begin{bmatrix} \quad\overline{\quad\quad\quad} \\ -\text{locative} \end{bmatrix} \\ \pm \text{reflexive} \end{bmatrix}$

3. *a.* − reflexive $\rightarrow \begin{bmatrix} \pm \text{abl-nominative} \ / \ \begin{bmatrix} \overline{\quad\quad\quad\quad} \\ +\text{nominative} \end{bmatrix} \\ \pm \text{abl-ergative} \quad / \ \begin{bmatrix} \overline{\quad\quad\quad} \\ +\text{ergative} \end{bmatrix} \end{bmatrix}$

   b. $\begin{bmatrix} \left\{ \begin{array}{c} +\text{stative} \\ +\text{nominative} \\ \begin{bmatrix} +\text{directional} \\ +\text{locative} \end{bmatrix} \\ \begin{bmatrix} -\text{causative} \\ -\text{reflexive} \end{bmatrix} \end{array} \right\} \end{bmatrix} \rightarrow \pm \text{oblique}$

4. $\begin{bmatrix} +\text{oblique} \\ +\text{abl-nominative} \end{bmatrix} \rightarrow \pm \text{abl-oblique}$

(If it were desirable to allow for the ambiguity of *He is cold* as suggested in §6.6 ($\begin{bmatrix} \text{nom} \\ \text{loc} \end{bmatrix}$ *vs.* nom), +reflexive in II. i. 2. *b* could be made dependent on $\left\{ \begin{array}{c} +\text{locative} \\ +\text{directional} \end{array} \right\}$ with consequent changes in II. ii.)

ii. 1. *a.* V $\rightarrow$ nom
    b. + locative $\rightarrow$ loc

2. *a.* + directional $\rightarrow$ abl // $\left\{ \begin{array}{c} \begin{bmatrix} \text{loc} \\ \overline{\quad} \end{bmatrix} \\ \begin{bmatrix} \text{nom} \\ \overline{\quad} \end{bmatrix} \end{array} \right\}$ / $\begin{bmatrix} \overline{\quad\quad\quad} \\ +\text{reflexive} \end{bmatrix}$

   b. + causative $\rightarrow$ V

3. *a.* + ergative $\rightarrow$ erg // $\left\{ \begin{array}{c} \begin{bmatrix} \text{abl} \\ \overline{\quad} \end{bmatrix} \ / \ \begin{bmatrix} \overline{\quad\quad\quad} \\ +\text{abl-ergative} \end{bmatrix} \\ \begin{bmatrix} \text{nom} \\ \overline{\quad} \end{bmatrix} \ / \ \begin{bmatrix} \overline{\quad\quad\quad\quad\quad} \\ \left\{ \begin{array}{c} -\text{abl-nominative} \\ +\text{nominative} \end{array} \right\} \end{bmatrix} \\ \begin{bmatrix} \text{loc} \\ \overline{\quad} \end{bmatrix} \end{array} \right\}$

$$b. \quad +\text{nominative} \rightarrow \text{nom} \; // \; \left\{ \begin{array}{l} \begin{bmatrix} \text{abl} \\ - \end{bmatrix} \Big/ \begin{bmatrix} \overline{} \\ +\text{abl-nominative} \end{bmatrix} \\ \begin{bmatrix} \text{loc} \\ - \end{bmatrix} \end{array} \right\}$$

$$c. \quad +\text{stative} \rightarrow \text{stat} \; // \; \left\{ \begin{array}{l} \left\{ \begin{bmatrix} \text{abl} \\ - \end{bmatrix} \Big/ \begin{bmatrix} \overline{} \\ \left\{ \begin{array}{l} +\text{abl-oblique} \\ -\text{locative} \end{array} \right\} \end{bmatrix} \right\} \Big/ \begin{bmatrix} \overline{} \\ +\text{oblique} \end{bmatrix} \\ \begin{bmatrix} \text{loc} \\ - \end{bmatrix} \\ \begin{bmatrix} \text{nom} \\ - \end{bmatrix} \end{array} \right\}$$

II. iii. 1. sequencing: $\left(\begin{Bmatrix} \text{nom} \\ \text{stat} \\ \text{erg} \\ \text{nom} \end{Bmatrix} \right)$ V (nom) (nom) (V) (abl) (loc)

The following conventions govern the operation of the sequencing constraints: (*a*) in the determination of the placement of a CS, each alternative is passed through from left to right—i.e. nom and erg take precedence over loc and abl; (*b*) erg represents both the erg introduced by +ergative and abl in a clause which does not also contain loc; (*c*) an unbracketed nom (or V) position in the rule is occupied by the obligatory nom (or V), unless, of course, it fails to meet other conditions (e.g. is not marked with stat for the first part of the rule) or it is otherwise pre-empted under (*a*) (e.g. is marked as erg). As noted in chapter 10, it may be that the final abl and loc should not be concatenated at this point (by the rule as it stands, at least).

conflation schemata: 1.   nom..., (abl)...[case (loc)

2. $\begin{Bmatrix} \text{loc} \\ \text{abl} \end{Bmatrix} \dots \end{bmatrix}$ abl

3.   V...[V

The square-bracketing in the schemata indicates the boundary of a subordinate clause; the elements represented are those which take part in conflation in each instance. The round brackets in 1 indicate that the enclosed elements may be conflated with each other; the comma, that the order of the elements so separated is irrelevant. Otherwise, conflation (of nom and case) under 1 is obligatory, though 'optional' in 2 and 3. 1 and 3 underlie the clauses in (xl), as compared with pre-conflation (xxxix). Under conflation, the sequence of the superordinate element is adopted. Schema 2 accounts for *The hat was sold (her) by John*, etc., in which the final *by* phrase is a conflation of (in this instance) abl and abl. As observed above, it may be that 3 is later than represented here. In all three instances, the superordinate V must also of course be +causative; and there are clearly further restrictions on 3.

cop-introduction: stat + V → stat $\begin{bmatrix} V \\ \text{cop} \end{bmatrix}$

III. ii. 1. case → N//case—

(this sequence is specific to Contemporary English)

It is likely that this set of rules is 'over-rich' with respect to the phenomena we have looked at: it is, for instance, not certain that the particular variants concerned should be allowed for in terms of ergativization of nom or nominativization of abl. Consider too the qualifications with which we conclude the final chapter.

12.2   Generating *It was sold to Mary*

I include here as an illustration of the intended operation of the proposed grammar a sample partial 'derivation', viz. that for the relevant structure of *It was sold to Mary*.

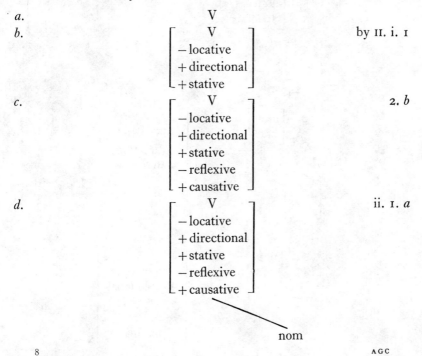

a.   V

b. $\begin{bmatrix} V \\ -\text{locative} \\ +\text{directional} \\ +\text{stative} \end{bmatrix}$ by II. i. 1

c. $\begin{bmatrix} V \\ -\text{locative} \\ +\text{directional} \\ +\text{stative} \\ -\text{reflexive} \\ +\text{causative} \end{bmatrix}$ 2. *b*

d. $\begin{bmatrix} V \\ -\text{locative} \\ +\text{directional} \\ +\text{stative} \\ -\text{reflexive} \\ +\text{causative} \end{bmatrix}$ ii. 1. *a*

nom

Notice that this and the following representations up to the operations
of the sequencing rule in *n* constitute 'wild trees' (in Staal's (1967*b*)
sense); by convention, each new category that is introduced is added on
the right.

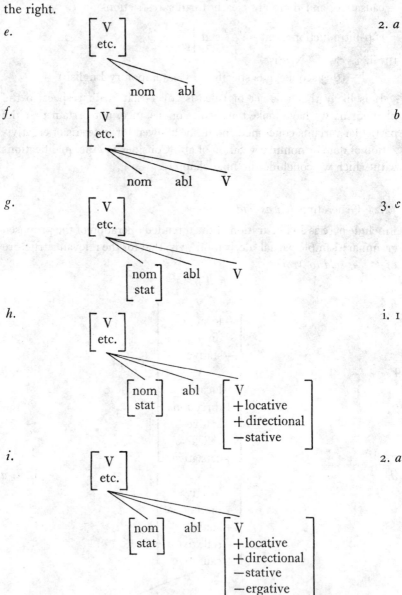

j.   *b*

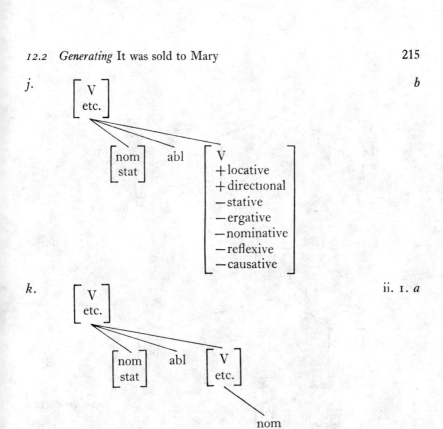

k.   ii. 1. *a*

l.   *b*

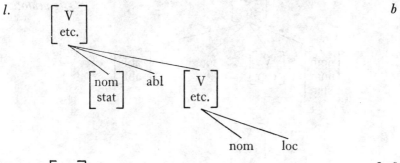

m.   2. *a*

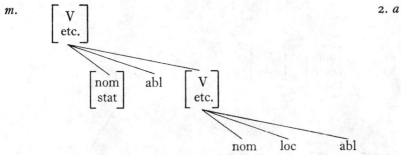

8-2

n.   *sequencing*

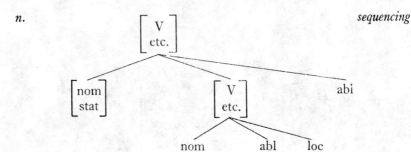

o.   *conflation*

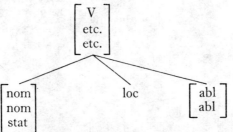

p.   *cop-introduction*
                                                                       and
                                                                 -segmentation

q.   III. ii. 1

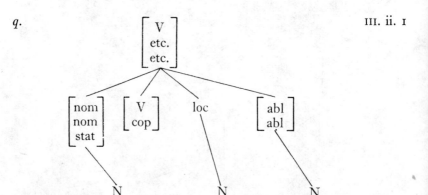

r.   *lexical insertion*

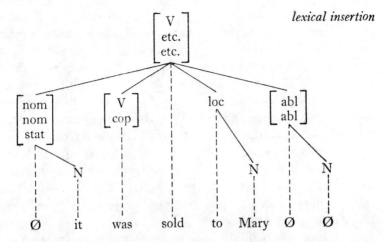

Under the alternative proposal for cop-segmentation suggested in §11.63, we would find the following in place of the representation in *p*:

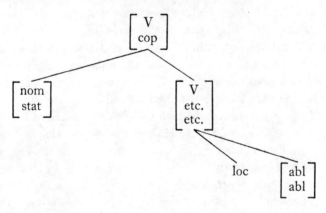

The representations in *q* and *r* would also require to be modified accordingly.

12.3   Final remarks

If abl and erg can be identified in the way I have suggested, and, further, a perhaps similar relation between loc and nom can be substantiated, then the views of the most radical localists will have been accommodated in a fundamental way. Nom and erg are reduced to the status of features accounting for the 'grammaticalization' (subjectivization and objectivization) of the basic cases loc and abl (and perhaps of the unmarked case

I have designated 'nom', if it is not identified with loc), which underlie both the non-'local' and 'local' cases (and, of course, 'abstract' uses of the 'local'). It would remain to examine the logical and diachronic relationship between the spatial and non-spatial instances of the two 'meta-cases'—loc and abl (say). The exploration of this may take us in quite different directions. It may be, for instance, that some other relationship than categorial identity exists between, in particular, loc and nom. What is clear is that there are many semantic and syntactic parallels between the concrete and non-concrete uses of the cases (and, of course, other categories) which require some more profound explanation than I have been able to formulate (though I have tried to indicate one starting-point for this). Such an explanation must be part of a ('panchronic') theory of language which would account for that relation between the representation of spatial and non-spatial phenomena that (as I have noted in chapter 1) has so often been remarked upon in the past. Although the structure of the argument must be rather different, it is possible to provide considerable evidence for a localistic interpretation of categories other than case. (It is likely that, in this respect, such a theory will be most fruitfully developed within a cognitional framework closer to that envisaged by (in particular) Locke and Condillac than some currently fashionable attitudes might allow.) Perhaps we must eventually try to proceed further than the localists in another direction also, and attempt to relate (what we have regarded as) the 'basic' concept of 'direction' (involving the difference between abl and nom/loc) to that of negation. We have already observed the correspondence between the representations of abl and (indirectly) of negation (*He is not at the meeting/He is absent from the meeting—He has gone (away) from the meeting*). It may be that an indication of the structure of *He has come (here) from London* is (to some extent) represented in the (in itself rather strange) paraphrase *He has come not to be in London and/but to be here* (cf. Binnick, 1968a; Leech, 1969: §8.7.2), with *from* derived as a conflation of what underlies *not + in* (though this parallel depends upon the particular distribution of *come*). But such a suggestion raises many further unresolved questions of fact and of principle (particularly concerning 'ergative' clauses—and including of course the many others associated with any antonymic pair) which I am in no position even to attempt to formulate precisely.

However, it is perhaps possible to discern at this juncture one manner in which it might be possible both to preserve the generalization concerning 'transitivity' and 'direction' embodied in the grammar formulated in §12.1 and yet to go some way toward capturing the (antonymic) relation between loc and abl. And this involves the abandonment of an assumption which has been implicit throughout the preceding discussion—namely that concerning the unitary, atomic character of case elements like loc. Suppose we reject this. Loc can then be regarded as a cover-symbol for, say, $\begin{bmatrix} +\text{locative} \\ -\text{negative} \end{bmatrix}$ and abl for $\begin{bmatrix} +\text{loc} \\ +\text{neg} \end{bmatrix}$. We thus give expression to the antonymy. Nom is then presumably − loc, and also − neg. This means that we can regard erg as $\begin{bmatrix} -\text{loc} \\ +\text{neg} \end{bmatrix}$. That is, erg is no longer identified with abl. However, we are still able to explain the similarity in semantics and in surface markers with reference to the presence of + neg; they are both negative cases. Similarly loc and nom are both − neg. In this way, it is possible to accommodate the relationship between transitivity and direction without having to suggest simple identity for abl and erg (with the consequent complications associated with cover-symbols, etc.). And the mutual restrictiveness of erg and the + locative cases can still be formulated in a quite natural way. In particular, the selection of + directional can be interpreted as introducing a case CS that is + neg, a CS that is also + loc (ablative) in a clause in which a + loc CS has already been introduced, but is otherwise − loc (ergative). Now, however, consider this suggestion in the light of the second alternative proposal for causatives offered in §11.4, whereby the subordinate V is dependent on either a loc or an abl in the causative clause. Assume that it is further the case that there are also non-causative clauses in which abl appears without loc (*Arnold was absent from the meeting*). Then it would be possible to substitute for the SRs in 11.i (as exemplified in §12.1) that determine which cases can co-occur, a simple condition on clauses that any combination of cases up to three per clause is permitted, though one case must be nom (or perhaps sometimes loc—cf. p. 50, n. 3). A causative clause is one in which erg and nom co-occur with either loc or abl; the notion 'causative' is thus not semantically primitive.

BIBLIOGRAPHY
INDEX

Bibliography

ABBREVIATIONS

AJPh	*American Journal of Philology*
AKAB(HP)	*Abhandlungen der Königlichen Akademie zu Berlin, historisch-philologischen Klasse*
AL	*Acta Linguistica (Hafniensia)*
AnL	*Anthropological Linguistics*
ASNS	*Archiv für das Studium der neueren Sprachen*
BGDSL	*Beiträge zur Geschichte der deutschen Sprache und Literatur*
BPTJ	*Biuletyn polskiego towarzystwa językoznawczego*
BSE	*Brno Studies in English*
BSL	*Bulletin de la Société de Linguistique de Paris*
CFS	*Cahiers Ferdinand de Saussure*
CJL	*Canadian Journal of Linguistics/Revue Canadienne de Linguistique*
ES	*English Studies*
FL	*Foundations of Language*
GL	*General Linguistics*
IC	*Information and Control*
IF	*Indogermanische Forschungen*
IJAL	*International Journal of American Linguistics*
IL	*Indian Linguistics*
JAF	*Journal of American Folklore*
JAOS	*Journal of the American Oriental Society*
JEGP	*Journal of English and Germanic Philology*
JL	*Journal of Linguistics*
JPsych	*Journal de Psychologie normale et pathologique*
KB	*Beiträge zur vergleichenden Sprachforschung auf dem Gebiete der arischen, celtischen und slavischen Sprachen*
KZ	*Zeitschrift für vergleichende Sprachforschung*
Lg	*Language*
MLN	*Modern Language Notes*
MSLL	*Georgetown University Monograph Series on Languages and Linguistics*
MSpråk	*Moderna Språk*
NTS	*Norsk Tidsskrift for Sprogvidenskap*
PhP	*Philologica Pragensia*
PMLA	*Publications of the Modern Language Association of America*

PPhS	*Proceedings of the Philological Society*
PSML	*Prague Studies in Mathematical Linguistics*
RRLing	*Revue Roumaine de Linguistique*
SAP	*Studia Anglica Posnaniensia*
SbAWW(PH)	*Sitzungsberichte der Akademie der Wissenschaften, Wien, philologisch-historischen Klasse*
SbPAW	*Sitzungsberichte der Preussischen Akademie der Wissenschaften*
SCL	*Studii şi Cercetări Lingvistice*
SL	*Studia Linguistica*
TCLC	*Travaux du Cercle Linguistique de Copenhague*
TCLP	*Travaux du Cercle Linguistique de Prague*
TLP	*Travaux Linguistiques de Prague*
TPhS	*Transactions of the Philological Society*
UJb	*Ungarische Jahrbücher*
VJa	*Voprosy Jazykoznanija*
VMKAW(L)	*Verslagen en Mededeelingen der Koninklijke Akademie van Wetenschappen, Afd. Letterkunde*
ZAA	*Zeitschrift für Anglistik und Amerikanistik*
ZDMG	*Zeitschrift der Deutschen Morgenländischen Gesellschaft*

Allen, R. L. (1966). *The Verb System of Present-day American English*. The Hague: Mouton.

Allen, W. S. (1956). Structure and system in the Abaza verbal complex. *TPhS* 127–76.

(1964). Transitivity and possession. *Lg* **40**. 337–43.

Anderson, J. M. (1968*a*). Ergative and nominative in English. *JL* **4**. 1–32.

(1968*b*). On the status of 'lexical formatives'. *FL* **4**. 308–18.

(1969*a*). A note on 'rank' and 'delicacy'. *JL* **5**. 129–35.

(1969*b*). Some proposals concerning the modal verb in English. (To appear in *Edinburgh Studies in English and Scots*.)

(1969*c*). Adjectives, datives and ergativisation. *FL* **5**. 301–22.

(forthcoming *a*). Dependency and grammatical functions. *FL*.

(forthcoming *b*). The case for cause: a preliminary enquiry. *JL*.

Anderson, T. R. (1968). On the transparency of *begin*: some uses of semantic theory. *FL* **4**. 394–421.

Asher, R. E. (1968). Existential, possessive, locative and copulative sentences in Malayalam. In Verhaar, J. W. M. (ed.), 88–111.

Bach, E. (1967). *Have* and *be* in English syntax. *Lg* **43**. 462–85.

(1968). Nouns and noun phrases. In Bach, E. & Harms, R. T. (eds.), 91–122.

Bach, E. & Harms, R. T. (eds.) (1968). *Universals in Linguistic Theory*. New York: Holt, Rinehart & Winston.

Bachmann, L. (ed.) (1828). *Anecdota Graeca*, II. Leipzig. (Reprinted 1965, Hildesheim: Georg Olms.)

Bacon, F.: see Robertson, J. M. (ed.).

Baker, H. G. (1931). Case in some earlier and later English grammars. *Papers of the Michigan Academy of Science, Arts and Letters* **14**. 525–35.

Bally, C. (1926). L'expression des idées de sphère personnelle et de solidarité dans les langues indo-européennes. *Festschrift Louis Gauchat,* 68–78. Aarau: Sauerlander.

(1932). *Linguistique générale et linguistique française.* Paris: Leroux.

Bazell, C. E. (1937). Notes on synchronic grammar (i): case in English. *ES* **19.** 20–3.

(1965). Semantics and non-semantics. *PhP* **8.** 131–3.

Beauzée, M. (1767). *Grammaire générale ou exposition raisonnée des éléments nécessaires du langage pour servir de fondement à l'étude de toutes les langues.* Paris.

Bendix, E. H. (1966). *Componential Analysis of General Vocabulary.* The Hague: Mouton.

Bennett, D. (1968). English prepositions: a stratificational approach. *JL* **4.** 153–72.

Benveniste, É. (1949). Le système sublogique des prépositions en latin. *Recherches structurales (TCLC* **5**). 177–84.

(1952). La construction passive du parfait transitif. *BSL* **48.** 52–62.

(1960). 'Être' et 'avoir' dans leurs fonctions linguistiques. *BSL* **55.** 113–34. (Reprinted as ch. 12 in *Problèmes de linguistique générale* (1966), Gallimard, Paris.)

(1968). Mutations of linguistic categories. In Lehmann, W. P. & Malkiel, Y. (eds.), *Directions in Historical Linguistics,* 83–94. Austin: University of Texas Press.

Bertschinger, M. (1941). *To Want: An Essay in Semantics.* (Swiss Studies in English **13.**) Bern: A. Francke.

Bhattacharya, S. (1954). Studies in the Parengi language. *IL* **14.** 45–63.

Bierwisch, M. (1969). On certain problems of semantic representations. *FL* **5.** 153–84.

Bierwisch, M. & Heidolph, K. E. (eds.) (1969). *Recent Developments in Linguistics.* The Hague: Mouton.

Binnick, R. I. (1968a). On transformationally derived verbs in a grammar of English. (Paper read at the L.S.A. Summer Meeting, 1968.)

(1968b). Transitive verbs and lexical insertion. (Paper read before the Chicago Linguistic Society, December, 1968.)

Blake, F. R. (1930). A semantic analysis of case. *Curme Volume of Linguistic Studies (Language Monograph* **7**), 34–49.

Boas, F. (ed.) (1911). *Handbook of American Indian Languages,* I. (Bureau of American Ethnology, Bulletin **40,** pt. 1.) Washington, D.C.: Smithsonian Institute.

(1911a). Introduction to Boas (ed.) (1911), 1–83. (Reprinted as pp. 1–79 in Holder (ed.).)

(1911b). Chinook. In Boas (ed.) (1911), 559–677.

(ed.) (1922). *Handbook of American Indian Languages,* II. (Bureau of Am. Ethnol., Bull. **40,** pt. 2) Washington, D.C.: Smithsonian Inst.

Boas, F. & Swanton, J. R. (1911). Siouan (Dakota). In Boas (ed.) (1911), 875–965.

Bolinger, D. L. (1952). Linear modification. *PMLA* **67**. 1117–44.

Bopp, F. (1829). Vergleichende Zergliederung des Sanskrits und der mit ihm verwandten Sprachen, IV: Über einige Demonstrativ-stämme und ihren Zusammenhang mit verschiedenen Präpositionen und Conjunctionen. *AKAB(HP)*, 27–47.

Bosworth, J. & Toller, T. N. (1898). *An Anglo-Saxon Dictionary*. London: Oxford University Press.

Bowers, F. (1968). English complex sentence formation. *JL* **4**. 83–8.

Boyd, J. & Thorne, J. P. (1969). The semantics of modal verbs. *JL* **5**. 57–74.

Brøndal, V. (1948). *Les parties du discours*. Copenhagen: Ejnar Munksgaard.

(1950). *Théorie des prépositions*. Copenhagen: Ejnar Munksgaard.

Brugmann, K. (1911). *Vergleichende Laut-, Stammbildungs- und Flexionslehre der Indogermanischen Sprachen*, II (=vol. 2, pt. 2 of Brugmann, K. & Delbrück, B., *Grundriss der vergleichenden Grammatik der Indogermanischen Sprachen*). Strassburg: Trübner.

Buyssens, É. (1950). La conception fonctionnelle des faits linguistiques. *JPsych* (special number: *Grammaire et psychologie*). 35–51.

Campbell, R. N. & Wales, R. J. (1969). Comparative structures in English. *JL* **5**. 215–51.

Chafe, W. L. (1967). Language as symbolization. *Lg* **43**. 57–91.

(1968a). Idiomaticity as an anomaly in the Chomskyan paradigm. *FL* **4**. 109–27.

(1968b). Review of Lamb (1966). *Lg* **44**. 593–603.

Chanidze, A. (1963). Le sujet grammatical de quelques verbes intransitifs en géorgien. *BSL* **58**. 1–27.

Chomsky, N. (1965). *Aspects of the Theory of Syntax*. Cambridge, Mass.: M.I.T.

(1966). *Cartesian Linguistics*. New York: Harper & Row.

(1968). *Language and Mind*. New York: Harcourt, Brace & World.

(1969a). Remarks on nominalisations. In Jacobs, R. A. & Rosenbaum, P. S. (eds.).

(1969b). Deep structure, surface structure and semantic interpretation. (Unpublished.)

Christie, J. J. (1969). Locative, possessive and existential in Swahili. (To appear in *FL*.)

Čikobava, A. S. (1969). Les problèmes de la construction ergative dans les langues ibéro-caucasiennes. *Langages* **15**. 108–26.

Collinson, W. E. (1937). *Indication*. (*Language Monograph* **17**.) Baltimore, Md.: Linguistic Society of America.

Condillac, É. B. de (1775). Cours d'études pour l'instruction du Prince de Parme, II: Grammaire. In LeRoy, G. (ed.), 425–513.

Corder, S. P. (1968). Double-object verbs in English. *SAP* **1**. 15–28.

Csink, J. (1853). *A Complete Practical Grammar of the Hungarian Language*. London: Williams & Norgate.

Curme, G. O. (1913). The proper subject of a passiv [*sic*—JMA] verb. *MLN* **28**. 97–101.

Curry, H. B. (1961). Some logical aspects of grammatical structure. In Jakobson, R. (ed.), 56–69.

Daneš, F. (1964). A three-level approach to syntax. *TLP* 1. 225–40.

(1968). The semantic structure of the sentence. *Lingua* 21. 55–69.

Darrigol, J. P. (1829). *Dissertation critique et apologétique sur la langue basque.* Bayonne: Duhart-Fauvet.

Davidson, W., Elford, L. W. & Hoijer, H. (1963). Athapaskan classificatory verbs. In Hoijer *et al., Studies in the Athapaskan Languages*, 30–41. (University of California Publications in Linguistics, 29.) Berkeley & Los Angeles: University of California Press.

Dik, S. C. (1968). *Coordination: Its Implications for the Theory of General Linguistics.* Amsterdam: North-Holland.

Donzé, R. (1967). *La grammaire générale et raisonnée de Port-Royal.* Berne: A. Francke.

Droescher, W. O. (1969). German verb types. *Lingua* 24. 19–32.

Einenkel, E. (1916). *Geschichte der englischen Sprache*, II: *Historische Syntax.* Strassburg: Trübner.

Ek, J. A. van (1967). A grammatical description of the accusative with infinitive and related structures in English. *ES* 48. 511–27, suppl. i–xvii.

Eliot, C. N. E. (1890). *A Finnish Grammar.* London: Oxford.

Erades, P. A. (1950). Points of Modern English syntax. *ES* 31. 153–7.

Erichsen, M. (1944). Désinences casuelles et personnelles en eskimo. *AL* 4. 67–88.

Fillmore, C. J. (1965). *Indirect Object Constructions in English and the Ordering of Transformations.* The Hague: Mouton.

(1966 a). A proposal concerning English prepositions. *MSLL* 19. 19–33.

(1966 b). Deictic categories in the semantics of 'come'. *FL* 2. 219–27.

(1968 a). The case for case. In Bach, E. & Harms, R. T. (eds.), 1–88.

(1968 b). Lexical entries for verbs. *FL* 4. 373–93.

(1968 c). Types of lexical information. *Ohio State University Computer and Information Science Research Center: Papers in Linguistics* 2. 65–103.

(1969). Review of Bendix (1966). *GL* 9. 41–65.

Finck, F. N. (1907). Der angeblich passivische Charakter des transitiven Verbs. *KZ* 41. 209–82.

(1910). *Die Haupttypen des Sprachbaus.* Leipzig: B. G. Teubner.

Firbas, J. (1964). On defining the theme in Functional Sentence Analysis. *TLP* 1. 267–80.

(1966). Non-thematic subjects in Contemporary English. *TLP* 2. 239–56.

Fodor, J. A. & Katz, J. J. (eds.) (1964). *The Structure of Language.* Englewood Cliffs, N.J.: Prentice-Hall.

Frachtenberg, L. J. (1922). Coos. In Boas (ed.) (1922), 297–429.

Frei, H. (1939). 'Sylvie est jolie des yeux.' In *Mélanges de linguistique offerts à Charles Bally*, 83–92. Geneva: Georg.

Fries, C. C. (1952). *The Structure of English.* New York: Harcourt, Brace & World.

Gaaf, W. van der (1904). *The Transition from the Impersonal to the Personal Construction in Middle English.* (*Anglistische Forschungen* **14.**) Heidelberg: Carl Winter.

  (1929). The conversion of the indirect personal object into the subject of a passive construction. *ES* **11.** 1–11, 58–67.

Gabelentz, G. von der (1891). *Die Sprachwissenschaft.* Leipzig: Weigel.

Gaifman, H. (1965). Dependency-systems and phrase-structure systems. *IC* **8.** 304–37.

Gardiner, A. H. (1927). *Egyptian Grammar: Being an Introduction to the Study of Hieroglyphs.* London: Oxford University Press.

Garnett, R. (1846–7). On the formation of words by the further modification of inflected cases. *PPhS* **3.** 9–15, 19–29. (Reprinted as pp. 260–81 in Garnett (1859).)

  (1848–50). On the nature and analysis of the verb. *PPhs* **3.** 159–64, 183–6, 213–17; **4.** 15–23, 95–100, 155–62, 173–82, 233–7. (Reprinted as pp. 289–342 in Garnett (1859).)

  (1859). *Philological Essays.* London: Williams & Norgate.

Gecaga, B. Mareka & Kirkaldy-Willis, W. H. (1953). *A Short Kikuyu Grammar.* London: Macmillan.

Gildersleeve, B. L. & Lodge, G. (1895). *Latin Grammar.* London: Macmillan.

Ginneken, J. van (1939). Avoir et être (du point de vue de la linguistique générale). *Mélanges de linguistique offerts à Charles Bally,* 83–92. Geneva: Georg.

Godel, R. (1950). Verbes d'état et verbes d'événement. *CFS* **9.** 33–50.

Gonda, J. (1957). The character of the Sanskrit accusative. In Catalan, D. (ed.) *Miscelanea Homenaje a André Martinet,* I, 47–65. Canarias: Universidad de La Laguna.

Goyvaerts, D. L. (1968). Towards a theory of the expanded form in English. *La linguistique* **2.** 111–24.

Grasserie, R. de la (1890). *Des relations grammaticales considerées dans leur concept et dans leur expression,* ou *De la catégorie des cas.* Paris: Maisonneuve.

  (1896). *Essai de syntaxe générale.* Louvain: J. B. Istas.

  (1901). *De l'anteriorité du génitif, & Des mots auxiliaires supplétifs et explétifs.* Paris: Maisonneuve.

  (1914*a*). *Du verbe comme générateur des autres parties du discours.* Paris: Maisonneuve.

  (1914*b*). *Du caractère concret de plusieurs familles linguistiques américaines.* Paris: Maisonneuve.

Green, A. (1914). The analytic agent in Germanic. *JEGP* **13.** 514–52.

Greimas, A.-J. (1966). *Sémantique structurale.* Paris: Larousse.

Groot, A. W. de (1956). Classification of cases and uses of cases. *For Roman Jokobson,* 187–94. The Hague: Mouton.

Gruber, J. S. (1967). Look and see. *Lg* **43.** 937–47.

Guillaume, G. (1964). *Langage et science du langage*. Paris and Quebec: Nizet and Presses de l'Université Laval.

Halle, M. (1962). Phonology in generative grammar. *Word* **18**. 54–72. (Reprinted in Fodor, J. A. & Katz, J. J. (eds.), 324–33.)

Halliday, M. A. K. (1961). Categories of the theory of grammar. *Word* **17**. 241–92.

(1964). Syntax and the consumer. *MSLL* **17**. 11–24.

(1966). Some notes on 'deep' grammar. *JL* **2**. 57–67.

(1967). Notes on transitivity and theme, 1 & 2. *JL* **3**. 37–81, 199–244.

(1968). Notes on transitivity and theme, 3. *JL* **4**. 179–215.

Hammerich, L. L. (1951). Kleinschmidt centennial 1: The cases of Eskimo. *IJAL* **17**. 18–22.

(1956). Contribution to the discussion 'What inferences can be drawn from the evidence of morphology and word-formation about the development of Proto-Indo-European?' *Proceedings of the Seventh International Congress of Linguistics*, 175–6. London.

Hanoteau, A. (1860). *Essai de grammaire de la langue tamachek'*. Paris.

Hansen, A. (1949). On the so-called indirect object in Danish. *Recherches structurales (TCLC* **5**). 198–202.

Harris, J. (1751). *Hermes*. London: T. Bolas. (Reprinted as vol. 55 in *English Linguistics 1500–1800*. Menston, England: The Scolar Press, 1968.)

Hartung, J.-A. (1831). *Ueber die Casus, ihre Bildung und Bedeutung in der griechischen und lateinischen Sprache*. Erlangen.

Hasegawa, K. (1968). The passive construction in English. *Lg* **44**. 230–43.

Hatcher, A. G. (1943). 'Mr. Howard amuses easy.' *MLN* **58**. 8–17.

(1956). *Theme and Underlying Question: Two Studies in Spanish Word Order*. (Supplement to *Word* **12**: Monograph no. 3.) New York: The Linguistic Circle of New York.

Havers, W. (1911). *Untersuchungen zur Kasussyntax der indogermanischen Sprachen*. (*Untersuchungen zur indogermanischen Sprach- und Kulturwissenschaft* **3**.) Strassburg: Trübner.

Hays, D. (1964). Dependency theory: a formalism and some observations. *Lg* **40**. 511–25.

Henry, D. & K. (1969). Koyukon locationals. *AnL* **11**. 136–42.

Heringer, J. T. (1967). Review of Gaifman (1965). *Ohio State University Research Foundation: Working Papers in Linguistics* **1**. 128–36.

Hill, A. A. (1958). *Introduction to Linguistic Structures: From Sound to Sentence in English*. New York: Harcourt, Brace & World.

Hill, L. A. (1968). *Prepositions and Adverbial Particles*. London: O.U.P.

Hirtle, W. H. (1967). *The Simple and Progressive Forms: An Analytical Approach*. (Cahiers du psychomécanique du language, no. 8.) Quebec: Les Presses de l'Université Laval.

Hjelmslev, L. (1928). *Principes de grammaire générale*. (*Det Kgl. Danske Videnskabernes Selskab, Historisk-filologiske Meddelelser* **16**, 1.)

(1935–7). La catégorie des cas. *Acta Jutlandica* **7**, 1 (i–xii, 1–184); **9**, 2 (i–vii, 1–78).

(1954). La stratification du langage. *Word* **10**. 163–88. (Reprinted as pp. 36–68 in Hjelmslev (1959).)

(1959). *Essais linguistiques*. Copenhagen: Nordisk Sprog- og Kulturforlag.

(1961). *Prolegomena to a Theory of Language*, 2nd edn. Madison, Wisconsin: University of Wisconsin Press. (Translated by F. J. Whitfield from *Omkring sprogteoriens grundlæggelse*. Copenhagen: Ejnar Munksgaard, 1943.)

Hockett, C. F. (1966). Language, mathematics and linguistics. In Sebeok, T. (ed.), 155–304.

Hofmann, T. R. (1968). Underlying vs. superficial grammatical relations. *Recherche sur la traduction automatique: 11ème rapport semestriel*, 35–55. Montreal: Université de Montréal.

Hoijer, H. (1945). Classificatory verb stems in the Appachean languages. *IJAL* **11**. 13–23.

(1959). Semantic patterns of the Navaho language. In Gipper, H. (ed.), *Sprache—Schlüssel zur Welt: Festschrift für Leo Weisgerber*, 369–73. Düsseldorf: Pädogogischer Verlag Schwann.

(1964). Cultural implications of some Navaho linguistic categories. In Hymes, D. H. (ed.), 142–9.

Holder, P. (ed.) (1966). *American Indian Languages*. Lincoln, Nebraska: University of Nebraska Press.

Holzweissig, F. (1877). *Wahrheit und Irrthum der localistischen Casustheorie*. Leipzig.

Householder, F. W. (1966). Review of Akhmanova *et al.* (1963), *Exact Methods in Linguistic Research*, University of California Press, Berkeley & Los Angeles. *JL* **2**. 237–42.

(forthcoming). *Linguistic Speculations*.

Huddleston, R. D. (1969). Some remarks on Fillmore's cases. (Unpublished.)

Hudson, R. A. (1967). Constituency in a systemic description of the English clause. *Lingua* **18**. 225–50.

(1969). On clauses containing conjoined and plural noun phrases in English. (To appear in *Lingua*.)

Humboldt, W. von (1829). Über die Verwandtschaft der Ortsadverbien mit dem Pronomen in einigen Sprachen. *AKAB(HP)*, 1–26. (Reprinted as pp. 304–30 in Leitzmann (ed.).)

Hymes, D. H. (ed.) (1964). *Language in Culture and Society: A Reader in Linguistics and Anthropology*. New York: Harper & Row.

Jacobs, R. A. & Rosenbaum, P. S. (1968). *English Transformational Grammar*. Waltham, Mass.: Blaisdell.

(eds.) (1969). *Readings in English Transformational Grammar*. Waltham, Mass.: Blaisdell.

Jakobson, R. (1936). Beitrag zur allgemeinen Kasuslehre: Gesamtbedeutungen der russischen Kasus. *TCLP* **6**. 240–83.

(1958). Morphological inquiry into Slavic declension (structure of Russian, case forms). In *American Contributions to the Fourth International Congress of Slavicists, Moscow, 1958*, 1–30. The Hague: Mouton.

(ed.) (1961). *Structure of Language and its Mathematical Aspects.* (Proceedings of Symposia in Applied Mathematics, **12.**) Providence: American Mathematical Society.

Jespersen, O. (1894). *Progress in Language, with special reference to English.* London: Swan Sonnenschein.

(1913). *A Modern English Grammar,* II. London and Copenhagen: Allen & Unwin and Munksgaard.

(1924). *The Philosophy of Grammar.* London: Allen & Unwin.

(1928). *A Modern English Grammar,* III. London and Copenhagen: Allen & Unwin and Munksgaard.

(1937). *Analytic Syntax.* Copenhagen: Ejnar Munksgaard.

(1940). *A Modern English Grammar,* V. London and Copenhagen: Allen & Unwin and Munksgaard.

(1949). *A Modern English Grammar,* VII. London and Copenhagen: Allen & Unwin and Munksgaard.

Jochelson, W. (1927). The instrumental and the comitative in the Aleut language. *Lg* **2.** 9–11.

Kahn, C. H. (1966). The Greek verb 'to be' and the concept of being. *FL* **2.** 245–65.

Kandiah, T. (1968). Transformational grammar and the layering of structure in Tamil. *JL* **4.** 217–45.

Katz, J. J. (1966). *The Philosophy of Language.* New York: Harper & Row.

(1967). Recent issues in semantic theory. *FL* **3.** 124–94.

Katz, J. J. & Postal, P. M. (1964). *An Integrated Theory of Linguistic Descriptions.* Cambridge, Mass.: M.I.T. Press.

Key, T. H. (1844). On the articles, etc. In *'The Alphabet'...and Other Philological Papers,* 116–19. London: Charles Knight.

(1846–7). On the origin of the demonstrative pronouns, the definite article, the pronouns of the third person, the relative, and the interrogative. *PPhS* **3.** 57–70.

(1850–2). On the nature of the verb, particularly on the formation of the middle or passive voice. *PPhS* **5.** 51–70.

(1874). *Language: Its Origin and Development.* London: Bell.

Kiparsky, P. (1968). Linguistic universals and linguistic change. In Bach, E. & Harms, R. T. (eds.), 171–202.

Kiparsky, P. & Staal, J. F. (1969). Syntactic and semantic relations in Pāṇini. *FL* **5.** 83–117.

Kirchner, G. (1937). The verbs with direct and indirect object re-examined, III. *ES* **19.** 97–112.

(1940). (*To be*) *due* as a (passive) verb-equivalent. *ES* **22.** 27–9.

(1952). *Die Zehn Hauptverben des Englischen.* Halle: Niemeyer.

(1959). Zur transitiven und intransitiven Verwendung des englischen Verbums. *ZAA* **7.** 342–99.

(1969). Detached observations on prepositional use in Modern, especially American English. *BSE* **8.** 105–10.

Kirkwood, H. W. (1969). Aspects of word order and its communicative function in English and German. *JL* 5. 85–107.

Koch, W. A. (1965). A semantic type of discourse analysis. *Linguistics* 12. 5–30.

Kohler, K. J. (1966). Towards a phonological theory. *Lingua* 16. 337–51.

Kruisinga, E. (1931). *English Accidence and Syntax*, 1. Groningen: Noordhoff.

Kuipers, A. H. (1962). The Circassian nominal paradigm. *Lingua* 11. 231–48.

Kukenheim, L. (1932). *Contributions à l'histoire de la grammaire italienne, espagnole et française à l'époque de la Renaissance.* Amsterdam: North-Holland.

Kuroda, S.-Y. (1965). Causative forms in Japanese. *FL* 1. 30–50.

(1968). Review of Fillmore (1965). *Lg* 44. 374–8.

Kuryłowicz, J. (1949). Le problème du classement des cas. *BPTJ* 9. 20–43.

(1964). *The Inflexional Categories of Indo-European.* Heidelberg: Carl Winter.

Lafitte, P. (1962). *Grammaire basque.* Bayonne: Amis du musée basque & Ikas.

Lafon, R. (1960). L'expression de l'auteur de l'action du verbe basque. *BSL* 55. 186–221.

(1963). Notes explicatives à Chanidze (1963). *BSL* 58. 27–40.

Lakoff, G. (1965). *On the Nature of Syntactic Irregularity.* (Report NSF-16, Mathematical Linguistics and Automatic Translation, The Computation Laboratory of Harvard University.)

(1968). Instrumental adverbs and the concept of deep structure. *FL* 4. 4–29.

Lamb, S. M. (1964*a*). On alternation, transformation, realization and stratification. *MSLL* 17. 105–22.

(1964*b*). The sememic approach to structural semantics. In Romney, A. K. & D'Andrade, R. G. (eds.), *Transcultural Studies in Cognition* (= *American Anthropologist* 66, 3, 2), 57–78.

(1965). Kinship terminology and linguistic structure. In Hammel, E. A. (ed.), *Formal Semantic Analysis* (= *American Anthropologist* 67, 5, 2), 37–64.

(1966). *Outline of Stratificational Grammar.* Washington, D.C.: Georgetown University Press.

Landar, H.-G. (1959). Four Navaho summer tales, III. *JAF* 72. 298–309.

Langacker, R. W. (1967). *Language and its Structure.* New York: Harcourt, Brace & World.

(1968). Observations on French possessives. *Lg* 44. 51–75.

Laroche, R. (1964). 'Agent' et 'object' chez Pāṇini. *JAOS* 84. 44–54.

Lass, R. (1969). Boundaries as obstruents: Old English voicing assimilation and universal strength hierarchies. (To appear in *JL*.)

Lee, P. G. (1966). The English preposition *with. Ohio State University Research Foundation: Working Papers in Linguistics* 1. 30–79.

Leech, G. N. (1968). Review of Bendix (1966). *JL* 4. 298–9.

(1969). *Towards a Semantic Description of English.* London: Longmans.

Lees, R. B. (1960). *The Grammar of English Nominalizations*, 2nd edn. (Publications of the Indiana University Research Center in Anthropology, Folklore and Linguistics, no. 12.) The Hague: Mouton.

Lehiste, I. (1969). 'Being' and 'having' in Estonian. *FL* 5. 324–41.

Lehmann, W. P. (1958). On earlier stages of the Indo-European nominal inflexion. *Lg* 34. 179–202.

Leitzmann, A. (ed.) (1907). *Wilhelm von Humboldt's Gesammelte Schriften*, VI: *Werke*, VI, I (*1827–1835*). Berlin: Behr.

LeRoy, G. (ed.) (1947). *Oeuvres philosophiques de Condillac*, I. Paris: Presses Universitaires de France.

Lewy, E. (1928). Possessivisch und passivisch. *UJb* 8. 274–89.

Lindkvist, K.-G. (1950). *Studies on the Local Sense of the Prepositions in, at, on and to in Modern English*. (Lund Studies in English, xx.) Lund and Copenhagen: C. W. K. Gleerup and Ejnar Munksgaard.

Livet, C.-L. (1859). *La grammaire française et les grammairiens au XVIe siècle*. Paris: Didier and Durand.

Lombard, A. (1929). Les membres de la proposition française: essai d'un classement nouveau. *MSpråk* 23. 202–53.

Longacre, R. E. (1964). *Grammar Discovery Procedures*. The Hague: Mouton.

Lunt, H. G. (ed.) (1964). *Proceedings of the Ninth International Congress of Linguists*. The Hague: Mouton.

Lyons, J. (1963). *Structural Semantics*. (Publications of the Philological Society, 20.) Oxford: Blackwell.

(1966). Towards a 'notional' theory of the 'parts of speech'. *JL* 2. 209–36.

(1967). A note on possessive, existential and locative sentences. *FL* 3. 390–6.

(1968a). *Introduction to Theoretical Linguistics*. London: Cambridge University Press.

(1968b). Existence, location, possession and transitivity. In van Rootselaar & Staal (eds.), *Logic, Methodology and Philosophy of Sciences*, III, 495–504. Amsterdam: North-Holland.

McCawley, J. D. (1968a). Concerning the base component of a transformational grammar. *FL* 4. 243–69.

(1968b). The role of semantics in a grammar. In Bach, E. & Harms, R. T. (eds.), 124–69.

Macdonell, A. A. (1916). *A Vedic Grammar for Students*. London: Oxford University Press.

McIntosh, A. (1968). The English comparative and some related problems. (Unpublished.)

Madvig, J. N. (1875). *Kleine philologische Schriften*. Leipzig: B. G. Teubner. (Reprinted 1966, Hildesheim: Georg Olms.)

Maejima, G. (1958). Some notes on English medio-reflexive verbs. *Anglica* 3. 101–26.

Manessy, G. (1964). La relation génitive dans quelques langues mandés. In Lunt, H. G. (ed.), 467–75.

Marache, M. (1967). Flexion casuelle et fonction grammaticale, I: Les fonctions grammaticales pures. *JPsych* 64. 279–96.

Martinet, A. (1958). L'ergatif et les structures de base de l'énoncé. *JPsych* 55. 377–92.

(1962a). *A Functional View of Language*. London: Oxford University Press.

(1962*b*). Le sujet comme fonction linguistique et l'analyse syntaxique du basque. *BSL* **57**. 73–82.

Maspero, H. (1947–8). Notes sur la morphologie du tibéto-birman et du muṇḍa. *BSL* **44**. 155–85.

Mathesius, V. (1929). Zur Ṣatzperspektive im modernen Englisch. *ASNS* **155**. 202–10.

(1964). On linguistic characterology with illustrations from Modern English. In Vachek, J. (ed.), 59–67. (Reprinted from *Actes du premier congrès international de linguistes* (1928), 56–63.)

Matthews, P. H. (1965). Problems of selection in transformational grammar. *JL* **1**. 35–47.

(1969). Review of Dik (1968). *Lingua* **23**. 349–71.

Matthews, W. K. (1953). The ergative construction in modern Indo-Aryan. *Lingua* **3**. 391–406.

Meillet, A. (1924). Le développement du verbe *avoir*. *Antidoron: Festschrift J. Wackernagel*, 9–13. Göttingen: Vandenhoeck & Ruprecht.

Meillet, A. & Vendryes, J. (1924). *Grammaire comparée des langues classiques*. Paris: Champion.

Mihailovič, L. (1967). Passive and pseudopassive verbal groups in English. *ES* **48**. 316–26.

Miller, R. L. (1968). *The Linguistic Relativity Principle and Humboldtian Ethnolinguistics*. The Hague: Mouton.

Moreux, B. (1968). Le rôle des cas dans les tours prépositionnels en attique et en latin classique. *CJL* **14**. 31–9.

Müller, F. (1876). *Einleitung in die Sprachwissenschaft*. Wien: Holder.

Murray, J. A. H. (1888). *A New English Dictionary on Historical Principles*, I. London: Oxford University Press.

Mustanoja, T. (1960). *A Middle English Syntax*, I. (*Mémoires de la Société Néophilologique de Helsinki* **23**.)

Naert, P. (1956). Le verbe basque est-il passif? *SL* **10**. 45–9.

Paul, H. (1886). *Principien der Sprachgeschichte*, 2nd edn. Halle: Niemeyer.

Pedersen, H. (1906). Neues und nachtragliches, 1: Exegetische und syntaktische fragen. *KZ* **40**. 129–73.

Perlmutter, D. M. (1969). On the article in English. In Bierwisch, M. & Heidolph, K. E. (eds.).

Planudes, Maximus: see Bachmann, L. (ed.), 1–166.

Pontoppidan-Sjövall, K. (1964). Categories of content and form. *SL* **17**. 65–93.

Porzig, W. (1934). Wesenhafte Bedeutungsbeziehungen. *BGDSL* **58**. 70–97.

Postal, P. M. (1966*a*). On so-called 'pronouns' in English. *MSLL* **19**. 177–206.

(1966*b*). Review of Longacre (1964). *IJAL* **32**. 93–8.

Pott, A.-F. (1836). *Etymologische Forschungen auf dem Gebiete der indogermanischen Sprachen*, II. Lemgo.

(1873). Unterschied eines transitiven und intransitiven nominativs. *KB* **7**. 71–94.

Poutsma, H. (1926). *A Grammar of Late Modern English*, II: *Parts of Speech*, II: *The Verb and the Particles*. Groningen: Noordhoff.

(1928). *A Grammar of Late Modern English*, I: *The Sentence*, I, 2nd edn. Groningen: Noordhoff.

Quirk, R. & Wrenn, C. L. (1955). *An Old English Grammar*. London: Methuen.

Ramamurti, G. V. (1931). *A Manual of the So:ra: (or Savara) Language*. Madras.

Redden, J. E. (1966). Walapai II: morphology. *IJAL* **32**. 141–63.

Reich, P. A. (1969). *The Finiteness of Natural Language*. (Linguistic Automation Project Report.) New Haven, Conn.: Yale University.

Robertson, J. M. (ed.) (1905). *Philosophical Works of Francis Bacon*. London: Routledge.

Robins, R. H. (1966). The development of the word class system of the European grammatical tradition. *FL* **2**. 3–19.

Roerich, R. de (1958). *Le parler de l'Amdo*. (Serie Orientale Roma, XVIII.) Roma: Istituto Italiano per il Medio e Estremo Oriente.

Rosén, H. B. (1959). Die Ausdruckform für 'Veräusserlichen' und 'Unveräusserlichen Besitz' im Frühgriechischen. *Lingua* **8**. 264–93.

Rosenbaum, P. S. (1967 a). Phrase structure principles of English complex sentence formation. *JL* **3**. 103–18.

(1967 b). *The Grammar of English Predicate Complement Constructions*. Cambridge, Mass.: M.I.T. Press.

Ross, J. R. (1967). Auxiliaries as main verbs. (Unpublished.)

(1969). On declarative sentences. In Jacobs, R. A. & Rosenbaum, P. S. (eds.).

Salmon, V. (1969). Review of Chomsky (1966). *JL* **5**. 165–87.

Sampson, G. (1969). Towards a linguistic theory of reference. (Unpublished.)

Sapir, E. (1917 a). Review of Uhlenbeck (1916 a). *IJAL* **1**. 82–6.

(1917 b). Review of Uhlenbeck (1916 b). *IJAL* **1**. 86–90.

(1922). The Takelma language of southwestern Oregon. In Boas (ed.) (1922), 1–296.

Sapir, E. & Swadesh, M. (1932). *The Expression of the Ending-point Relation in English, French and German*. (*Language Monograph* **10**.) Baltimore, Md.: Linguistic Society of America.

Sastri, M. I. (1968). Prepositions in 'Chemical Abstracts'. *Linguistics* **38**. 42–51.

Šaumjan, S. K. (1965). Outline of the applicational generative grammar for the description of language. *FL* **1**. 189–222.

Sauvageot, A. (1951). *Esquisse de la langue hongroise*. Paris: Klincksieck.

(1953). Caractère ouraloïde du verbe éskimo. *BSL* **49**. 107–21.

Schane, S. A. (1969). A theory of natural phonological rules. (Paper read at the UCLA conference on Historical Linguistics in the Perspective of Transformational Theory.)

Schmitt, A. (1956). Der nominale Charakter des sogenannten Verbums der Eskimosprache. *KZ* **73**. 27–45.

Schuchardt, H. (1896). Über den passiven Charakter des Transitivs in den kaukasischen Sprachen. *SbAWW(PH)* **133**. 1–90.

(1905–6). Über den aktivischen und passivischen Charakter des Transitivs. *IF* **18**, 528–31.

(1921). Possessivisch und passivisch. *SbPAW* 651–62.

(1922): see Spitzer (ed.).

Sebeok, T. A. (1946). *Finnish and Hungarian Case Systems: Their Form and Function.* Stockholm: Acta Instituti Hungarici Universitatis Holmiensis, Series B: Linguistica, **3**.

(ed.) (1966). *Current Trends in Linguistics,* 3: *Theoretical Foundations.* The Hague: Mouton.

Sechehaye, A. (1926). *Essai sur la structure logique de la phrase.* Paris: Champion.

Sedláček, K. (1968). Khongs and its grammaticized usage in Modern Written Tibetan. *ZDMG* **118**. 367–72.

Seuren, P. A. M. (1969). *Operators and Nucleus: A Contribution to the Theory of Grammar. (Cambridge Studies in Linguistics* **2**.) London: Cambridge University Press.

Sgall, P. (1967). Functional sentence perspective in a generative description. *PSML* **2**. 203–25.

Šimko, J. (1957). *Word-Order in the Winchester Manuscript and in William Caxton's Edition of Thomas Malory's Morte Darthur (1485)—A Comparison.* Halle: Niemeyer.

Small, G. W. (1924). *The Comparison of Inequality.* Baltimore, Md.: The Johns Hopkins University.

Sommerfelt, A. (1937). Sur la notion du sujet en géorgien. *Mélanges offerts à J. van Ginneken,* 183–5. Paris: Klincksieck.

Sonnenschein, E. A. (1927). *The Soul of Grammar.* London: Cambridge University Press.

Sørensen, H.-C. (1949). Contribution à la discussion sur la théorie des cas. *Recherches Structurales (TCLC* **5**). 123–33.

Southworth, F. C. (1967). A model of semantic structure. *Lg* **43**. 342–61.

Spitzer, L. (ed.) (1922). *Hugo Schuchardt Brevier.* Halle: Niemeyer.

Staal, J. F. (1967a). Some semantic relations between sentoids. *FL* **3**. 66–88.

(1967b). *Word Order in Sanskrit and Universal Grammar. (Foundations of Language Supplementary Series* **5**.) Dordrecht: Reidel.

Steinthal, H. (1863). *Geschichte der Sprachwissenschaft bei den Griechischen und Römern.* Berlin: Dümmler.

Sundén, K. F. (1916). *The Predicational Categories in English,* and *A Category of Predicational Change in English. (Uppsala Universitets Arsskrift (1918),* I.) Uppsala: A.-B. Akademiska Bokhandeln.

Swanton, J. R. (1911). Tlingit. In Boas (ed.) (1911), 159–204.

Tagliavini, C. (1937). Osservazioni sull'ergativo georgiano. *Mélanges offerts à J. van Ginneken,* 187–92. Paris: Klincksieck.

Taylor, F. W. (1953). *A Grammar of the Adamawa Dialect of the Fulani Language,* 2nd edn. London: Oxford University Press.

Tesnière, L. (1959). *Éléments de syntaxe structurale.* Paris: Klincksieck.

Thalbitzer, W. (1930). The absolute and the relative in Eskimo. *A Grammatical Miscellany offered to Otto Jespersen on his Seventieth Birthday,* 319–29. Copenhagen and London: Levin & Munksgaard and Allen & Unwin.

Theban, L. (1968). Perspectiva liniară a propozițiilor trimembre. *SCL* **19**. 307–15.

(1969). Review of Staal (1967*b*). *RRLing* **14**. 504–10.

Theban, M. & Theban, L. (1969). Propoziția romanică și universaliile sintactice. *SCL* **20**. 55–62.

Thorne, J. P. (1966). English imperative sentences. *JL* **2**. 69–78.

Tooke, J. Horne (1798–1805). *Epea pteroenta, or The Diversions of Purley.* London. (Reprinted as vol. **127** in *English Linguistics 1500–1800.* Menston: The Scolar Press.)

Trabalza, C. (1908). *Storia della Grammatica Italiana.* Milano: Ulrico Hoepli.

Traugott, E. (1969*a*). Toward a grammar of syntactic change. *Lingua* **23**. 1–27.

(1969*b*). Simplification versus elaboration in syntactic change. (Paper read at the UCLA Conference on Historical Linguistics in the Perspective of Transformational Theory.)

Traugott, E. & Waterhouse, J. (1969). Already and yet: A suppletive set of aspect-markers? *JL* **5**. 287–304.

Troubetzkoy, N. (1929). Notes sur les désinences du verbe dans les langues tchétchénolesghiennes. *BSL* **29**. 153–71.

Uhlenbeck, C. C. (1901). Agens und Patiens im Kasussystem der indogermanischen Sprachen. *IF* **12**. 170–1.

(1907*a*). Karakteristiek der baskischen Grammatica. *VMKAW(L)* **4**, 8. 4–42.

(1907*b*). On Finck, 1907. *KZ* **41**. 400.

(1916*a*). Het passieve Karakter van het Verbum transitivum of van het Verbum actionis in Taalen van Noord-Amerika. *VMKAW(L)* **5**, 2. 187–216.

(1916*b*). Het identificeerend Karakter der possessieve Flexie in Taalen van Noord-Amerika. *VMKAW(L)* **5**, 2. 345–71.

(1948). Le langage basque et la linguistique générale. *Lingua* **1**. 59–76.

Uhlířová, L. (1966). Some aspects of word order in categorial and transformational grammars. *PSML* **1**. 159–64.

Vachek, J. (ed.) (1964). *A Prague School Reader in Linguistics.* Bloomington, Indiana: Indiana University Press.

Vaillant, A. (1936). L'ergatif indo-européen. *BSL* **37**. 93–108.

Valin, R. (1954). *Petite introduction à la psychomécanique du langage.* Quebec: Presses de l'Université Laval.

Vasiliu, L. (1968). Some methodological remarks concerning a semantics of prepositions. *RRLing* **13**. 541–9.

Velten, H. V. (1931). On the origin of the categories of voice and aspect. *Lg* **7**. 229–41.

(1932*a*). The accusative case and its substitute in various types of language. *Lg* **8**. 255–70.

(1932*b*). Sur l'évolution du genre, des cas et des parties du discours. *BSL* **33**. 205–23.

(1962). On the function of French *de* and *à*. *Lingua* **11**. 449–52.

Vendler, Z. (1967). *Linguistics in Philosophy*. Ithaca, N.Y.: Cornell University Press.

Vendryes, J. (1921). *Le langage*. Paris: La Renaissance du Livre.

(1932). Sur les verbes de mouvement en indo-européen. *IL* **2**. 21–5. (Reprinted in *Choix d'études linguistiques et celtiques* (1952), 127–31. Paris: Klincksieck.)

Verhaar, J. W. M. (ed.) (1968). *The Verb 'Be' and its Synonyms*, 2. (*Foundations of Language Supplementary Series* **6**.) Dordrecht: Reidel.

Vinson, J. (1903). *Manuel de la langue tamoule*. Paris: Leroux.

Visser, F. T. (1963). *An Historical Syntax of the English Language*, 1: *Syntactical Units with One Verb*. Leiden: E. J. Brill.

Vogt, H. (1938). Esquisse d'une grammaire du géorgien moderne. *NTS* **10**. 5–188.

(1944). Le système des cas en ossète. *AL* **4**. 17–41.

(1949). L'étude des systèmes des cas. *Recherches structurales* (*TCLC* **5**). 112–22.

Wagner, K. H. (1968). Verb phrase complementation: A criticism. *JL* **4**. 89–91.

Weinreich, U. (1966). Explorations in semantic theory. In Sebeok, T. (ed.), 395–477.

Whitney, W. D. (1893). On recent studies in Hindu Grammar. *AJPh* **14**. 171–97.

Whorf, B. L. (1956). *Language, Thought and Reality*. New York: Wiley.

Wijk, N. van (1902). *Der nominale Genitiv Singular im Indogermanischen in seinem Verhältnis zum Nominativ*. Zwolle.

Winkler, H. (1889). *Weiteres zur Sprachgeschichte*. Berlin: Dümmler.

Worth, D. S. (1964). Ob otobraženii linejnyx otnošenij v poroždajuščix model jax jazyka. *VJa* **3**. 46–58.

Wüllner, F. (1827). *Die Bedeutung der sprachlichen Casus und Modi*. Munster.

Wundt, W. (1900). *Völkerpsychologie*, 1: *Die Sprache*, 11. Leipzig: Wilhelm Engelmann.

Yamakawa, K. (1958). On the construction '*have* (or *get*)+object+past participle'. *Anglica* **3**. 164–96.

Zubatý, J. (1906). Die 'man'-sätze. *KZ* **40**. 478–520.

Index